BIG shoes

A Young Widowed Mother's Memoir

Lisa Bradshaw

3 george
media

For information address:

3 George Media, Inc.
331 Valley Mall Parkway #213
East Wenatchee, WA 98802

Info@3georgemedia.com

Cover design by Evan Earwicker
Cover photo by David Clark
Interior design & production by Joel Friedlander
www.TheBookDesigner.com

Printed in the United States of America

To Hunter.

I love you to Daddy and back.

And to Brian.

You are the shelter.

Contents

Acknowledgments — vii

Foreword — xi

Prologue: It's Time — xv

1. The Garage — 1

2. Oxygen — 9

3. Titration — 19

4. Call an Ambulance — 35

5. Second Look — 47

6. The Decision — 61

7. The Guardian — 81

8. Cowboy Up — 91

9. The Walk — 103

10. Three-Day Wait — 121

11. OnStar — 139

12. Slip On Shoes & My Best Friend — 153

13. Move Something — 171

14. Goodbye To a Stranger — 189

15. 24/7 — 199

16. Easter Sunday — 217

17. Day One — 233

18. You're Here, Aren't You? — 241

19. Training Wheels — 255

20. Hero — 275

21. Heading West — 279

22. The Longest Winter — 305

23. Getting James'd — 315

24. Ignoring the Voice — 333

25. Crossing the Abyss — 345

26. Thoughts from My Father — 353

27. Big Love — 365

Epilogue: The DON'T WAIT Project® — 377

Acknowledgements

Without the support of my community, this book and The DON'T WAIT Project® would not have unfolded the way they did. My day job enables me to interact with philanthropic and innovative thinkers who serve and help shape our community every day, including Central Washington Hospital, Wenatchee Valley Medical Center, Total Travel, Solomon Financial, Ruth & Clyde Ballard and M & M Productions.

I thank Dan Conway for giving me the opportunity to produce and host *The Life with Lisa Show*, and I thank Dave Bernstein for teaching me what I have needed to know along the way. I remain grateful to Cherry Creek Radio and its leaders, not only for the show but also for their continued encouragement of the work I do outside of the building.

Betty Teller and Norma Petersen edited the book with patience, empathy and good humor. Thank you for helping me fill in the blanks.

Joel Friedlander of Marin Bookworks has been instrumental in the outcome of this book and the entire project. From our first phone consulation to the very font chosen for the title chapters of this book, he is a true crusader of bringing books from concept to creation.

When searching for the jewelry design to best represent The DON'T WAIT Project®, I found the talented Brooke Mortensen of Ritzy Misfit. Together, we created a beautiful pendant for supporters of the project and the story.

Heather Urich contributed the foreword—a sequel to Bob's earlier work. We never could have known what was to come.

I am thankful for the competent medical team members who did their best to save Wesley, especially Drs. Patel, Wille, and Young, and our ever hopeful nurse, Alyson.

My dear friends, each of them have made a difference in the outcome of my grief, my progress, and my life. I thank them all for being patient with me when I had so little to give in return.

Wayne, Tara, Jenny, Heather and Bubba—I love my Texas brothers and sisters.

Jay, the Godfather, never forgets Hunter's birthday. Wesley would be grateful, just as I am.

Wesley's parents, Donna, Roger and Jimbo, supported my decision to move thousands of miles away when life was already changing so quickly. I am thankful we remain part of Wesley's endearing family.

My mom helped take care of Hunter throughout Wesley's illness, enabling me to care for Wesley when he needed me most. I have become the wonderful mother she has been to me. I am grateful for the lessons I have learned from her in times of tragedy and joy.

My dad wrote a chapter in this book. He poured out his heart and revisited a time in our lives he did not want to recall in such detail, but he did it for the reader and for me. As a result, he helped heal himself.

My brother Vance has become my dear friend. We share what matters most in common and are not so different after all.

Konnor and Brooklynn have made me stronger, more patient and a better manager of my time out of necessity, and, most of all, they have expanded my capacity for love and have given Hunter what he never would have had without them: a brother and a sister.

I have said it before, it is a privilege and a joy to share my life with my son Hunter. His daddy would be proud, and I remain forever grateful for the miracle of him.

I thank Brian (a.k.a. Hot Guy) for understanding and sharing in the work we know I am meant to do. May we be blessed to live long lives and grow old together—the two of us raising our children and enjoying our grandchildren and their children. I love him BIG.

Foreword

When my late husband Robert Urich was diagnosed with cancer in August 1996, the news was all over the place. It was on the CNN wheel and the cover of just about every newspaper and magazine in this country and beyond. Consequently, he received many books relating to anything at all to do with cancer, along with hundreds of letters and cards full of encouragement, including a card from Lisa Bradshaw. That was when Lisa first came into our lives.

Two years after Robert was diagnosed with cancer and had finished treatment, he met Lisa at a conference in Houston at MD Anderson Cancer Center in September of 1997 when he was the keynote speaker at their annual patient conference. At the time, Lisa was writing her first book based on the journal she had kept while going through her own cancer experience. She had been diagnosed with cancer at the age of twenty-four, and she chronicled her journey as a survivor. My husband was taken with the courage she exuded as she successfully battled this insidious disease. At the time, she gave Robert's assistant sample chapters and a request to have Robert write the foreword. At first, Robert declined because he was in the middle of writing his own book. Lisa persisted, asking him to reconsider with a letter from her father and her husband Wesley. Robert soon replied to Lisa with a handwritten note and asked her to send him the book when it was ready and agreed to write the foreword. Lisa still keeps that notecard near her desk today.

Looking back now, Lisa and I never could have imagined what was to come in her life as we continued a valued long distance friendship. One year after my husband died, Wesley began to get sick. Throughout Wesley's illness, Lisa sent me emails with updates about what she and her family were enduring. However, I was stunned beyond measure reading *Big Shoes* as she was writing it. I had no idea of the enormity of pain in the details of Wesley's struggle. This is a brilliant, soul-wrenching book written with electric honesty and passion. It is a universal experience: a portrait of a marriage during good times and bad. It speaks to anyone who has loved and lost.

Big Shoes is a true story of love. It is the story of Lisa and Wesley's battle with the biggest demon imaginable. It is one thing to have a disease that can be diagnosed and treated accordingly. It is quite another to be at the mercy of an unknown beast and the best medical experts available can do nothing but scratch their heads in wonder. This narrative is delivered with raw truth in remarkable, beautiful language.

I recall the first time I met Lisa. It was six months after my husband died. I walked into my kitchen and she was there. She showed up to volunteer for The Robert Urich Fund Golf Tournament at Sherwood Country Club to raise money for cancer research. It is a fund Robert started before he died and one I continue to champion today. She recalls how shattered I was during that time. After Wesley died she and Hunter came to visit me in Los Angeles. She said she wanted to spend time with someone who understood.

Lisa's son Hunter and my daughter Allison are one year apart. During that first visit, we reveled in the fun they had together. We never imagined either one of us would become widowed mothers, let alone our two children would have a lemonade stand together and become friends during their visit. It was then we began to realize through our children's joy and laughter that eventually we would make it. We would be all right.

We have done the widow walk together.

Heather Menzies Urich

Prologue

One day, when I was eight years old, I climbed to the top of a pine tree in front of our neighbor's house. I do not know where the rest of the kids from the neighborhood were that day, but I remember being bored and silent and curious.

I fearlessly climbed the tall tree and planted myself firmly on a strong branch near the top, then watched cars drive past, people pull in and out of nearby driveways, and critters play in neighboring trees. Everything was quiet. No one knew I was in the tree, and I observed without being disturbed.

As I sat there, a feeling came over me, a knowledge of something greater than myself, something I was just beginning to grasp when I followed our neighbors to church every Sunday, but did not yet fully understand. I did not recognize it at the time, but I was finding God in that moment in the tree.

I remember feeling I was being told something, that there was something I was to do with my life. Something told me I had chosen to be born—and I chose birth while knowing my fate was a life that would be arduous but equally rewarding.

Sixteen years later, when I was diagnosed with cancer, it was devastating, but in time, I understood the balance. I learned to accept what had come from it and using my voice to write a book and help other people better cope with their own cancer journey made sense to me.

Eight years later, when my husband died, I was too paralyzed with grief to even contemplate this way of thinking. I believed I would never find a balance between what had been lost and what could be gained from the experience. Without considering an alternative, I was convinced the truth was and would remain that no matter how much I learned from the devastation of losing Wesley—even if I eventually found happiness—Hunter losing his father would be impossible to accept.

In the months after Wesley died, I searched for understanding, and I had many questions. How was I going to live the rest of my life without Wesley? How was I going to be enough for Hunter? How was I going to find greatness in the heap of sadness piled high around and inside of me?

I read books written by people who had lost their great love. I read books about surviving grief. I read books about finding my purpose but those pages just made me wonder: what was the purpose of Wesley's short life, and how had I influenced his outcome? Everything in the year after Wesley died was about filling the gap he left behind, not only in the everydayness of life but mainly in the gaping, wounded heart of our little boy, who was now my fatherless son.

One day, about three years after Wesley died, I ran across some pictures taken when we were visiting our family in California. The pictures were taken on a hot summer day. Many members of our family were at the park, and we were having a water fight. It was spontaneous and wonderful, and even our parents joined in the fun.

Hunter had been three years old at the time. He knew to stay out of the street and was standing in the grass, close to a sidewalk and surrounded by adults when a man sped by in his car, driving at least ten miles over the speed limit in the park. My immediate impulse was to yell to Hunter, "Stop! Don't move. Stay where you are."

Wesley's reaction was to yell at the man to slow down, while flipping the driver his middle finger. The guy yelled something back at Wesley about keeping our kid out of the street, showed his middle finger to Wesley, and kept driving. Hunter was not in any danger, but the driver was because I am sure Wesley would have punched him a few times if the man had turned around and come back for more.

When I saw the photographs, I remembered that day clearly, but it was not until a photo of Hunter and Wesley near a water fountain surfaced in the pile of pictures that I lost my footing. As I stared at the photograph, I began to weep. I crumbled to the floor, holding the picture, barely able to see it through the tears. The image on the paper was simple: Hunter was squirting my brother Vance with a water bottle and smiling a mischievous smile at Wesley while he did it, and Wesley was smiling back at Hunter. In that painful moment alone, while looking at the photograph and seeing my boys together that day, it was as if I could hear them laughing in that joyful moment etched in time, and I wanted it back. All of it—our family, Wesley's protection, easy moments of laughter and joy.

I cried and cried, wishing with all of my might Wesley would come back to me. I wanted somehow to return to that day when Wesley was strong and steadfast and the man he had always been— protective and capable. I had always believed nothing bad would ever happen to Hunter or to me in Wesley's presence—but what would become of us in his absence?

After sobbing for several minutes, sitting on the bedroom floor holding the photograph, and petting our dog Emma while she stood by with concern for my sadness, I began to consider what Wesley's presence meant to my life and what gifts I had been given by being so loved by this man of such great measure, and the tears began to slow.

As I considered his presence in my life, I felt his absence. Then I pondered: Was I missing something in the enormity of my grief, something that would only be my own once I was willing and able to accept his departure? Had I forgotten about that day in the tree when I was eight years old? Had I forgotten I chose to be born? Had I forgotten I knew there would be strife but there was also the promise of balance? It was in this moment of agony and reflection I began to experience clarity.

The only path I had in front of me was to find my way through the grief—and to bring Hunter with me. My sole purpose in life was to bring to fruition the only answer that made sense: There had to be an enormous reason for Wesley not to be alive, and it was up to me to discover and live what that was, even if it took my lifetime to do it. I knew I was blessed to understand I was gifted with my own purpose, but it was still painful to understand my purpose could only exist if Wesley did not. It was my job to bring to my life everything waiting for Hunter and me, not in spite of losing Wesley but because of losing Wesley.

Wesley and I had been on both sides of the vows we made to each other when we married. I was sick with cancer early in our marriage, and Wesley had to face the reality I might not survive. Just eight years after cancer, I was faced with the reality Wesley might not survive. In only ten years of marriage, we had started from the beginning and found ourselves at the end.

During his illness, I fought for Wesley's life, and the fight was not always mild-mannered and polite. I pressed for answers, and I demanded exceptional care during an impossible situation—so in the end, no matter the outcome, there would be answers to complicated questions. It was all part of the journey and part of the importance of leaving no stone unturned, so our son would know what we were willing to endure for the chance of another day in the park on a hot summer day.

I have the picture of Wesley and Hunter in front of me as I write these words. In it, I see love. I see no matter how short Wesley's time here was, it was well spent. I am grateful and honored to share our story, in the hope of helping even one person better cope with loss and make full use of the time we are given.

I tell the truth here. Some things I would rather not admit, but feel compelled to share. I fall down along the way, but I get back up and start again. None of this has been easy. It has been painful to write Wesley's name in the past tense. Many times I was certain I would perish from a broken heart, but I eventually began to understand that though I would never get over Wesley's death, I could get through it.

It took years for me to decide to write these words in a form that would be shared with others. All along I have had Wesley and Hunter's permission and encouragement. This story is private, but it is also necessary to tell it because it is part of the beginning of all things for us. What is our own, I keep for our own; what can and should be shared in these pages, I willingly share.

I write this book not only because Wesley trusted me to write it, but because he asked me to write it. And because I believe it helps serve *his* purpose.

CHAPTER ONE

The Garage

Some moments are absolute, forever etched into the mind as a turning point, a pivotal experience that lends its weight to almost everything that follows. For me, there have been a few moments like this: When I was diagnosed with cancer. When I found out I was pregnant after being told we might never be able to have children because of my cancer treatments. And the moment Wesley came inside the house to take a break from cleaning our garage.

"I'm having trouble breathing," he gasped, leaning against the washing machine in the laundry room.

Everything from that moment on changed the course of life for me and for many others: People who loved him, people who loved us, and people I had yet to meet.

Every spring, during the last weekend in February, we prepared for our son Hunter's birthday party in March by freshening our flower beds, raking the winter's leaves, and mowing the lawn for the first time after a short and mild Texas winter. Then, the following weekend, we would celebrate our miracle child with a fabulous birthday party. Nothing particularly extravagant—we did not rent a circus or hire clowns and face painters—but we always had a theme and made it fun for the whole family.

This year, Hunter was turning four. We had waited five years after we were married to have a child. Wesley had his reasons for wanting to be sure we were solid in our marriage before having children because his own parents divorced, and he wanted to give our marriage time to be solid before having children of our own. I wanted to wait until the fear of cancer returning to my body was no longer at the forefront of my thoughts.

The doctors told us to wait at least a year after cancer to try to get pregnant, but said two years would be better, because the threat of recurrence would be drastically reduced. We waited two years to the month of my recovery—and three weeks later found out I was pregnant. The moment I found out, the fear I had of cancer left me, and I finally felt I had truly healed. I knew there was no room for fear in the presence of our miracle. Nine months later our healthy son was born.

We had taken Hunter to Sea World when he was three, so we decided to have a Shamu theme for his fourth birthday party. Wesley got it in his mind to find a Shamu moonwalk for the kids to jump in during the party. It took him two hours and dozens of phone calls, but he did eventually find a company that had one and ordered it for the party.

I am always amazed when some mothers plan and execute every aspect of what is wonderful about the celebrations in a child's life while the dads are merely spectators. This fascinates me because it does not have to be that way, and that was not how it was in our house. Wesley paid attention and held our attention. He lived and breathed us, as we did him. We were a solid family, and when it came time to throw a party, he was the one who always extended the guest list, wanted and prepared more food, and made sure everyone's glass was full once the guests arrived. I made things look good; he made things taste good.

The year before, we had a jungle theme for Hunter's third birthday, and Wesley spent two evenings spray-painting strands of rope different colors of the jungle so we could hang them in our dining room where the lion cake I was baking and decorating would be displayed. This year was no different. Teamwork and good times made our lives richer and worth everything we had lived through to get the family we celebrated.

That day, the pivotal day, one week before the party, Wesley was cleaning out the garage, including an old cabinet that had never been opened. We had bought the house from his stepdad Jimbo six years before and even he did not remember ever having opened the cabinet. Inside, Wesley found droppings, mold, and a bag of fertilizer that was soaking wet but should have been dry.

I was in the kitchen cleaning when Wesley walked into the laundry room next to the garage door. He leaned against the washing machine and said, "I'm having trouble breathing."

"Then please stop cleaning," I told him.

Usually, Hunter was outside helping his dad while I was working inside, but on this day he was not. He was in his room playing with his toys.

"I'm going to finish up, but keep Hunter inside until I am done," Wesley told me, wanting to make sure Hunter was not exposed to whatever had caused his own shortness of breath.

"I will."

His shortness of breath continued. By the next day, when the mulch for our flower beds was delivered, he tried to shovel and spread it, but it was too difficult for him. I usually helped him, but this time he helped me—and he was not happy about it.

Later that afternoon, he started to mow the lawn but could not finish, so I did it. I told him he needed to go to the doctor, and he said he would see how he felt the next day.

The next day he was not better, but he still resisted going to the doctor. The day after that he was better, but two days later he was worse. This pattern continued for a few weeks until his heart started beating rapidly one day while playing softball with friends. The next day, he finally went to the doctor.

The first doctor gave Wesley an inhaler and told him to come back in two weeks if he did not feel better. In two weeks he was not better, so the doctor scheduled him to see a cardiologist, because his chest X-ray of his lungs looked cloudy and his heart was enlarged. The visit to the cardiologist would include a stress test, which was terrifying. Wesley would be expected to walk on a treadmill at a rapid pace, and I knew he was not capable of it given his extreme shortness of breath.

There was never a moment when either of us truly believed whatever was causing his shortness of breath and now an enlarged heart was going to be something minor or something that could even be treated. It was not because we were not optimistic, because we had always been people who held that the glass was half full, but we feared the worst. Wesley's dad had died nine years before after being diagnosed with an idiopathic lung disease—which meant the doctors did not know what the disease was and never would.

In recent months, even before that spring day, when Wesley occasionally mentioned he felt short of breath when using the stairs at work or walking long or uphill paths, I told him to do more cardiovascular exercise. I dismissed it as a result of his not following a regular exercise regimen. After all, he was young and strong. I realize now that deep down he was worried something was wrong.

Wesley said he wanted to go to the cardiology appointment by himself and asked me to stay home. My mom was visiting and planned to leave the next day, so I did stay with her and Hunter for a while, but after an hour, I left and went to sit with Wesley while he waited for the test. I knew I needed to be there, just as he had been there for me through cancer eight years before.

He could not finish the stress test. It was too difficult for him—he could barely breathe when he was exerting himself. As a result, the doctor wanted to admit him to the hospital for further testing, and we were scared. Wesley asked him if he could at least go home for a few hours and be with his family before he returned for admission later in the afternoon. Since he was in no immediate danger, the doctor agreed.

Wesley and I left the doctor's office and drove to a nearby restaurant. Neither of us was hungry. We did not even order food to eat. We just held hands and tried not to cry. As we sat at the restaurant, during that stolen hour away from everyone, we talked about the second baby we had planned to start trying for when Hunter was four. We said when Wesley got better, we would continue our family. He told me how much he loved me and reassured me he would not let anything bad happen to our family. I wanted to believe him, but somehow I knew we would not return to our life as it had been, and this necessary man was starting to slip away from me.

When we left the restaurant, Wesley asked me to go on ahead of him and said he would be a few minutes behind me in his car. I understood he needed a few extra minutes to collect his thoughts before facing Hunter. When I got home, Hunter was in the living room watching a movie, and my mom was in front of the house. Her reaction to the look on my face was instantaneous; she was crying before I could reach and embrace her. She had watched Wesley's dad die, as we had.

"I'll stay. I won't leave tomorrow," she promised, holding my hands in hers. My mom was the first person to learn that Wesley was having trouble breathing and needed to be hospitalized. When I told her—with my eyes, not with words—she was terrified.

Ten minutes later, Wesley pulled into our driveway. My mom went inside to check on Hunter, and I stood in front of the house, trying to smile at Wesley through the car window. Wesley forced a smile in return. There were no words. Together we went inside and played with Hunter, helping him stack his building blocks, then knock them down, only to stack them up and knock them down again.

I went into our bedroom to pack a small overnight bag for Wesley to take to the hospital. I left my boys playing with Hunter's blocks as they had so many times before, and I thought about when I was eight years old and first met Wesley. He was on top of a pile of boys playing football in my front yard with my brother and other kids in the neighborhood. When I saw him, I had this overwhelming feeling that has always been difficult to describe. I did not love him at that age, but he did become important to me, and I wanted to be important to him.

I could not have known back then we would grow up and spend years apart, then come together as adults and fall in love. I never could have known as a child that as a woman I would marry him and become the mother of his son. I could not remember a time when he and his family were not a part of my life. Together, we had built the family I had always wanted to have with Wesley. Our marriage had always prevailed, even during the dark period when I had cancer or in the struggles married people experience together. Now, we were in this familiar place of fighting for our lives. Only this time it was not just the two of us, because there was Hunter to consider.

When I was finished packing, we said goodbye to Hunter. We lied and told him his dad was going to the ranch to help Papa

Jimbo and would be back in a few days. Hunter believed us, and we left our beautiful four-year-old son to play with his blocks. My mom would get him through the rest of the day and night.

As we drove to the hospital, we held hands but did not speak. We stopped at a traffic light near the hospital, and I saw a very old man in the car next to us. His skin was wrinkled, what little hair he had was white, and he had age spots on his head. He wore thick glasses and a plaid shirt with large buttons like my grandpa used to wear. What I noticed most was the simple wedding band on his left ring finger as he held onto the steering wheel tightly.

Seeing the old man, I considered what his body had survived in his lifetime to bring him to this stoplight at this very moment. How long had he been married? How many children did he have? Did he have grandchildren and great-grandchildren? What about his body had enabled him to escape death for so many decades? Did he know the gift he had received in growing old? Did his wife realize the gift she had been given by growing old with the person she had vowed to love?

As the light changed, I looked at the old man in my side mirror and watched him as we drove away. I would never know any of the answers to my questions. I looked at Wesley; he stared ahead as we turned into the parking lot of the hospital.

"We can do this," I firmly told him.

"We already are," he responded, never taking his eyes off the road in front of him.

CHAPTER TWO

Oxygen

Wesley casually paced the emergency waiting room vinyl tiles. He walked from one end of the room to the other twice, crossing the twelve-inch squares while we talked about everything except the reason he was pacing.

When the nurse asked Wesley about his symptoms and he told her of his shortness of breath, she attached a white clip that had a red light on the top of it to his fingertip. It is called a pulsox. It lightly squeezed the tip of his finger and measured his oxygen levels. It was the first time we found out his saturation level was in the low nineties while he sat in a chair exerting absolutely no energy. She called this his "at-rest" level and asked him to walk across the room with the pulsox on his finger to see if his oxygen decreased. As he walked from one end of the emergency room to the other, we watched the number dive to the mid eighties. She said this was his oxygen level when moving, which she explained is called "ambulant." Normal oxygen level for someone with healthy lungs is 99 to 100 while breathing room air.

Wesley and I were trying to concentrate on something other

than our reasons for being in the ER.

"Did you call Christi?" Wesley asked me.

"No, I figured it could wait until we get you checked into the hospital."

"You still have a business to run," he insisted.

Christi had been working for me for a few months as my assistant, handling much of the daily operations of my newly formed company. In September, when Hunter had started attending preschool two days a week, I decided to take some of my children's decor ideas to buyers of local high-end children's boutiques to see if I could sell my custom pillows and other products. Originally, I just wanted to start a small business that would allow me to work part time and contribute a nominal amount monetarily to our household while still being able to make Hunter my first priority. To my surprise, every buyer I met during Hunter's first two weeks of preschool placed orders. The business was on its way.

Working from home was a priority for me, and within a few more months I figured out I could still work from home while providing work for other women who also wanted to work from home. I did not have a budget for growth with traditional advertising, but it occurred to me if I could get the pillows I had designed used on a popular sitcom as set decoration, it would help me get third-party endorsements in magazines, on television, and in other media. I knew Jennifer Aniston's character Rachel on the hit show *Friends* was having a baby, so I got in touch with the set decorator of the number one sitcom—and he accepted my offer of our custom pillows. I had already decided if he agreed to using them on the set, I would launch a website, making the products available through custom online orders. That is exactly what happened.

Through a friend, I met a woman named Melody who was a self-taught web developer, and she agreed to design the website for me. We worked together for several weeks, creating a logo, designing the website, and solidifying the brand. It was an exciting time of growth and possibility. The website was up and running in time for our product premiere on the set of the *Friends* show—and we started getting orders within hours. I will always remember the excitement of receiving my first order.

While I was enjoying the early success of the business, promoting it in the media and contracting with seamstresses who were also working from home, Christi was doing an amazing job organizing, fulfilling, and shipping orders. We were receiving write-ups in numerous local and national publications, ranging from the local business journal to *ePregnancy* magazine, but what was happening to Wesley and how it affected our family was more important than any newfound success. It was too soon to know how this booming business would be impacted by Wesley's illness or how the business would also impact all of us.

I stepped outside of the ER to call Christi. She immediately put me at ease about our workload and made me feel confident she could handle things until I could check in with her in a few days, once we knew what we were up against with Wesley.

It took almost two hours, but Wesley was eventually admitted to the hospital. The pulmonologist referred to us by the cardiologist was to visit us in Wesley's room by the end of the day. It was just before 5:00 p.m. when he came into the room and told us he was concerned by whatever was causing Wesley's depleted oxygen levels. He said he was prescribing oxygen for him, which meant Wesley would be given oxygen through a nose cannula and have continuous flow until they could figure out what was causing his difficulty breathing.

The pulmonologist examined Wesley and ordered several tests. He said it was possible the only way they could get the answers they needed was to do an open lung biopsy, but I wanted no part of it. It felt premature—and dangerous. Wesley was braver and said he needed to know what was wrong so he could know what he was fighting. We agreed to consider it but not to make a decision until the next day.

I stayed with Wesley until he started to get tired. I did not want to leave him, but he wanted me to go home so I would be there when Hunter woke up. I was terrified to face Hunter, but I did as Wesley asked and promised to be back in the morning.

When I got home, Hunter and my mom were asleep. I knew they would be—I was counting on it. I could not sleep myself, though, because my mind was racing with worry over Wesley. Nothing was distracting me. I called my dad, knowing he already knew what was happening—my mom had told him when she let him know she was not coming home the next day as planned. Her priority would be Hunter. There was enormous comfort in knowing Hunter would not only be in good, safe hands in the days to come, but he would also be happy. He liked being with my mom and would not miss Wesley and me as much with her there.

By the time I called my dad, it was nearly three in the morning, but he was awake. When he answered, I started to cry.

"You're going to find your way through this," he tried to reassure me. "I promise you will. You have to, for Hunter's sake."

"I can't face Hunter in the morning. I don't know how," I sobbed.

"You will find the strength. What you need to do right now is try to get some rest because Wes is going to need you. You let your mom take care of Hunter. You take care of Wes. You be the strength he needs you to be. I'm sure he is scared right now, and he needs to know you can keep it together for Hunter. Your mom is here for you. I'm here for you. You have amazing friends and family who love you and Wes and Hunter. You know that. When you walk into a room with Wes in it, you need to be strong for him," he lovingly said, trying to help renew my strength.

I knew how to be strong for Wesley because Wesley had taught me how by his devotion and care of me when I was sick. I knew I could be there for him in the ways he needed me to be, but I was most terrified of losing him.

I cried and cried and cried. I could barely speak. My dad continued to encourage me to be strong and rely on my faith to get me through, but what I never heard from him in our conversation was that he believed everything would be okay.

"You're the rock now, Lisa."

He never said it would turn out to be nothing or Wesley could beat whatever was lingering. Wesley's dad was one of my dad's best friends and my dad was there when he died. My father, the man whose glass was always half full, was as scared as I was about what was happening to Wesley and how that would affect his daughter and grandson.

I said what was in my heart, and he told me his own truth.

"Wesley and I aren't going to grow old together, are we, Dad?" I asked, not really wanting to know the answer.

The words that came next from my father were so unexpected I could not deny what I was trying to deny.

"No, you probably aren't," he answered honestly.

I was shocked by his admission but not angry with him for saying it. I loved him for telling me the truth.

"Wes probably isn't going to live to be an old man, but he could live long enough to help you raise Hunter and prepare you for life without him," he told me, fighting back tears of his own.

I listened and cried and asked him how to face Hunter in the morning.

"You give him your love," my dad plainly said, knowing how much I loved Hunter. My love would be enough.

That is what I did. In the morning, when Hunter woke up and called for me from his bedroom, I mustered the strength to greet him with the same love and enthusiasm as every other morning of his life. I got him ready for preschool, walked him to his classroom, and I kissed him goodbye. Then I went to the hospital to be at his dad's side.

As far as Hunter knew, his dad was at the ranch, and I had a business meeting, so grandma would be picking him up from preschool and taking him to the park. That morning was the beginning of my learning to show Hunter only what he needed to see and to tell him only what he needed to know. No child with the wonderful life he had and the love he experienced needed to know his daddy was sick or learn everything he knew about the life we shared had already changed.

Nothing in the next day's tests could explain the symptoms Wesley was suffering, but they showed he had depleted lung function, so we agreed to the open lung biopsy. However, the results told us nothing more than we knew before they cut a piece of his lung out of his body to slide under a microscope searching for answers. His biopsy showed irregular tissue but the pathologist who studied the slides could not make a diagnosis and reported the biopsy was inconclusive. We were scared and Wesley was frustrated, not only with not knowing what was causing him to require oxygen twenty-four hours a day, but also with me, for constantly trying to explain away his symptoms and deny what was really happening. I wanted to believe it was asthma or even a heart problem hindering his lung function, something that could be fixed.

The day after the lung biopsy, I looked for the cardiologist and found him in the parking lot as he was about to leave for the day.

All the questions they had asked us had focused mostly on Wesley's dad; no one was paying any attention to the onset of his symptoms brought on by cleaning out the old cabinet in the garage. I stood at the doctor's car door in the parking lot and told him again of the day Wesley cleaned the cabinet and explained the immediate effect it had on his breathing. The doctor listened but he still dismissed it, saying it did not explain the continued symptoms.

We finished our polite debate, and he got in his car and drove away. As I stood in the parking lot alone, I looked in the direction of Wesley's hospital room in the west wing of the hospital and watched the sun as it slowly hid behind the hospital rooftop.

I wanted to be anywhere but there. We had endured my cancer years before, but this was different. As scared as we were when I was diagnosed, I was diagnosed, and there is something to be said for knowing what is wrong and how to fix it. We did not know that the treatment would work and save my life, but at least there was a treatment that could lead to a cure. There was an explanation for what ailed me, and over time our lives could be restored.

Two days later, after Wesley's chest tube was removed, he asked if he could go outside. The nurse said it was not allowed because he was on a heart monitor, but Wesley pressed her and promised I would stay with him. She agreed as long as he went with oxygen and a wheelchair, so I wheeled him to the hospital's courtyard. We sat quietly. After a few minutes, I broke the silence.

"I think when you get better we should simplify our lives. Hunter is young, we should buy an RV and travel for a few years before he has to start school, or maybe we should buy a boat and visit ports along the coasts of the United States," I suggested, wanting to get as far away from the hospital and what it represented as possible.

He was quiet for a moment, then added, "We could sell our

house and use the money to just live and teach Hunter the importance of taking the time to be a family."

"Just think of the life lessons he could gain from such an experience. While everyone we know is busy working to pay a mortgage, we could just sail away. We could make another baby and just pick a place for her to be born," I continued, keeping our dream to sail away alive, even if just in conversation.

"Her?" Wesley asked with a smile.

"Yep, one of each," I smiled back.

We just smiled at each other, then both of us fell silent. As I considered our contemplated escape from the reality of this hospital courtyard, the bandages across his chest from the inconclusive open lung biopsy, the oxygen tube in his nose, and our aching hearts, I wrapped my arms around his shoulders and leaned my head on his head. He held my arms with his hands.

"I'll go anywhere you want to go," I promised him. "Just say the word."

Five days after Wesley's lung biopsy, he was released from the hospital, but we had no more answers than when we arrived. The most common lung diagnoses for those with his symptoms were chronic obstructive pulmonary disease (COPD), cystic fibrosis, and pulmonary fibrosis, none of which showed up in his biopsy. One report suggested the early onset of a condition called pulmonary veno-occlusive disease, an extremely rare capillary disease of the lungs, which at end-stage leads to lung transplant, but the report was inconclusive and there was no way we were going accept it as a possibility.

The pulmonologist suggested Wesley start on a medication called Flolan. We read about it in detail, but given the health risks of the medication and the fact that once Wesley started taking it he could never stop, we adamantly declined until we had more answers. I was less than impressed with the doctor's lack of a plan, but Wesley and I agreed to wait a week and see if he would improve with the oxygen the doctor prescribed. Maybe Wesley would rebound and all of this would disappear. Maybe we would get our lives back and sail to a welcoming harbor off a coast far away.

It was a long week. When we went to Wesley's follow-up appointment with the pulmonologist, he still had no plan. Wesley was not better but he also was not worse; the doctor seemed content to leave things as they were and wait to see what would happen, responding accordingly. We refused to stand still. When we got home from the appointment, I started looking for alternatives.

I spoke to a neighbor who worked at the medical center downtown known for its comprehensive health care. She put me in touch with one of the best pulmonologists in the city, Dr. Bela Patel. We made an appointment with her for the following week, but Wesley got worse two days before the appointment, so I called to ask what we should do. She requested we go to the emergency room of her hospital, where he was admitted the same day. Only this time, he improved. She prescribed steroids and within two hours he felt better and required less oxygen than he had needed since his first hospital stay. Then she put him on blood thinners.

Dr. Patel was not sure what was wrong with Wesley but was treating him as if he had pulmonary emboli, a showering of tiny blood clots in both lungs. She explained the X-ray looked like tiny blood clots that could have occurred when he was hospitalized a few weeks before and said the steroids could bring his lung function back to where it was before the garage incident, giving his lungs time to rebound from the hit they took when he cleaned out the cabinet. Considering how much better he was feeling, she sent him home on oxygen and steroids the next day and told us he would likely improve over the next few weeks; we could hope for a full recovery.

Dr. Patel acknowledged the garage incident as the perfect storm and said any talk about Flolan was premature. We were happy with this assessment and stopped searching for another answer.

When we got home from the hospital, I found the bill from the first pulmonologist. He had charged us a ridiculous amount of money for his courtesy visits at the end of every afternoon. I wrote him a five-paragraph letter letting him know what I thought of his care and told him we had no intention of paying the amount he was charging; we would pay a third of the bill for the time he took to visit us daily and for not doing Wesley any further damage during the open-lung biopsy.

When he received my letter, he called me directly. I told him about Dr. Patel and described how much Wesley had improved. I also let him know that if he was in over his head he should have said so and helped us find a doctor who could help. He agreed Wesley's case was complicated and wished us the best.

When I called the next day to pay the one-third amount we had promised him, his office told me there was no bill. The doctor had asked for it to be removed from the system.

Cancer had taught us years before to build a strong medical team we could trust, and when something did not feel right, to say so. We learned doctors were human. They did not have all the answers, and they made mistakes. It was our job, as the patient and the patient's family, to pay attention to our health care and to ensure our own safety.

Even though we still did not have a diagnosis for Wesley's condition, he was doing better and that made us all breathe easier.

CHAPTER THREE

Titration

Competent medical care is essential: vital to the body and to the mind, critical to the spirit in crisis.

As confusion circled us, it was quickly evident the search for more answers would not be easy. We would fight every step of the way for the answers we needed even if they were not what we wanted to hear. I would rework the words in my head until I could speak them aloud in a manner that did not steal every ounce of hope I had for Wesley's survival, because his survival was essential to me, vital to our family, and critical in every way.

His breathing was worsening again. I tried not to panic, but it was impossible to remain calm.

Fortunately, Dr. Patel meant it when she gave us permission to call her cell phone when she released Wesley from the hospital nearly two weeks before. She told us to call if Wesley worsened or if we had questions. Now he was getting worse, and we did have questions. Many questions.

We called her and she did her best to arrange a room for Wesley before we arrived at the hospital. She let them know we were coming and asked that he be admitted to the ICU. Wesley did not want Hunter to come with us, but it was late and we did not want to ask anyone to keep him for us. My mom had left a couple weeks earlier, when it looked as if Wesley were improving. She had been away from my dad for weeks, and we knew she needed to go home. We decided to take Hunter along because he was used to being with us, and he would rather be with us, in an emergency waiting room, than anywhere else without us.

I packed an overnight bag for Wesley, loaded up a spare oxygen tank in case his ran out while we waited for him to be admitted, and drove downtown, hoping we would not have to wait long for a room.

No such luck. We waited three hours. Each doctor who saw us asked the same questions, then left the room, looking perplexed by Wesley's case. Dr. Patel had assured us she would be in to see Wesley first thing in the morning unless he needed to be seen by her that night. She prescribed a higher dose of steroids to give his breathing the bump it needed to improve quickly until she could assess him in the morning and come up with a new plan.

Wesley and I both grew tired of answering the ER doctors' questions. I finally told the last doctor who came in to review Wesley's chart to come back in the morning and ask our doctor instead—we were done answering questions.

"Our son is tired, and I promise you there is nothing we can tell you tonight that is going to change what will be done for Wesley tomorrow. It's complicated. We know this. We also know and appreciate that this is a teaching hospital. Believe me, I want you to learn from my husband, but right now we are tired, and we need you to get us into a room," I told him, growing agitated with the doctor, even though I knew he was only doing his job.

"Happy to. It won't be long now," he replied.

Within fifteen minutes, Wesley was admitted and in his room for the night. I did not want to leave him, but we had made the decision to not let our son see Wesley in the ICU. I then took Hunter home and called my good friend Peggy to ask her to help with him in the morning so I could be at the hospital before the doctors did their morning rounds.

Dr. Patel could not explain why the blood thinners and steroids were not working. She did another chest X-ray, which looked the same: cloudy and impossible to use as a diagnostic tool. She did another CT scan. It also looked the same. His breathing had improved since she had bumped up his steroids the night before, but this was not a long-term solution; Wesley still required six to ten liters of oxygen at all times.

Within a few days, he stabilized. She sent him home and asked us to give him a little more time to recover from the injury to his lungs from the garage exposure. We agreed and went home, waiting for Wesley to get better.

I asked her to prescribe a pulsox machine we could use at home. She said she had never before done that; I told her I understood, but we needed to know if he was making progress. Just because it had not been done before did not mean it should not be done. She said she would do her best.

The insurance company denied her request, so I called them and asked to speak with a supervisor. I explained our plight.

"At times my husband requires more oxygen than what can be released through the nose cannula. Sometimes his life is in danger, and the next step beyond the oxygen provided at home is hospitalization and possible intubation. If you approve the pulsox machine for our home use, we can better limit his activities based on the information the pulsox provides. His oxygen levels could remain higher, and he would not be at such a high risk for complications at home. This, to me, sounds a lot less expensive for you than another trip to the ICU for a week at a time," I told her.

She agreed and a pulsox machine was delivered to our home the next day. Sometimes you just have to ask. When you do not get the answer you are seeking, state your case and ask again.

When the pulsox machine arrived, I created a chart for Wesley so he could keep track of his progress. I wanted him to see the numbers on the days he felt better, and I thought the chart could prove to him there were minor improvements, as well as pinpoint what caused his relapses. I hoped we could point to overexertion as a cause and limit his movement to keep his oxygen levels higher. I also hoped prolonged optimum oxygen levels would speed up his recovery.

Although he resisted, Wesley agreed to keep a journal of his numbers and rate how he felt according to the chart I made for him. After nearly two weeks of his charting numbers and levels of exertion, it was obvious to him he was not improving, but I refused to admit it.

I started keeping the log for him. After nearly two more weeks, I finally acknowledged to myself that Wesley was right. He was not getting better. All my prolonged charting had done was prove he was getting worse again. In addition, the high-dose steroids were making him incredibly moody. The shortness of breath did not help, but what we struggled with most was fearing the worst and not knowing what was causing his complications.

One night, Wesley was reading Hunter a bedtime story, as we often took turns doing. When he was done, he found me doing laundry and said to me, "He's ready for a kiss goodnight."

After I kissed Hunter good night, I did not see Wesley in the family room, so I went to our bedroom. He was sitting on the edge of the bed.

"What's the matter?" I asked him, concerned about his increased difficulty breathing.

"I could barely finish," he said, still trying to catch his breath.

"Finish what?"

"Finish reading the story. It was too hard to breathe and read at the same time," he answered, looking down at the floor, avoiding eye contact with me. He looked terrified.

I did not know what to say. I was also terrified. Too sick to read our son a bedtime story? What was happening to him?

By now it was August. His shortness of breath had begun in March; he was first hospitalized in April, then again in May and in July. Every time, he managed to stabilize, but there were still no answers. He had only been able to work two days in the past four months. He should not even have tried to do that, but he was determined to make himself better and to try to live his life as if he were getting better, but it was not working.

By the end of the summer, Wesley needed my help showering and getting dressed. He refused help for as long as he could, but he was not capable of doing it on his own without his oxygen dropping so low it took him longer to recover than to shower.

The first time I helped him I tried to rush through showering to get it done quickly, because there were so many other things I needed to do. I figured he would not complain and would just be glad it was getting done. When he stopped me more than once to show me how to do it his way, I was surprised at first. As time went on and he continued to need my help showering—because there was not a day he felt well enough to do it himself—I felt selfish for ever expecting him to settle for less than the way he wanted to be cleaned on a daily basis. The fact he even needed my help was hard enough on him without me making him feel as if he were inconveniencing me. I bought a bench to place in our shower and tried to make him as comfortable as I could.

Wesley was also having increased mood swings caused by the steroids. The smallest things that were part of everyday living would set him off. He would yell at me for the most insignificant reasons, only to apologize a few hours later.

Finally, one afternoon when Wesley yelled at me in front of Hunter because he could not find his slippers that should have been by the bed where he thought he had left them—then apologized later when he found them by his chair in the family room—I had had enough.

"I can take this from you because I understand it isn't who you are and it's the medicine that is making you this way, but Hunter doesn't understand. I don't need your apology right now, and I don't want your apology right now. The person you owe an apology to is Hunter," I firmly told him.

Without saying another word to me, he found Hunter in his room playing. I was standing nearby cleaning the bathroom and heard Wesley say, "I'm sorry I yelled, Buddy. I should not have yelled at Mommy like that and especially in front of you."

"Especially you shouldn't yell at Mommy," Hunter told him.

"I know, Buddy. I'm sorry," he apologized again, giving Hunter a hug.

"Give Mommy a hug, too," Hunter told him, pulling on Wesley's hand, leading him over to me.

Wesley hugged me and I forgave him again, but I knew as long as he was on steroids and sick without knowing why, I would be the person he felt safe venting to, and he would have to fight it out. It was not right, but it was not going to change. I could accept that as long as I could protect Hunter. It was not Hunter's job to protect me.

Preschool was starting for Hunter the following week. We had planned for him to go only two days a week, just as he had done the year before, but Hunter did not like his new teacher, Miss Michelle. He said she yelled at the kids a lot, and she was not nice to them. Hunter had always loved his school and was well beyond separation anxiety, so when he cried the first three times I dropped him off, I had to believe him when he told me why.

I did not care for his teacher either, but the only other option was to enroll Hunter in the Monday through Friday program in another teacher's class. I thought it might be too much time away from home for him. It was not until the latest outburst from Wesley, combined with Hunter crying again when I dropped him off at school the fourth day, that I decided to make the move.

While Hunter sat crying in Miss Michelle's class the fourth morning of the new school year, I walked down the hall to Miss Gayle's classroom. She was the teacher with the Monday through Friday class. I asked her if she had room for Hunter, and she said she would be happy to have him.

I left Miss Gayle's classroom and went to the school director's office to speak with her about moving Hunter out of Miss Michelle's class.

"I am and have always been supportive of this school and the teachers, but I do not feel Miss Michelle's classroom is the right place for Hunter at this time. He needs a place that he looks forward to going. Right now in his life there is enough stress at home that this has to be a safe, comfortable place for him," I explained.

She knew Wesley was sick and realized what a struggle it had been for our entire family. She agreed and said if Miss Gayle wanted to add Hunter to her classroom, he could be moved that very morning.

With that, I walked into Miss Michelle's classroom and told her Hunter would be switching to a five-day-a-week class. The teacher looked slightly confused, but also as if she knew why I was removing Hunter from her classroom. There had been other complaints from parents about the way she was treating the kids; I was just the only parent who was doing anything about it at that point. It is true Hunter probably would have settled into her classroom if I had given it more time, just as the rest of the kids in her classroom eventually would, but time was not a luxury we could afford when it came to Hunter's everyday happiness and stability at home or at school given our current circumstances.

When I took Hunter to Miss Gayle's classroom down the hall, she greeted him with a smile and open arms, and he never cried again when being dropped off at school.

That night, Wesley started his new routine of staying up late, as late as 2 a.m., so he would sleep until noon and have more energy when Hunter got home from school at 2 p.m. However much we did not want to admit it, we had a new life now and needed to make adjustments to it. We could not stop trying to fight whatever was slowly taking away the man I loved, but for Hunter's sake we had to accept our limitations and give him the best we could every moment we could.

The next day, after I finished helping Wesley shower, he was in the bathroom blowing his nose when he yelled for me to come to the bathroom. He sounded alarmed.

"Look at my nose! Look inside my nose!" he screamed.

I could see exactly what he was trying to show me. Most of the cartilage in the middle of his nose was gone. He stood there with Q-Tips inside each of his nostrils that he could touch together. So much of his nose was missing inside I was amazed the bridge had not collapsed.

"What is going on? What is happening to me?" he exclaimed.

"I don't know. I'll call the doctor. I'll call her now," I said and left the room to find the phone. I knew he was inconsolable.

I left Dr. Patel a message and got on the Internet to try to figure out if this was a side effect of steroids or what other possible explanation there could be. Trying to diagnose or gain understanding of Wesley's condition and symptoms by researching on the Internet was not always the best thing to do, but at times it had helped me gain a better understanding. This was one of those times.

I started reading about a disease called Wegener's Granulomatosis and discovered how loss of nose cartilage is a symptom. It was one of the diseases Dr. Patel had ruled out after she ran the first battery of tests on Wesley when we met her in May.

When Dr. Patel retuned my call later that morning, I told her what I had read and asked if we should revisit the possibility of Wegener's. Although it was a complicated disease and the prognosis could be grim, there were treatment options, and it could explain his disease process. She agreed to look into it and said she would call us back later that afternoon.

When she called back as promised, she had scheduled Wesley for an appointment for the following day with the ear, nose, and throat doctor in her building. The doctor would remove tissue from Wesley's nose and biopsy it to see if they could detect Wegener's. She explained the biopsy might be inconclusive, but it was a good place to start. She scheduled us for an appointment in her office for the day following the biopsy to discuss the results and take another chest X-ray to see if there had been any improvement in his lungs.

Wesley had the biopsy as scheduled. At our appointment with Dr. Patel, she told us the biopsy did not show Wegener's but it was possible the results could be a false negative. After looking at Wesley's X-ray results and assessing Wesley's condition based on what we told her, she concluded he had not improved and gave us the option of trying the treatment for Wegener's. She explained the treatment was a chemotherapy drug called Methotrexate. If it worked, we could hope for improvement within days to weeks, and long-term remission was possible. Treatment would have to continue until a year of remission had been achieved, but it could work and Wesley could make a full recovery.

Dr. Patel also made it clear if he did not have Wegener's, then the chemotherapy would not work and could make him worse. Given the many months of slow deterioration with no answers leading to another diagnosis or treatment option, we understood she was giving us hope and the option to try something that was a risk but could be worth it, so we agreed to the chemotherapy. She scheduled it for the following Tuesday morning.

When Tuesday came and it was almost time to leave for chemo, I remembered Tuesdays were the day I used to have chemo treatments. We took it as a good sign Wesley's chemo was on Tuesday at 9 a.m., just as mine had been. I survived. Maybe he would, too.

My mom was back with us by that time, so she took Hunter to preschool shortly before we were ready to leave for chemo. When she had arrived the week before, after spending time with my dad and visiting both of my grandmas in California, she had brought back several gifts from our friend Rod, wrapped in a cloth. Rod is a member of the Me-Wuk tribe of Indians, and he had given my mom, among other things, Blessing Sage for Wesley. It was not a typical practice in our home, but Rod had given me similar gifts when I had cancer, and each had given me comfort.

Wesley said he wanted to use the Blessing Sage before we left for the hospital, so as he stood outside in front of our house, I did what Rod had told me to do and circled Wesley with the smoke from the burning sage.

As the smoke surrounded Wesley, he said, "I believe this can be the answer for us. Chemo can help save me like it helped save you."

I continued to wave the sage around Wesley, and when he started to cough from the smoke because his lungs were so compromised, we laughed.

"We've done everything we know to do," he smiled, walking away from the smoke and toward the car. "The rest isn't up to us."

Neither of us said a word during the drive downtown to the hospital. We listened to Bob Seger and The Cure and silently said our separate prayers to God. Wesley was right; we had done everything we could do.

Wesley was stronger than I was and always had been. He was not easily shaken. The idea of chemo did not seem to scare him the way it scared me when I had cancer. If it did scare him, he did not show it. He was logical and knew we had little hope and few options; he would do whatever it took to save his life and preserve our family. So when the nurse started the chemo IV drip, he did not seem to care and played cards with me while we watched television.

The chemo infusion took about an hour. When it was over, Wesley stood up, thanked the nurse for her help and walked out of the hospital, hoping the medicine that might make him sicker would instead make him well.

Three days later, he was not any better. A week later, he was worse. Two weeks later Dr. Patel said if it were going to work, he should have improved by now. She said we should not continue chemo and risk him getting even sicker. We spent the next two days trying to get through the disappointment.

Then, three weeks after chemo, he got sick enough that he needed to be hospitalized again.

*

In our minds, we had absolute categories: the things that we were certain we could accept and the things that added up to more than we could bear. One of the things we tried to completely deny was the need for Flolan. This drug had first been recommended by the pulmonologist who performed Wesley's biopsy back in April. Now it was October, and Flolan was on the table again, only this time the recommendation was coming from Dr. Patel, whom we trusted and who had held as much hope as we did of finding other options. So far, there just were not any.

With Flolan came enormous responsibility. We would have to be visited by a home nurse who would teach us how to administer the medicine; we would not be cleared to begin using it until the nurse felt confident we could handle all it required. Our insurance also had to approve it, and the company providing the Flolan needed to give us a letter stating they guaranteed the ongoing supply of the drug even if we did not have health insurance for any reason in the future, because once Wesley started taking it, it could not be stopped.

Flolan is a lifetime therapy that requires uninterrupted infusion because of its short effect—three to five minutes, and it is incredibly expensive. If it worked for Wesley, Flolan would dilate blood vessels in his lungs and throughout his body. The drug would be administered intravenously directly into his bloodstream through a surgically implanted catheter by a battery-operated pump attached to a belt Wesley would wear around his waist or carry in a small shoulder pack. Since the drug's effect is so short, it must be infused constantly: it is slowly and continuously pumped into the body through a permanent catheter placed in a vein in the chest. The pump is filled daily with the mixed Flolan solution we had to prepare, which must be changed at the exact time each day. The drug requires special handling, including a constant, controlled temperature and protection from light.

There is no set dose. The dosage to be used would be based on the amount of relief it provided Wesley and his ability to handle Flolan's side effects. The dose would need to increase during his therapy to remain effective.

Side effects can include headache, flushing, jaw pain, nausea, diarrhea, and vomiting. Even a brief interruption of the drug infusion can be life-threatening and can result in a sudden reoccurrence of symptoms. The central IV line through which the pump delivers the Flolan requires methodical maintenance; infections can be serious.

Even with all that Flolan would require of us and the side effects Wesley would have to endure, we agreed to the medication and all that it implied. That is how desperate we were. We were told of numerous people with pulmonary hypertension who had responded well to this form of therapy. If Flolan worked for Wesley, he would not need oxygen prescribed, and he might be able to resume some of his normal activities, including reading Hunter a bedtime story and much more.

Nothing about our decision to go forward with Flolan felt like a hopeful option. It was not going to save him, and it might do more damage than good. It would change our lives and once it did, we could not go back.

Dr. Patel told us Wesley would be checked into the ICU and monitored closely as they began the Flolan titration.

"How do you determine when he has enough?" I asked.

Dr. Patel gave me a blunt answer. "When he can't take it anymore we will stop, give him time to adapt to it, send him home and try to increase the dosage over time."

Since Wesley's condition had not been diagnosed, yet all the more common lung diseases had been ruled out, we still did not know the primary cause of his symptoms. There was no way to know if Flolan would help him. Pulmonary hypertension is often a

primary cause for illness, but Wesley's pulmonary hypertension—
the measure of the pressure in his pulmonary artery—was considered secondary to whatever was causing it. Most people never
know their pulmonary pressure but a healthy pressure is between
fifteen and thirty. Wesley's was measured through his pulmonary
artery catheter, an invasive and complicated way to read the pressure; it was 112. Whatever was causing this high pressure was the
reason he could not walk from our living room to the kitchen without requiring up to ten liters of oxygen, then needing to rest and
recover before walking back to the living room.

Before Wesley could be admitted to the ICU, Dr. Patel arranged
for a home nurse to come to our house and teach us how to inventory, store, and administer the medication. There were several steps
to mixing it; any mistakes could cause an overdose and put Wesley's
life in danger. She told us what to do in an emergency and suggested we get a medical bracelet for Wesley in case he were ever
found unconscious for any reason, from a car accident to a complication of his illness, so the health care professionals would know he
was on Flolan. She explained that many nurses and even doctors
are not familiar with Flolan but would at least be aware of it being
prescribed to him and could find out how to care for him and for
the battery pack of medicine attached to his person.

By this time in Wesley's illness, he was no longer driving, because
there was nowhere he could go on his own. He could not get in
and out of the car without my help or walk far enough even with
oxygen to make an outing on his own realistic. There were times
when he stayed home alone for short periods of time, so we ordered
a medical bracelet and signed the papers she brought showing we
agreed to the medication and to the risk involved when taking it.

After she taught us all we needed to know to responsibly take
care of Wesley on Flolan, she cleared us for the medication. She

said it usually took a few visits to a home to train patients and their caregivers in how to use the medicine before she signed off that the patient was ready, but she cleared us after two hours.

"You guys know what you are doing and seem to know what you may be in for," she told us.

I did not mind her being so direct. We needed direct.

A few days later, Wesley was admitted to the ICU. Wesley was a strong man, physically and mentally, so seven hours into the titration of Flolan, when he told me, "I'm done. Make them stop," I believed him.

I told the doctors to stop. He had had all he could take.

He went home two days later. Our lives were changed—limited and complicated by the medicine. The doctors told us to chart his progress from day to day, not knowing I had already reprinted my blank progress reports from months before. They seemed convinced he would respond to the Flolan over time because of the testing they did at the onset of the medication.

So we waited. We waited for any improvement at all. While we waited, we prayed for progress. I took little time to consider what we would do if the medicine did not work because I knew we were running out of options. I was too afraid to consider what would become of Wesley if the Flolan failed to help him return to a quality of life recognizable to both of us.

Waiting can be the hardest part.

CHAPTER FOUR

Call an Ambulance

When I was twenty-four years old, my family doctor—the man who had delivered both my brother Vance and me—told me I had cancer. He looked me in the eye and told me that my family should pray for Hodgkin's disease because, based on the tests he ran, I had advanced lymphoma, either Hodgkin's or non-Hodgkin's, and the latter was much more difficult to treat. I remember thinking how very sad it was that the best we could hope for was a better kind of cancer.

When Wesley and I agreed to Flolan, I felt the same way. Wesley, only thirty-four years old, was fighting a monster inside of his body not even the top specialists could diagnose. And the best we could hope for was a positive response to a medicine that, even if it worked, would be limiting and debilitating. At least when I had cancer we had a diagnosis and a treatment. By now, I knew my own suffering and illness did not compare in magnitude to Wesley's. I had stopped trying to understand what he was going through—a thirty-four-year-old man facing what could be the end of his life, without a physical explanation of why. We still did not know what was causing his body to deteriorate so quickly. We might never know.

When he first became sick, I thought that because of what I had experienced myself, I was especially able to offer Wesley support. I believed I could be understanding and empathetic in a way that would make a difference, but I soon realized I could not. Two distinct differences between Wesley's and my illnesses existed: first, I was diagnosed within an hour of my biopsy with one of the most treatable forms of cancer, while Wesley still did not have a diagnosis. Second, from the day I started treatment, I began to get better. Wesley was not getting better. Most of the time, he was getting worse.

It had been a week since Wesley started taking Flolan. He had improved slightly since starting the medication, but he still needed ten liters of constant oxygen through his nose. He was not struggling quite as much with the simple task of walking across a room, and he was able to read a short bedtime story to Hunter again. With eight to ten liters of oxygen, his blood oxygen levels were reaching 97 to 99 a few times a day, a few days in a row—when at rest, but if he tried to walk across the room, his oxygen levels would quickly fall to the mid eighties. For a person with normal lung function, this would be a drastic hit to the body's functions and abilities, but not for Wesley, because by now his body was used to functioning on considerably less oxygen than the average person.

After he recovered from the hospital stay, Wesley tried to walk on our treadmill. He even started using the progress charts I had created to track his progress when he first got sick, months before. He could not walk faster than one mile per hour, and even at that pace he could not walk longer than three minutes at a time. He wrote it down the first day and the second, but when he did not improve on the third day, I saw him quietly put the progress chart in a kitchen drawer, go to our bedroom and shut the door.

It seemed there was one hurdle after another. Wesley told me he was experiencing blurred vision, but had a hard time describing it.

"I can see everything around you clearly, but your face is blurry," Wesley told me.

We decided to see if his vision would improve over the next couple days before calling Dr. Patel. The next night, I was watching one of my favorite television dramas, *ER*. Bob Newhart was a guest star playing a heart patient who was taking a drug called Digoxin. Wesley was taking the same medication for his heart failure.

During one of the scenes, the camera showed the view from Bob Newhart's character's perspective. He was looking at his doctor and she was blurry, but everything around her was clear. I was recording the show in case I was interrupted and would need to finish watching it later, so when the scene was over, I asked Wesley to come watch it with me and played it again so he could see it.

"That's it! That's exactly how things look to me!" Wesley exclaimed, relieved for an explanation.

Bob Newhart's character was experiencing an overdose of Digoxin. The doctor on the show referred to it as an oculotoxic effect, which caused generalized blurry vision as well as seeing a halo around each point of light.

I called Dr. Patel and explained Wesley's symptoms and what we had just watched on *ER*. She told us to go in for a blood draw the next morning to check his "dig" levels, as she called it.

Sure enough, Wesley's were at a toxic level, so she immediately adjusted his medication and his symptoms eased within two days. Who knew we could learn from a television drama?

Wesley still had stitches where the catheter for the Flolan medication had been placed. The area surrounding the stitches was red and felt warm to the touch. I suspected an infection, so I called Dr. Patel. She asked me to take him to the hospital immediately. Wesley was in constant danger of infection from the catheter because he had high pulmonary pressure. She feared an infection in the catheter line could cause him critical, life-threatening harm.

By now, we had been to the ER numerous times. Every doctor we had met during the months of Wesley's illness, particularly those in the ER, was fascinated by his case. Often when we arrived at the hospital, Wesley's oxygen levels were visibly compromised. His lips were purple and his now slender extremities were pale blue and showed poor circulation. Honestly, sometimes he looked dead.

The doctors were interested in the case, but they did not always understand how to treat him. During two of our past visits to the ICU—where his blood gases were always taken through the arterial vein in his wrist, for accuracy—the doctors had determined the dosage of his blood thinning medication was too high. They said he needed plasma to quickly reverse the effects of the medication, because he was in danger of internal hemorrhaging.

On those ICU visits he had received plasma, a blood product used to thicken his blood. The first time he received it, he crashed. His oxygen quickly fell into the low seventies and the ICU nurse had to give him an oxygen mask with a fifteen-liter flow along with the nose cannula of ten liters he constantly needed even when at rest.

While the ICU doctors waited for him to improve, they suggested he might need to be put on a ventilator to help him breathe. They said it would be temporary, just until he recovered from this episode, but I resisted the idea. I had read about people with severe lung disease who were not able to be weaned off a ventilator once being put on it. Instead, I could see Wesley was shivering and deduced he was struggling with the cold temperature of the plasma. I thought the cold plasma was likely causing his compromised breathing, so we covered him with warm blankets—and he recovered rather quickly, his oxygen returning to the high eighties from the low seventies.

Because of this experience, the second time he needed plasma I insisted the nurse titrate it slowly to avoid another crashing episode and cover him again with warm blankets. Wesley did not like it when I gave the nurses instructions, but my suggestion worked, and we narrowly escaped another crashing episode. His oxygen remained in the eighties that time, and there was no threat of Wesley needing a ventilator.

Even something as routine as a transfusion was not simple for him—but we did not have the luxury of time to contemplate alternatives. With Wesley at risk for brain bleeds and other serious complications from a common blood-thinning medication, we only had one option. We had to do whatever was necessary to save him on that day, to try to keep him alive until we could find a way to turn this around.

This time, in late October, when we arrived at the hospital to determine if Wesley had an infection in his catheter line, he was doing quite well. His oxygen levels were in the high nineties at rest, so Dr. Patel called ahead and asked the ER doctor to admit him to a regular room until it could be decided what to do about his catheter line. For the first time since the biopsy in April, there was no need for the ICU when being admitted to the hospital.

It was a Friday evening and most specialty doctors had left for the weekend. The interventional radiologists were not around to surgically move the catheter line, so Dr. Patel asked Wesley to stay until Saturday. She was out of town, but she ordered his blood to be drawn twice. Although his white count—the blood level often measured to determine if the body is fighting infection—was slightly elevated, she wanted to see if removing the stitches would remedy the mild infection without the need for another invasive procedure.

The stitches were removed, and until a decision could be made about Wesley's catheter line, the doctor caring for Wesley in Dr. Patel's place moved his Flolan medication from the catheter line to a vein in his arm. I knew this was not an ideal solution. Flolan should be administered through an arterial line, but I trusted the doctor knew what he was doing. I figured one night would not hurt him. I would watch him closely in the hospital and be able to get help quickly if needed.

We had planned to take Hunter to the children's museum downtown on Saturday. We were trying to make sure to the best of our abilities that Hunter was able to do the things we had always done as a family. Wesley asked me to take Hunter without him. I rarely left Wesley in the hospital alone, and I felt even more reluctant to do so since he was on Flolan and staying in a regular room without the constant monitoring he usually received while staying in the ICU, but I did as he asked. My mom and I took Hunter to the museum as we had promised.

That Saturday, his white count was the same: not better, but not worse. In Dr. Patel's absence, a young resident from Florida State University was overseeing Wesley's care, so I called him Dr. Florida (but never to his face). He was inexperienced, which made me nervous because Wesley's condition was critical even when he was not being admitted to the ICU. Dr. Florida assured me he would let me know when he heard from the radiologist about Wesley's catheter line and said nothing would be done until I returned later in the afternoon.

While at the museum, I had a bad feeling in my stomach. I was more worried than usual, and I could not shake the feeling something bad was about to happen to Wesley. I called Dr. Florida, and he was happy to talk with me. He told me Wesley was doing fine and was even resting comfortably, sleeping in his hospital room.

I asked if a decision had been made to move the catheter in case of infection, or if infection had been ruled out and the line could be used again. I voiced my concerns about Flolan needing an arterial line.

What happened next explained the sinking, frightening feeling I had in the pit of my stomach.

"Tell you what. This is what I was thinking I'd do," Dr. Florida said. "Why don't I put in orders to stop the Flolan until Monday? That way, we don't have to worry about infection or make a decision without the radiologist, and we can decide what to do when the other doctors return on Monday."

There was not a hint of hesitation in his voice. Dr. Florida was completely serious.

"I'll tell you what," I replied with steel in my voice. "Why don't you hang up the phone, find your superior, and tell him exactly what you just told me about my husband's Flolan medication. Tell him I said I will be there in twenty minutes, and nobody should touch my husband before I get there. And while you wait for me, read up on Flolan."

"I don't understand," said Dr. Florida, the idiot.

"Just don't touch him. I'm on my way," I insisted and hung up the phone.

We immediately left the museum. Within five minutes Wesley called me.

"What did you do?" Wesley asked curtly. I could tell he was angry, assuming I had upset the doctors by being too forceful.

"Why?" I asked him, not sure if he knew what had just happened with Dr. Florida.

"Because I was sleeping and all of a sudden there were three doctors in my room. They said you had called, and they're waiting in the hallway for you to arrive," he exclaimed, angry about my interference.

"Don't get mad at me!" I snapped. "Dr. Florida, the damn idiot, thought it would be a good idea to stop your Flolan until he could get an answer from a real doctor on Monday. If I had not prevented him, some nurse would have come into your room while you were sleeping and stopped your Flolan without you even knowing it, and you would have been dead in five minutes!"

"What?" he yelled. Now he was upset, too.

"Yes, there you are in a regular room with no monitors and no one would have known your heart just stopped. So don't yell at me!"

When I arrived at the hospital, Dr. Florida's superior was there to smooth things over with us. He apologized profusely and assured us that they would have an answer within the hour from Dr. Patel and the radiologist who was on call.

Dr. Florida asked to speak with me.

"I'm so sorry," he apologized. "I had no idea."

"Today I decided to take our son to the museum because I figured Wesley would be safe here for just a few hours," I told him, beginning to illustrate how complicated even a simple outing with our son had become.

"I understand," Dr. Florida started to interrupt.

"No, you don't," I continued, cutting him off. "You can't possibly understand. You are going to meet a thousand more wives like me in your career, and you need to remember this day for as long as you are a doctor. This man is no longer your patient. He is my husband, and he's Hunter's father. There is no room for mistakes. He's got too far to fight to come back from even the simplest setback, let alone from cutting off the medication you should know his life depends on."

"I'm so sorry."

"I accept your apology, but you still aren't taking care of Wesley.

You're not ready. This is as simple as knowing and understanding the medication your patient is taking."

I left Dr. Florida standing in the hallway, and I never saw him again.

While waiting for a response from the radiologist and Dr. Patel, Dr. Florida's attending physician made the decision to move the Flolan from Wesley's arm back into the catheter line, realizing it never should have been moved.

Wesley's white count had not returned to normal by Saturday afternoon, so the radiologist on call came in and moved Wesley's catheter line to the other side of his chest. He said we could go home the next morning, but in the morning the incision site was still slightly bleeding when it should not have been, so the radiologist came back to the hospital to repair it, and Wesley was released Sunday afternoon.

Two days later, repeat blood tests showed a normal white count. There was no longer an infection.

After that stay in the hospital, Wesley told me he wanted Hunter to sleep with us.

"I want us to be together as much as we can," he shared. "When I can't sleep, I want to be able to see you both in our bed."

I agreed without question.

The high-dose steroids made it difficult for Wesley to sleep; by now he was sleeping sitting up with pillows propped behind his back and head to help him breathe more comfortably. He was in early congestive heart failure, so he was also taking diuretics to try to eliminate some of the fluid buildup on his heart and lungs.

The pills made him urinate frequently. I bought a plastic urinal container with a lid for him to use, to help him avoid the difficulty of getting out of bed during the night when he needed to use the bathroom. I had bought it at the same time as the bench for the shower, but he had refused to use it then. He finally started using it a few nights after starting the water pills. This was another concession that was not easy for him—but he was learning to choose his battles and allow for a few conveniences.

It was still October. We were nearing two weeks with Flolan, but after the first week there was no noticeable improvement. By the third week in October, Wesley was starting to feel worse again. His breathing was more labored, and he was back to barely being able to walk across the room. The Flolan had ruined his appetite, and he was losing weight more quickly than before. I did everything I could to make him more comfortable, but nothing worked. He was miserable, and it was heartbreaking to watch.

The morning of the last day of the third week after starting Flolan, Wesley called to me from our bedroom.

"Lisa!" he yelled.

We used Hunter's baby monitor to help us communicate on the days Wesley was too ill to get out of bed. We had started a code between us, because it was so difficult for him to yell for me and not lose his breath his calls to me always sounded urgent. Our code was that he called out "Honey" when it was not urgent, and he just needed me to come to our bedroom when I finished doing whatever I was doing. He yelled "Lisa" when he needed me right away.

When I heard him yell for me by name, I was playing with Hunter in his bedroom.

"Wait right here, Hunter, while I go check on Daddy."

Hunter stayed in his room, and I walked quickly toward our bedroom door. I was almost afraid to open it. From one morning to the next, we never knew how Wesley was going to feel. Some days he could manage to participate in our family life, and other days he could barely get out of bed. Waking up to a new day brought more fear than hope.

When I opened our bedroom door, I saw Wesley sitting on the edge of our bed trying to catch his breath. His ankles were horribly swollen due to heart failure, and his lips were purple.

I shut the door behind me as I waited for Wesley to speak. I did not want Hunter to see his dad this way.

"I need you to listen to me. I need you to listen to me and not panic." He said it calmly, but I was already starting to panic, not knowing what he was going to say.

"Okay, I'm listening."

"You need to call someone to pick up Hunter, and get him out of here."

"Okay, I'll call Christi," I told him, still trying not to show my fear.

"After Hunter leaves, you need to call an ambulance."

He had never asked for an ambulance before.

"Because I'm going to die today."

CHAPTER FIVE

Second Look

I stood frozen. I tried to move, but I could not. I tried to speak, but no words would come out of my mouth. Tears began to well up in my eyes.

"Don't cry. There is no time to cry. Just call Christi to pick up Hunter and do what I ask," Wesley quietly insisted.

I looked deep into his tired green eyes and touched his right shoulder with my left hand. With every breath he struggled to take, I considered what this moment must feel like for him. How incredibly frightened he must be if he was willing to call an ambulance—but at the same time how incredibly honorable he remained, still making Hunter his number one concern.

I stood in front of him, still unable to speak.

"Please. Go." Wesley asked me, so I did.

I called Christi, and she quickly came to pick up Hunter. Wesley called Hunter into our bedroom before he left.

"I love you, Buddy," Wesley told him. "You be good for your mommy."

"But I'm not going with Mommy; I'm going with Miss Christi!"

Hunter said, as he giggled at his daddy.

Then Hunter kissed him goodbye and happily left our house with Christi.

I waved to Hunter from the front door. I knew what Wesley meant when he told Hunter to be good for me, even if Hunter did not understand. His dad feared he might not make it back from the hospital this time.

When the ambulance arrived, we explained to the two medics that we needed to be taken to the medical center downtown. I told them I had already called Wesley's pulmonologist, and the ER was waiting for him and would immediately admit him to the ICU.

The medics were very kind but said they could not take us downtown because they were required to take us to the nearest hospital.

"But the nearest hospital is where all of this began. They won't know what to do with him and will eventually have to transport him downtown. We don't have time for that," I explained to the medics.

Again, they kindly told us they could not take us anywhere but the nearest hospital because they could not risk being liable for what might happen to Wesley in the time it took them to drive him to the medical center downtown.

"Isn't there something you can do to help us?" I pleaded.

They looked at the pulsox machine again and saw his oxygen was in the low eighties at rest.

"Is his oxygen usually this low?" one of the medics asked me.

"Sometimes, but not usually when at rest," I answered.

"Can you sustain this oxygen level at rest long enough for your wife to drive you downtown?" he asked, trying to access the level of immediate danger Wesley was in.

He had been directing most of his conversation toward me so

Wesley could save his energy, but he wanted Wesley to answer this question for himself.

"I think I can, if nothing changes," Wesley assured him.

"Are you refusing to go with us to the nearest hospital?" the other medic pressed.

"If that's what we need to do, then we are refusing your help," I answered. I knew he needed us to refuse their help before he could offer any other suggestions. "Now can you help us?"

"We can help you load him up, put at least three tanks in the car with you in case you hit traffic, and you can drive him directly to the medical center," the other medic told us. "If he gets into trouble, don't try to find a hospital, just pull over, park on the shoulder of the freeway, and call 911."

The two men loaded three oxygen tanks in the car and helped Wesley into the passenger seat. Before closing the car door, they wished us luck and sent us on our way.

Fortunately, there was no traffic that morning and nothing happened en route. When we arrived at the hospital, Dr. Patel had already given orders to have Wesley immediately admitted to the ICU. Even so, no matter how many times we had shown up at the ER since April, we were still met with questions and chaos. I had learned how to minimize the wait time by insisting they refer to his chart for the answers to their questions and admit us to the ICU as Dr. Patel had requested. By now, we had visited the ER nearly a half dozen times in the past six months and had grown tired of the process.

As much as we tried to maintain a balance in our lives that was not always about fighting for Wesley's life, it was proving nearly impossible. If only he could breathe, maybe we could have denied how sick he was, at least some of the time. Wesley wanted normalcy as much or more than I did. The previous week, when he was feeling good, he had grilled dinner for us two nights in a row. He played music loudly from the family room into the kitchen while he cooked and hugged me tightly on his way out the door to our patio. He stood in one place near Hunter's swing set and pushed him on the swing for as long as he could manage to breathe comfortably. He stood by the tub while I bathed Hunter and talked to both of us instead of sitting in the living room resting on the overstuffed chair he could never quite get comfortable in. He set a Wiffle ball on Hunter's T-Ball tee for him while Hunter practiced hitting the ball. Wesley could not chase or catch the ball for Hunter, but he did his part for as long as Hunter was willing to do his.

He also insisted on walking Hunter to his preschool class one day, even though I was certain he would not be able to make it without fainting, or worse.

"I haven't even been able to see his classroom yet this year," Wesley told me, trying to convince me that was enough of a reason for him to compromise his health and walk Hunter to class.

"But it's at the very end of the second hall and you won't be able to keep up with Hunter even with extra oxygen," I argued. "And I know you. You won't stop to catch your breath because you won't want anyone to see you struggling."

"I'm doing it," he insisted, as he got in the car with me to take Hunter to school.

I was the first one to encourage Wesley to remain positive and do what he was capable of doing on a daily basis, but this was different. He was in danger of irreversible consequences caused by walking Hunter to class, and I could not bear the thought of him fainting or having a heart attack just because he was too stubborn to heed his limitations.

He did walk Hunter to his classroom. When he came back to

the car where I was waiting for him, his face was pale white, his lips were purple, he was shaking and struggling considerably to catch his breath.

"I… Did… It…" he managed to say to me.

Just six months before, Wesley had been coaching Hunter's first year of T-Ball and reveling in fatherhood. I recorded him on our video camera the night he called each parent to introduce himself as their child's new coach. He went to the YMCA every day for a week to get the updated list of parents' names and phone numbers to call, so he could welcome each child and parent to the team. He even bought baseball pants for every kid on the team. He did not want anyone to feel bad about not being able to afford them, so he just bought pants for everyone.

When he first got sick and could no longer coach the team, Wesley would leave thirty minutes before Hunter and me to attend the games, because he needed to be able to walk and rest for as long as it took to get to the ball field on Saturday morning. When he quickly got worse and could not walk to the field anymore, he had to stop attending Hunter's games. He was not yet ready to accept the wheelchair then.

The morning of the first game Wesley would have to miss, I forgot my keys. I ran back inside the house to get them and saw Wesley in our bedroom. He was quietly crying as he looked out the window at Hunter already buckled up in his car seat. I started to walk toward him, but he raised his hand as if to say, "Stop."

"He'll be late. He can't be late," Wesley insisted, more worried about Hunter than himself.

I left him there, knowing there was absolutely nothing I could do or say. The only thing he needed I could not provide. He needed to be able to breathe.

Most of us take the simple, involuntary bodily function of

breathing for granted from the moment we are born. For him it was a constant struggle and a reminder of everything he was not able to do, and even more, what he was not able to be—fully and completely engaged in our family.

Wesley had always wanted a son. The day we had the ultrasound and found out we were having a boy is when it all began for him. I did not really want to know the sex of our baby in advance, but he so badly wanted a son he felt he needed a little time to prepare if we were having a girl. I assured him it would not matter at the moment the baby was born, or in any moment after, but he needed to know. He promised me the next baby could be a surprise, so I agreed.

During the ultrasound, when the doctor told us the baby was a boy, Wesley literally jumped up and down in the doctor's office. Tears welled up in his eyes. He was elated (I was just trying not to pee).

We had already agreed he could name our son (within reason) and I would name our daughter, if we had one. That week he started looking through the baby name book. Page by page he skimmed, looking for the name that made the most sense for our son.

Each evening he looked through the book, one page at a time, then marked where he left off. He called out a few names he had never heard of and commented on how sad it was parents gave their children such ridiculous names.

By the end of the week, Wesley was still looking through the baby name book, as he had every evening. I was in the kitchen making dinner, and he was in the family room. One letter of the alphabet at a time, he slowly made his way to the letter H.

"Is Hunter a name?" he called out to me.

"It is," I answered.

"That's it," he proclaimed. He closed the book, set it down on the table next to him and never opened it again.

Wesley was an avid fisherman and hunter. He loved spending time outdoors and was driven by the time in between. Hunter's name was never going to be anything else.

From the start, from the moment Wesley knew of our pregnancy, he was present. He was actively involved. He was doing his best to replicate what he knew of his own father and stepdad that seemed to work and leave behind what did not.

On this day, when Wesley woke up convinced he would not survive another day—and his first thought was to get Hunter out of the house so he would not see him leave in an ambulance—I was reminded of the man I married. My husband was not the man who was sick and angry at the world because he could not breathe; steroids and Flolan were making him miserable. This was the man I loved, the father of our child, who in the face of everything, dealing with the reality of being incapable of even the natural yet complicated task of breathing, was still looking out for us. He was putting us first.

More than anything, I wanted to fix what was broken inside of him. I wanted to bring him back to the day when breathing was as easy for him as it was for me, but I could not. Instead, I answered the ER doctor's questions and told Dr. Patel what Wesley had said to me about dying that day.

I kept recalling the sight of our son leaving the house that morning without a care in the world—not knowing his dad believed he might never see him again. Two months before, when Wesley had been hospitalized because he caught a cold that his body could not manage to fight efficiently, Hunter overheard me telling my friend Peggy that Wesley caught a bug but was finally starting to feel better. The next day I heard Hunter tell his friend Natalie, Peggy's daughter, his dad swallowed a fly—his four-year-old interpretation of what he had heard me say.

As the doctors drew Wesley's blood to check his blood gases, a new doctor in the unit started asking me the questions the rest of the doctors knew I no longer answered. I respected this was a teaching hospital and Wesley was a fascinating case, but he was also my husband. Every minute they spent asking me questions when he was being admitted to the ICU took away time they could spend finding a way to help him breathe better and relieve some of our anxiety and terror.

"His breathing is significantly compromised," the new doctor informed me.

"Yes, it is. It always is," I responded politely.

"What do you attribute to this onset of complications?" he questioned.

"With all due respect, we keep concise notes. We are compliant and diligent in our efforts to know what sets off an episode and what doesn't, but the truth is he is very sick and no one seems to know why," I informed him, already exhausted by the line of questioning.

"I understand," he replied.

No, he didn't.

If I had had an accurate diagnosis from every doctor who did not understand but told me he or she did, Wesley would have been healed by then, or we would at least know why he could not be.

When Wesley was settled into his room and resting more comfortably, I started to leave to call Peggy to check on Hunter. Peggy was helping us with Hunter until my mom could return the following week.

"Can you wait to call?" Wesley asked.

"Yeah. What's wrong?" I asked, confused by his request.

"Is Dr. Patel still in the building?" he wanted to know.

"She already left. She said she would check in on us tomorrow."

"I think we need to talk with her about another biopsy. I don't know how much longer I can last like this," Wesley ventured, knowing his suggestion would be met with considerable opposition.

"That's not an option," I insisted, caught off guard.

"It's always been an option," Wesley reminded me.

"But she told us you might not survive another biopsy, and it isn't worth the risk because the results would likely be inconclusive," I argued, not wanting to even consider a procedure that could do him any further harm.

"I know, but not surviving the biopsy is no different from the way I am living now. This isn't living, and there is no end in sight."

"But your dad. He didn't survive his biopsy, and you are much sicker than he was."

"I can't not know anymore," Wesley said, looking me straight in the eye, letting me know he was very seriously considering a second biopsy.

"But knowing may not change the outcome," I protested. I was not willing to risk losing Wesley to a dangerous procedure just to find out what might eventually kill him.

"If I have the biopsy, then at least we know we did everything we could to find out and fix whatever is wrong with me," Wesley explained, accepting the risk.

"But it doesn't change anything. They've tried everything. You may just be moving all of this along too quickly," I said, standing my ground.

"There is nothing about this that is moving along quickly. It's a slow and miserable existence. It's not fair to Hunter or to you." It was clear Wesley was feeling more and more like a burden on us.

"Don't worry about us. I can take care of us," I assured him, never wanting him to make a decision like this based on how long

I could endure his ongoing illness. "This is about our family and we aren't a family without you."

"Then it's not fair to me," he pleaded. I could hear in his voice how weary he had become. He was growing tired of the fight.

"But I can take care of you, too."

"You are taking care of me. I can't even dress myself anymore. I'm peeing in a urinal next to our bed. I can't make love to my wife. I can't read a bedtime story to my son. Everything that makes us who we are is slipping away, and if this is how I am going to go out, then I feel like I need to know what it is inside of me that is going to force me to leave you and Hunter. Don't you think it's important to know?" he pressed. He wanted me to think beyond what we were living with everyday and consider how knowing what was making him sick might help us move forward, even if he did not survive the biopsy.

"It doesn't change anything. It's not worth knowing to me," I resisted.

My mind could not be changed. The biopsy was a risk I was not willing to take. By now, I was in tears, sitting on the edge of his hospital bed. Wesley was holding my hand.

"When you had cancer, we did what we had to do so we would always know we did everything we could to save you," Wesley said, trying to appeal to me.

"This is different. I was always getting better. You wouldn't have wanted me to take this risk," I insisted.

"You're right. I wouldn't have wanted you to, but I would have let you decide." He was determined to make me see things his way. "You have to let me decide. I have to know you're okay with it."

I was silent. I could not give him what he wanted. Not yet. I was not ready.

"How long have you been thinking about a second biopsy?" I

questioned him. It was obvious this had been on his mind for a while.

"Since last night, when I started feeling worse again."

"So you've had a day to think about this?" I asked.

"Yes," he quickly answered.

"Then please give me the same. We can talk to Dr. Patel about it when she comes tomorrow, but let me have another day to think about it," I begged him.

"That's fair, but you need to know, this is what I have decided, and I need you to get behind me on it," he finally agreed, but under the condition I know he expected my full support at the end of the day.

I told him I would be back after calling to check on Hunter and walked quickly to the empty waiting room. I was shaking with fear. I prayed for a solution that would save both of us from choosing something we could not take back. I did not know how to give Wesley what he was asking of me. I had an overwhelming feeling if he had the second biopsy, he would die during or soon after the procedure. I feared the results would come back—after his death—as "idiopathic," giving us no answers. Even if, without a diagnosis, Wesley only had months left to live, I knew I could not be part of a decision to end his life any sooner, even for the sake of understanding what was killing him slowly. I was not capable of giving up any of the time Hunter and I had left with Wesley.

I knew I could not agree to the biopsy, and one more day to think about it was not going to change my mind. It would have to be his decision, but I prayed another day would bring an alternative, even if it was just Wesley changing his mind.

The next morning, Wesley was still adamant about wanting the biopsy. He felt it was his decision to make. Although he gave me the option to speak my mind, he could not promise my opinion would change anything. He told me he wanted the procedure sooner rather than later. He did not want to spend another day not knowing what was so terribly wrong with him.

I got to the hospital early enough to give Wesley a sponge bath before Dr. Patel made her rounds in the morning. It was a struggle to bathe him in the ICU, not just because it was time-consuming and did not give him the relief a real shower did, but because he was not even well enough to bathe. Every step of our well-orchestrated effort was plagued with his struggles to manage the limits of oxygen deprivation. His skinny legs were blue. His lips were purple. His enlarged heart was breaking.

"I'm not letting you talk me out of this," he told me as I washed his backside. "You need to let people know."

I did not argue with him. There was no point in arguing.

When I finished bathing him, I left the room to call Hunter before he left for preschool, and started making the other calls Wesley had asked me to make to our family and a few close friends.

I stood in the parking lot and called his best friend Mike. I told him what Wesley wanted to do and explained I had no choice but to let him.

Mike is a strong man whose troubled life had hardened him to most things and most people, but never to Wesley or to me. They were misfits and opposites in high school, but Mike had a difficult home life and lived with Wesley and his family in times of trouble. Their differences did not matter; they were like brothers, and he loved us like we were his family. Watching Wesley suffer this way was breaking his heart. Other than his own children, there was no one Mike loved more than Wesley.

"What will happen to him?" Mike asked.

"He'll probably die," I answered, holding back my tears.

Mike started to cry and was silent for a few minutes.

"I will let you know when the biopsy is scheduled, if you want to see him," I told him, sensing he wanted to get off the phone.

"Okay… Okay," Mike said, hanging up the phone in tears.

When I hung up the phone, I stood in the parking lot for a few more minutes. I could see Wesley's hospital window. I could not see him, but I knew he was in there, watching television, trying to eat breakfast despite his lack of appetite and, as always, trying to breathe.

After calling my parents and Wesley's, I went back inside and sat in the waiting room for a few minutes before going back into Wesley's room. Dr. Patel saw me sitting on the couch before walking into the ICU, so she sat down next to me and asked me what was wrong. I told her Wesley wanted a second biopsy and shared his reasons why. She understood his need to know what was causing his illness, but she explained again it might be inconclusive, and he probably would not survive it.

We walked to Wesley's room together, and she repeated her explanation of why a second biopsy was not a good idea.

"We could open you up and find nothing more than we did the first time, but with your severely high pulmonary pressure, even if you survived the procedure, it is unlikely that you would recover enough to be taken off the ventilator after surgery. Your lungs couldn't recover. You might never breathe on your own again," Dr. Patel explained.

"What is the other possibility?" Wesley asked.

"That we go in and find what is wrong and come up with a way to treat it that we have not yet tried," she firmly replied. "But, again, it's not likely and not worth the risk to you."

"How long can I go on like this? How long until I am brought in here as I was yesterday and die without an explanation of why?" he asked her, knowing he could not live this way much longer.

"There is no way to know that," she answered, unwilling to level with him about how right he might be.

"Dr. Patel, you and I both know each time I come in here, I am getting worse. It's only a matter of time before I don't make it through one of these episodes," Wesley responded, growing frustrated with Dr. Patel.

Wesley was even better than I was at convincing anyone about anything he wanted to do. That is what scared me most.

"I hadn't mentioned this to you yet, because I am not sure it will make a difference, but tomorrow I'm taking part in a two-day conference here with several leading pulmonologists from around the world. I am presenting your case to them," Dr. Patel explained.

An answered prayer.

"Consider giving me until tomorrow to see what we come up with. Then we can revisit a second biopsy," she negotiated. I hoped she had a plan in place that would help us avoid a second biopsy. Even if she did not, at least she was stalling and giving Wesley time to reconsider.

Wesley was determined to have the biopsy. I could not figure out if he wanted it so badly because he needed to know what he was fighting against—or if he was doing it to give up the fight. I am not sure he knew either. He just knew he did not want to live like this any longer. I wanted him to live, so I was selfishly willing to let him continue to suffer, as long as he was still alive. I did not want to know what was wrong with him if it meant he would not be here when I found out.

At this pivotal time, after enduring six months of confusion, catastrophe, and anguish, all I could do was pray tomorrow would bring us what we had lacked for so very long—answers.

CHAPTER SIX

The Decision

That night in the hospital, Wesley and I talked in detail about the possibility of the biopsy and the reality he probably would not survive it. Through our conversation, I was beginning to understand his reasons for wanting it. I could see what it represented to him: He was taking control and making decisions. For the first time in months, he was having a say about what was and was not going to happen to him. He knew he was dying. I think it scared him more to die in an ambulance on the way to the nearest hospital than to opt for this surgery and take a chance we would get some answers and a more controlled outcome. I do not know if I would have made the same choice, but I knew I needed to give him what he was fighting for—some sort of closure to an experience he had never expected to endure.

As he talked, I listened. He told me what he wanted if he died. He told me he wanted to be cremated and described where he wanted his ashes to be spread. He told me he loved me and thanked me for all I had done for him since becoming his wife and the mother of his only child. He told me to be strong—he knew I could get through everything if I held on to what Hunter needed.

I felt numb. I wanted to stop him from telling me these things because I did not want to admit the likelihood of his eminent death, his nearing departure. Simultaneously, I wanted to respond to him, to reply, to say the words he may have needed to hear. My head was spinning with uncertainty during Wesley's intermission of clarity.

People who have never been through watching a loved one die, while fighting for every last hope of survival, think these conversations, like the one Wesley was having with me as I listened and tried to deny its implications, are common and expected. It is just not always true because no matter how debilitating the illness, no matter how unlikely survival may be, hope becomes all there is, and when there is hope, there is still time. I was nowhere near to saying goodbye to Wesley or wrapping my brain around where I would lay his ashes. I was still in survival mode. Not denial, but survival.

As much as I wanted to respond to Wesley and his requests, I did not know how. All I could tell him was how much I loved him and reassure him Hunter would always be okay. I had hoped that would be enough.

We decided I should go home to Hunter that night because the next few days might be difficult, and I needed to spend time with him while I could. We stuck to our rule that Hunter would not see Wesley in the ICU, so instead of visiting him, I told Wesley I would have Hunter call him before bed and the next morning when he got up.

I kissed Wesley and held onto him for a few minutes before leaving the hospital room. I left the room and started on my long walk from the ICU wing to the garage where I was parked. As I walked, I thought about our ten-year wedding anniversary approaching in December.

Only our closest friends and immediate family had attended our wedding. For years I had planned to surprise Wesley by inviting them all back to the place we were originally married to witness us renew our vows. Before he got sick, he was simultaneously planning an anniversary vacation for us, but I knew he would rely on me to buy and confirm the tickets once he arranged the flights and hotel, so I planned to cancel his reservations, switch locations, and make sure no one who planned to attend our renewal of vows told Wesley.

Thinking about this plan I had kept a secret for at least two years, I stopped in the hallway near the elevator and exit to the parking garage. The elevator door opened and closed several times as I stood in front of it, wondering if I should go back to Wesley's hospital room and tell him everything I had planned for us that we would not be able to do now. I did not want to him to feel bad about it. I just wanted him to know how much being married to him for ten years had meant to me.

I was not sure I should go back, but something inside told me to do it.

When I reentered his room, he smiled at me.

"What are you doing? Why'd you come back?" he asked.

I smiled back at him, sat next to him on the bed, and held his hand.

"I have something to tell you. I didn't want to leave tonight without telling you."

As I told him of my plans, he pulled me to him and buried my head in his chest and started to cry. We both cried. Not only because we still loved each other enough to fight for his life and see him through, no matter what, but also because we still loved each other enough to each be planning a special way to celebrate a decade of marriage.

"You will always be the best choice I ever made," Wesley whispered to me through our tears. "Always."

When I left that night to go home, I was thankful I had done what my heart told me to do. I decided to never leave him in a room without saying what was in my heart if I felt compelled to share it.

I woke up the morning of the conference with hope the doctors attending it would discover something that had been missed. It was still October. Still the month Wesley started Flolan and still the month he woke up certain he was going to die two weeks after starting the medication. There were times I saw improvement in Wesley and hoped it was the Flolan that was helping him. At other times I quietly thought the Flolan was not making a difference and could even be making him worse. Either way, it could not be changed.

I spent the morning with Hunter before taking him to Peggy's house. Wesley called to talk to Hunter, but I did not hear the phone ring because I was giving him a bath.

I later heard the message.

"Hunter B, are ya there, Buddy? It's Daddy," Wesley said to Hunter. I could hear the sound of his oxygen flowing through the nose cannula on the phone.

We've called him Hunter B since the day we brought him home from the hospital.

"Hunter Beee, Beee, Beee, Beee," Wesley sang into the phone, then giggled and hung up.

When I heard the message, I saved it and had Hunter call him back.

Until Wesley's illness, we had rarely left Hunter with anyone, and he was not adjusting well to being forced to accept the care of others. My mom later told me it took her weeks to even convince

Hunter she knew how to tie his shoes because he always insisted he wanted me to do it.

Little by little, Hunter was learning to accept other people in his life. Even though everyone who was helping take care of him, including our parents and my dear friend Peggy, were the closest people to us and the ones we trusted the most, we had been raising him to count on Wesley and me. We had raised him to know we would see him through anything, and he was still counting on us to do that.

After a few hours at home, I called Dr. Patel to leave her a message. I let her know I would be back at the hospital for the rest of the day and night, and we were eager to hear the outcome after her meeting with the pulmonologists from the conference.

I was on my way to the hospital when she called me back. It was just after noon. I was surprised to hear from her so soon.

"Did meeting with the other pulmonologists help?" I asked, feeling hopeful about the possibilities with such brilliant minds all working together on Wesley's case.

"Yes, it did help," she answered, but not elaborating in what way.

"Oh, good! Were you able to reach an understanding of what to do?" I asked, relieved the meeting seemed to be productive.

"We did. I'm actually on my way to the hospital now. Why don't we meet in Wesley's room in an hour? I can explain a few things to you both then."

"Okay! Thank you so much. We'll see you in an hour," I cheerfully agreed, hoping she had answers about how to treat Wesley and avoid a second biopsy.

"I need you to understand that what we came up with is not ideal, but it is an answer," she explained.

She sounded apprehensive, as if she did not want to get my

hopes up, but I was just thankful an agreement had been met based on their findings.

I arrived at Wesley's hospital room before Dr. Patel and told Wesley she was on her way.

"Did the meeting help?" he asked.

"She thinks so," I answered but also did not elaborate.

Dr. Patel soon arrived and began explaining what conclusions had been drawn based on the information she shared with the panel of doctors. Each of them reviewed Wesley's pathology reports from the biopsy in April, his chart since the day Dr. Patel started seeing him as her patient in May, and the titration record from the day Flolan was first administered in the ICU earlier in the month. Apparently, based on the pulmonary pressure markers noted during the initial titration of Flolan, the panel decided Flolan could indeed help prolong Wesley's life.

We were not prepared for what came next.

"Because of his initial response to Flolan, it is apparent to us he could sustain even minimal progress and Flolan could prolong his life. He could survive long enough," she began.

Then she paused.

"Long enough for what?" I asked, completely oblivious to the enormity of her response to my obvious question.

"Long enough to receive a lung transplant," she cautiously replied.

I immediately looked at Wesley, but he would not look at me. He was looking out the ICU window.

"This is what it's come to?" Wesley asked Dr. Patel, without looking at either one of us.

"We feel every other possibility has been exhausted," she assured him.

"And a second lung biopsy?" he continued, sensing his argument was futile.

"We agree a second lung biopsy would not provide any new information that would lead to a treatment option we have not tried. End stage lung disease like what you are fighting, no matter the cause, leads to transplant," she explained.

End stage lung disease. It was the first time anyone of medical authority had used that term with us. This was the end.

"How long?" he asked.

"How long before you have the transplant?" Dr. Patel responded.

He did not answer her. He was still looking out the window.

"You need to start thinking about getting on a transplant list and what your options are."

Questions were running through my mind, but I could not manage to ask them. I did not know how to face what was happening. I did not think I could handle more information.

After one of Wesley's initial hospital stays, when we discovered his pulmonary pressure was ten times what it should be, we had read about lung transplants. All I remembered at that moment was of the organ transplants available in these times of medical progress, lung transplant had the lowest long-term survival rate.

"Wesley?" I tried to get him to look at us, but he would not.

What Dr. Patel had just told us was Wesley had only a few years to live—and that was only if he survived long enough to receive a transplant, and if his transplant was successful. Even a successful transplant meant he likely would not live long enough to see Hunter grow into a man, or even a teenager. We would not grow old together. I would not share in the pleasures and trials of life with Wesley beyond his fortieth birthday. Most agonizing of all, I would have to raise our beautiful son without his father.

All of these thoughts were running through my mind, and Wesley still had not looked at me.

"Wesley?" I said to him again.

Slowly, he looked away from the window, looked passed Dr. Patel and straight into my eyes.

"What?" he answered sharply.

He was angry.

I do not know what I expected to see in his face at that moment. A part of me wanted to crawl into his hospital bed and tell him everything was going to be okay, but that would be a lie. When he looked at me, his eyes were filled with tears but not one had fallen down his face. He looked sternly into my eyes, almost begging me to say something positive just so he would have an excuse to scream. To fight. To let go of everything stirring within him.

I looked down at the floor and did not say a word.

"I'm going to give you both some time to talk this over. It's a lot to take in," Dr. Patel interjected.

Wesley and I remained silent. He was looking out the window again, and I was still looking at the floor when Dr. Patel left the room.

I waited for Wesley to say something. I did not know what to say.

Several minutes passed without a word spoken. I was still waiting for Wesley to speak, or for words I could say that would not make this worse to come to my mind.

I broke the silence. I could not help it.

"Maybe you'll be the exception and live long enough for progress to be made in lung transplant patients."

When I finished that sentence, I knew I should not have said the words, but I did not know how else to be. I could not imagine anything but Wesley being the exception to the rule of statistics clobbering us in this moment of anguish and defeat.

"Stop! Just stop! Don't you get it? This is it, Lisa! There is no maybe this or maybe that! This is it! No matter what a lung transplant gives us, it will never be enough!" he yelled at me.

I knew the nurses and doctors could hear him outside the door, but I had also heard Dr. Patel talking quietly with one of the nurses outside our door after leaving the room. I knew she had told the nurse to give us our privacy, and why. Any emotion Wesley was having in this moment would have been acceptable, and anger was expected.

Several minutes of silence and mindless television watching had passed when Wesley told me he needed to use the bathroom. I knew that meant I needed to watch the door for him because in the ICU the bathrooms did not have doors, they were just a cabinet with a toilet and minimal plumbing.

As I stood outside the door, waiting for him to finish, his dietician came walking toward me. Wesley's body was showing symptoms of diabetes brought on by the high-dose steroids. Dr. Patel had arranged a consultation with the dietician to help control this so he would not need insulin shots when going home from the hospital.

I told her Wesley was resting, but we could talk at the nurse's counter if she liked. It was only a few feet from Wesley's door, so I spoke with her and kept an eye on the door to make sure no one entered.

I turned my back for just a moment, and in that time a nurse knocked and entered his room without waiting for him to invite her in. I saw her back out of the room, then she apologized to me.

I told the dietician we would have to continue our consult later and bravely walked into Wesley's room. He was furious, as I knew he would be.

He had always been a very modest person. A nurse walking into his room while he was going to the bathroom in a cabinet was unacceptable to him, and the only one he could blame for his discomfort was me.

He yelled at me again. This time I told him I should probably just go home for the day. He told me that was a good idea, so I grabbed my purse and walked out the door. I wanted to stay with him. I needed to stay with him. But he was inconsolable.

He was so worked up, I literally feared he might have a heart attack. I did not want to make it worse for him, so I started to leave the ICU. I wanted to call and ask his mom and stepdad not to come visit as planned, but it was too late; Donna and Roger were walking into the ICU wing as I was leaving.

I pulled them aside and told them what Dr. Patel had told us about the possibility of transplant. They were concerned about the risks of a second lung biopsy, so to them this seemed like a better alternative. And it was—but they had not researched lung transplants as we had, so they did not yet know Wesley's life expectancy or the complications that would come with this decision.

I warned them Wesley was very angry, but they were not leaving. Donna said she was going to watch the football game on television with Wesley whether he liked it or not. That was the best thing she could have said.

I walked back into the room with them. Wesley still looked furious.

"You guys might want to just go home. I'm not up for watching the game today," he told them.

"Well, you don't have to watch it if you don't want to, but we didn't drive all the way here to turn around and go home," Donna said, as she sat down in a chair next to his bed.

He needed someone to stand up to him from time to time, and she was about the only person who could get away with it.

I quietly left the room and walked to my car. I tried to make myself drive away, but I could not. I did not want to leave things as they were, so I just sat in the car and tried not to cry.

After about fifteen minutes, Wesley telephoned me from his hospital room.

"Why are you sitting in the car?" he asked, pressing his hand against the ICU window.

I looked up at his hospital room window and saw him standing there in his hospital gown with the phone to his ear. He waved to me.

"I have nowhere else to go," I answered, refusing to cry.

I waved back.

"You can come back up here."

"It's probably best if I just stay in the car for a while."

"I'm sorry I yelled at you," he apologized. "But, man, you know I hate it when the nurses barge in like that. I asked you to stay by the door."

"I was standing by the door, but the dietician asked to talk to me, and I didn't want to be rude to her."

"I understand that, but she can wait. Everyone can wait. This is about what we need to do for us at any given moment. I would do the same thing for you and I have," he continued, reminding me of the many times during my treatment he made sure I was comfortable in my care, no matter what.

"You're right. I'm sorry," I apologized. "I'll be up there in a minute."

"Love you," he said, forming "I love you" in sign language through the window.

"Love you, too."

We were both devastated by the only option we had left. I had never let myself believe that Wesley's illness would lead to a lung transplant. I could no longer deny it as our last hope.

I went back up to Wesley's hospital room and, after Donna and Roger left, I fell into his lap and sobbed in his arms. He held me tightly and cried with me.

"But... Hunter," I whispered softly through my tears.

"I know," Wesley agreed, holding me even tighter against his chest. "I know."

Without another word between us, we both knew the greatest tragedy was what Hunter would endure in the weeks, months and years to come. Wesley would not grow old with us, and even though every part of that reality was excruciating in every way, Hunter losing his Daddy hurt us both the most.

*

Wesley was released from the hospital two days later. Dr. Patel told us our first step was to contact our health insurance company to find out about our options. There were transplant hospitals across the country, but not all of them were approved by our insurance carrier. We had hoped to stay close to home and get on a list there, but our hospital in Houston did not perform enough transplants each year to be on the list of approved facilities. So we started our search from a different perspective. We knew the more transplants that were done by any given approved facility, the better chance Wesley had of getting one sooner, and surviving it once he did get it.

The first thirty days after a lung transplant are critical. Survival depends on how ill the patient is going into the surgery, how comprehensive his care is after the surgery, and how quickly he recovers. We would not know until we tried, but we did our best to make an informed decision.

Over the next several weeks, Wesley had his ups and downs. He was hospitalized in November but made it out in time for his thirty-fifth birthday. I bought him a recliner, and he loved it. He did not like the idea of needing a recliner to make him comfortable, but he enjoyed the ability it gave him to be in the family room more often and to take short naps without having to go to bed.

He said he did not want any visitors for his birthday, but I insisted he let me invite his mom and Roger, as well as his other stepdad, Jimbo. Donna and Jimbo had been divorced for years, but he had been a big part of Wesley's upbringing and Wesley considered him his dad. All three of them came for Wesley's small birthday party.

Wesley was incredibly private and rarely let anyone come visit. He had a hard time understanding he did not need to entertain our close friends and family when they came. They just wanted to sit with him and spend time with him. He did not even need to talk to them, but he was stubborn and refused guests most of the time.

For Thanksgiving, his mom invited us to stay the weekend with them, along with Wesley's siblings, their spouses, and their children. They lived less than two hours away, so we went, but it was a big mistake. Wesley hardly left the guest bedroom and did not have the energy or appetite to join the family for Thanksgiving dinner.

That getaway set Wesley back, but we still tried to get into the holiday spirit. Dr. Patel discouraged us from having a live Christmas tree because of the risk of mold growing on the tree and how it could affect Wesley. When his uncle JB (Jimbo's brother) and his cousin Jay heard about us not having a tree, they bought a fake one. They surprised us by showing up at our house one evening ready to set it up. Wesley insisted on helping, and Hunter and I decorated it right away.

There were intermissions of happiness, moments when we resembled the family I remembered us being. Hunter brought us the most joy and laughter. Wesley was able to attend Hunter's swim lessons when it was not too hot and humid outside. He was there when Hunter finally worked up enough courage to jump off the diving board for the first time. Hunter squealed with delight as he swam to the edge, saying, "I did it, Daddy! Did you see? I did it!"

"Yeah, Buddy! Good job!" Wesley cheered, clapping for Hunter.

Wesley and Hunter also still enjoyed watching football together on television; college football in particular still mustered joy from Wesley when his team was winning.

Most of the time, no matter how much we tried to let the light shine in, the cloud of darkness was always looming overhead. When Hunter reached a milestone, I secretly wondered if Wesley would be around for the next one. When Wesley laughed, it was often followed by dead silence, deafeningly familiar, as his reality crept in.

There were times when I tried to share my optimism, but it was often met with opposition. Like the time I told Wesley that Hunter's teacher had mentioned there was a little girl at Hunter's school who had a crush on him, and the feelings seemed to be mutual.

"You never know about those two," I laughed as I told Wesley. "I made my mind up about you when I wasn't much older than them."

To which Wesley sarcastically replied, "Yeah. I'll be sure to tell my grandchildren about that."

I do not think he said that because he felt sorry for himself. He had a right to be angry and to express it with sarcasm. He would not be around to see his grandchildren, and I knew for every time he said something sad or negative out loud, there were so many more times he kept his hopelessness to himself.

Knowing the reality of Wesley's drastically shortened lifespan forced me to live in the moment because our future was so uncertain. We could not know what would happen to him, but we knew how hard it had been so far, which made it difficult to hold hope.

Wesley was hospitalized again before Christmas. Dr. Patel let him out on Christmas Eve, even though he still was not doing well. She thought he would recover better at home than in a hospital over the Christmas holiday. My parents were visiting for a few weeks and helping with Hunter.

My brother Vance, Wesley's friend since we were kids, flew into town to visit over New Year's. By then, Wesley was feeling better, but Dr. Patel had bumped up his steroids to help him recover during his most recent episode. The increased steroids made him more irritable and Wesley was incredibly difficult to get along with, as he had been since this all began.

On New Year's Eve he was on the backyard patio with Vance and my dad. I could not believe it when I saw a rum and coke in his hand. I was furious with him and let him know it.

Throughout the years we had been together, almost thirteen years, Wesley had a drinking problem. He did not drink everyday and we did not keep alcohol in the house on a regular basis, but when he did drink, he rarely knew when to stop. If there was one thing I knew coming into our marriage, it was that we would struggle with his drinking. It had been and continued to be the biggest conflict in our marriage. He had definitely slowed down after Hunter was born, and he had not drunk in months. This was no time to start again.

This time, though, it was different from me being tired of having to be the designated driver, even on my own birthday. We were beyond fighting over how much he could spend on an alcohol tab at a bar or restaurant. This was life and death. He was in heart failure, and any damage drinking might cause could be irreversible.

I went into our bathroom to start getting ready for bed. He came in and told me I had no right to be angry with him because it was his choice to drink if he wanted to relax and enjoy himself. After all, he said, it was New Year's Eve.

"Enjoy yourself?" I replied. "Seriously, you think this is about enjoying yourself because you think you deserve to have a good time?"

"What's wrong with that? I haven't had a moment of rest, to just relax with old friends and enjoy the moment."

"When was the last time you saw me relax? When was the last time I woke up in the morning not worried about it being your last? This has nothing to do with what the two of us deserve. Do you deserve to be able to sit with my brother and my dad and get stupid drunk if you want? Sure, why not, but are you capable? Is your body capable? Absolutely not!" I snapped.

"Then I will deal with whatever consequences I face tomorrow morning for choosing to have a few drinks tonight!" he yelled.

"No, you won't! Hunter and I will! Because I will be working twice as hard around here trying to help you recover and avoid another trip to the hospital, and Hunter will deal with it because you won't be able to get out of bed for two days and he'll miss his daddy! You will have made the choice, but Hunter and I will suffer the consequences of that choice," I shouted at him, gesturing with my hands. "Not to mention if the insurance company approves us and we try to get on the list soon, you know they test for alcohol. They have the option to deny you because you pose a risk as someone who isn't committed to the long-term responsibility of being a transplant patient."

"There is no talking to you," he said, turning his oxygen cart around and walking out of the bathroom.

He knew I was right. It was a ridiculous sight, him pushing an oxygen cart with one hand and holding a cocktail in the other, but I was not going to argue with him anymore. I just washed my face, brushed my teeth, and climbed into bed with Hunter, who had been asleep for hours, and prepared myself for what would come in the morning.

I heard Wesley crawl quietly into bed about an hour later, but I acted as if I was asleep. It was obvious he had decided not to stay up late and party with Vance and my dad. He did what was right, even though he hated to admit it.

Two days later, it was time for Vance to go back home.

"I tried to mind my own business during this visit, but I had a hard time not telling him to treat my sister better," Vance told me, as I walked him to the car before my dad drove him to the airport. "I know this isn't who Wesley really is, and you seem to be dealing with it."

"We are all doing what we have to do right now and hoping the transplant will bring a change for the better," I assured him, not wanting to send him home worrying about Hunter and me.

It was hard on my brother to see Wesley that way. The last time we had all been together, he and Wesley had arm wrestled and Wesley had won. It was a rematch Wesley had prepared for after losing to my brother during our previous visit with him. Seeing Wesley now, Vance, too, wanted it all to go away and for Wesley to resemble the person he had known for more than twenty years.

It was always hard when our guests left because Wesley welcomed only the people closest to us—which meant when we had company we were surrounded by loving, helping hands who brought balance to our otherwise increasingly miserable existence. When they were gone, the only constants that remained in our home were oxygen tanks, Flolan, and Hunter's happiness. Without all three of those, we would not make it through another day.

By now our search for the right transplant hospital had ended. We had made the decision. Wesley had a rare blood type; we chose the University of Alabama Hospital (UAB) in Birmingham, Alabama because it was a reputable transplant hospital, and it did not have a waiting list for Wesley's particular blood type. We had no way of knowing how long it would take to go through the necessary tests and get listed if he were accepted, but we had decided to move there and start the process.

It was frustrating to try to deal with the details by phone. UAB was ten hours away, and they would not take us seriously about getting on the list if we did not relocate and live within an hour of the hospital. We would have to be able to get there quickly in case lungs became available for Wesley.

We had done our research and were trying to remain positive, even though we knew lung transplants were complicated, life afterward could be arduous, and from what we had read, we would likely be trading one set of problems for another. We also knew life after a transplant, when managed well and under the best circumstances, meant no more oxygen tanks and no more wheelchairs, and we could prolong Wesley's life while trying to attain a quality of life more recognizable to all of us.

In my research I read about a lung transplant performed on a sixteen-year-old boy during the blackout in New York City months before. The *New York Times* quoted the young patient's mother, so I looked her up and called her on the telephone.

Her name was Kim, and she was happy to talk with me. She told me her son had been the thirty-eighth person diagnosed with a rare lung disease I could barely pronounce. She used the acronym PCH and said many of Wesley's symptoms sounded similar to her son's, from the severe onset of his illness and the cloudy X-rays to the degree of his illness and daily struggles to survive.

Kim said her son was doing very well and welcomed me to call her anytime if I needed to talk or had additional questions. Before we hung up, she suggested I ask Wesley's doctor about PCH. She understood it would not change anything, but it might be helpful to know what was causing the nightmare we were living in. I later mentioned PCH to Dr. Patel, but she said the pathology from Wesley's April biopsy did not show it, so we moved on.

Wesley found a furnished, corporate apartment in Birmingham that would be available in the middle of February and a one-bedroom hotel with a kitchen we could move into in the meantime. We would take with us only what we needed to get through the next months, not knowing how long we would be there or what it would be like for us once we arrived. Our insurance would reimburse us for living expenses in Birmingham, so we decided not to rent out our house. With Wesley's long-term disability insurance and the money I was making with my business, we could afford to maintain it. My business was still doing well, and because our products were mostly sold on the Internet, I could live anywhere and operate it successfully, with Christi's continued help.

We were doing what we had to do. We rented a U-Haul trailer and made every advance arrangement at our destination we could. Hunter had a going away party at his school. We were leaving the first weekend in February.

I was terrified of going—and equally terrified of not going. If we stayed, Wesley would die within months, maybe weeks. If we uprooted our entire lives and moved to a city ten hours away with a hospital that performed dozens of lung transplants each year, we had a chance at a few more years with Wesley. We had no choice but to go.

I knew our lives were forever changed. I no longer held hope we would be able to return to the life we shared before the day Wesley cleaned out the garage and started getting sick. I knew every day would be spent counting pills and being cautious, because after the transplant Wesley would be at constant risk of infection due to the high-dose anti-rejection medications he would have to be on for the rest of his life. I also knew lung transplant patients struggled more than any other type of transplant patients because the lungs are not like the kidneys or the heart, safely tucked within the body and protected from outside elements. Lungs are exposed to the elements of everyday life, from common colds to toxins in the air. Life would be complicated and beyond our control.

In time, I hoped the responsibilities and the burdens of being a transplant family would be lessened as we adapted and made the best of the precious gift we hoped to receive—healthy lungs in Wesley's failing body. But right now, it felt like a part of us was dying, and I feared no matter how hard I tried, I could not save us.

CHAPTER SEVEN

The Guardian

I made a list of things I had to do before we could safely leave for Birmingham, Alabama. Wesley was too sick to help and Hunter was too young. The forty-seven items on the list were not simply menial tasks, like taking out the trash or turning off the cable service, although those items were included. They were things like acquiring medications and oxygen accessories that could be a matter of life and death along our journey. In the months leading up to our transplant decision, I had learned that medicine and oxygen came before anything else, because without both, the end was imminent.

When I look back at the list now, I realize how much detail went into each item and how critical most of them were. It is unimaginable that I had to simultaneously handle shutting off the main water line to the house and signing our Last Will and Testament.

In the midst of working through the list, an important decision had to be legalized: naming a guardian for Hunter in our will. We had chosen a guardian for Hunter when he was six months old, and informed the family members who needed to know of our decision, but we had not had a will drawn up yet. The will we drew up named our original choice, but I suggested to Wesley we also name a second person because circumstances had changed, both in our lives and in the life of the guardians we would be choosing. Wesley would not give me an answer when I brought it up to him, so I waited a few more days then brought it up again. Still he ignored my request, without giving me a reason, so I told him I was going to have our lawyer name the additional guardian unless he disagreed. Again, he did not respond.

My friend Christine, who was also our estate lawyer, had been at our home the evening before, as well as our two witnesses, to finalize the documents. When she arrived, she discussed the details of the will with me in the dining room while Wesley was in the kitchen.

"He really should be listening to this before he signs anything," Christine told me.

I approached Wesley in the kitchen, where he was making dinner for Hunter and me. He did not have much of an appetite to eat with us, but he still liked to cook.

"Christine needs to explain the documents before we sign anything," I told him, knowing he was ignoring us on purpose.

"You can listen for me. I am making dinner," Wesley said to me, without looking away from the stovetop where he was watching pasta boil.

"She needs you in there. This is a legal document that she has taken a great deal of time to prepare. We should show her our appreciation by following her instructions," I told him again.

Christine was a family friend. She had insisted on compiling our will at no charge before we left for the transplant.

Wesley reluctantly agreed to join us in the dining room.

As we read through the details of what we owned and who would have the rights to our belongings if either or both of us died, it was hard to imagine either of us not seeing the other through life. As we initialed each page and signed our names where the stickers prompted us, neither of us looked up from the document. I could not bear to look Wesley in the eye. Because, short of something tragically and accidentally happening to me that would abruptly end my life, we knew the immediacy of the will and its necessity was due to his illness and what might happen to him in the coming weeks and months.

Seeing Hunter's name in the will made choosing a guardian that much more real. It is not an easy choice to make. Many people avoid even having a will drawn up because of having to make that choice, but we did not have the luxury of denial. While it made us take stock of our closest friends and our extended family, it also forced us to acknowledge no one was better suited to raise Hunter than we were.

Every day, no matter how much Wesley came at me emotionally and verbally with every possible complaint, I listened and fixed whatever I could. I suffered the agony of what it felt like to be constantly fighting for a man I could not possibly fight against. I told myself the illness was unbearable to him and the lack of oxygen and the high-dose steroids were the reason for his behavior. It had nothing to do with how he truly felt about me.

There were times of reprieve from the relentless conflict his illness often brought when I would hear him tell someone on the phone he could not get through a day without me. I listened with an open and full heart because I knew the words he said to others were the emotions he truly felt. His agony was my own, and I loved him enough to see beyond the heartache his suffering caused all of us. I avoided arguments whenever I could, and I did not pick this fight, but I could not compromise, either. As much as I tried never to argue with Wesley while he was sick, some things were worth fighting about.

Ultimately, there was nothing in the will Wesley did not know about. I had known him most of my life. I knew when I suggested to him more than once we name an additional guardian, his lack of response was his way of telling me to handle it without having to say it to me out loud. He did not want to think about it. When he signed the will, he was not angry with me for making the addition; he was angry because seeing it in writing made our circumstances incredibly real to him. Hunter's guardian, no matter who we chose, was a relevant and immediate reality.

Wesley screamed at me that night after everyone left, and I countered. I could not give in because it was too important. It is obvious to me now the argument was more about what he was losing in that decision than about the decision itself. He could have refused to sign the papers. He could have negated the whole will. It was not unlike him to fight a good fight and not care what anyone else thought as long as he truly believed in what he was fighting for, but he did not do that. He just fought me.

I understood even then that this was not really about whom we chose to care for Hunter if we both died; it was about how real this was for both of us. This was not hypothetical. This was reality. Facing the journey we were about to take, I could not compromise on a legal and binding document that would matter if anything happened to both of us.

The argument was escalating, and Wesley was having trouble breathing. He started to yell, and each breath got more difficult. He grabbed his oxygen mask to add fifteen liters to the ten liters already flowing through his nose cannula.

We argued for just a few minutes about the decisions that were made. It would have dragged on and on, but Wesley did not have the strength, and I did not have the heart. I see now that maybe

I was beginning to take charge of a life I might be leading on my own, but I never would have been able to admit that to myself at the time.

"You're going to give me a damn heart attack!" he yelled.

I looked him in the eye. With my whole heart I was sorry for what he felt, but I could not change this for him. I could not fix it, so I said nothing.

Wesley glared at me through the mask, not only the actual oxygen mask on his face but also through the invisible mask he wore trying to cover his fear and despair, because he did not want his son, our son, to end up with anyone but us. He did not want someone else to teach his son how to fish or how to throw a baseball. He did not want someone else to buy him his first car or take him to visit colleges when the time came. He wanted us to do it. Every bit of it. Anything short of that was impossible for him to imagine.

The fight he had in him that night was not about Hunter's guardian, or even about me. It was about Hunter and how much this father loved his son and wanted to be there for him at every turn in his life. It was about the possibility, and even the reality, Wesley was not going to experience being a father who was present in Hunter's life.

I walked out of the room. He did not follow me. Instead, he walked into our bedroom where Hunter was sleeping. I could see them both from the foyer. Wesley was watching Hunter sleep. I could see Wesley's shoulders rising and falling; he was gasping for air, and in the deep breaths it took for him to recover in that moment, I cannot begin to imagine what he was thinking.

He soon went to bed and I finished working from the list of things that had to be done before his parents arrived in the morning to begin our two-day drive to the new city and hospital we had chosen. I did not go to sleep that night. There was not time.

In the morning, when Wesley saw me taking inventory of his medication in the bathroom, he stood in the doorway.

"Can you cut my hair before we go?" he asked me.

"Sure."

I finished what I was counting and got out the clippers from the linen closet. While I did that, he wrapped a towel around his shoulders and sat down on the small ice chest he had brought in from the garage to sit on while I cut his hair.

"You never slept," he said. It was not a question. He knew there was too much for me to do to get ready to go.

"There wasn't time," I replied, as I began to slowly move the shears over his thinning hair.

"I need you to know you will make no mistakes. You'll do everything right," Wesley began. "If I don't make it, you'll make no mistakes with Hunter."

This was a discussion I did not want to have. I did not want to consider our lives without Wesley.

"I can't even imagine it, Wesley." I did not look up but I could feel him looking at me in the bathroom mirror. I just kept trimming his hair.

"You have to know this. You have to know that I believe in you. I trust you," he continued. "And for a dad where I am, that means everything."

"This family doesn't work without you. I can't begin to imagine it. I don't want to do this alone. I don't even want to talk about it."

"But if you have to do this without me, raise our son alone, you are the most capable woman I've ever known."

"That's enough. Now I know." I tried to stop him from saying anything more.

"I'm sorry about last night. You don't need to be, but I'm sorry," Wesley apologized.

"Sometimes you have to know I am still here, and I can't always agree with you just because you are sick," I told him.

"I know," he agreed.

I looked at his reflection in the mirror.

The haircut was done.

We had done this so many times before. This time was no different. Even though we would be leaving in a few hours for the two-day trip to Birmingham, we tried to stick to the routine of things. He picked up the ice chest and brought me the broom. I swept his short, fine hairs from our bathroom floor into the dust pan while he held the small trash can for me. I put the towel in the hamper while he turned on the shower. He sat on the shower chair while I got a clean washcloth and body wash. I draped his oxygen tube over the shower curtain rod while he held onto the shower nozzle and sprayed himself with hot water.

I washed his body from the tips of his toes to the top of his fingers. He lifted his arms as I worked my way to the top of his body. We had to stop three times for him to catch his breath. Even though he only had to sit on the shower bench while I did the rest, the steam in the shower made it hard for him to breathe, and once he got short of breath it was difficult for him to recover.

We did not speak as I showered him. I think we both knew this might be the last time he showered in our bathroom. It was more than we could manage to acknowledge. At least out loud.

I held the shower nozzle and sprayed his shoulders and back until the water in the drain ran clear of soap suds. Then he turned off the water. He stood up from the shower stool and turned toward me. It was only then I looked him in the eye. I smiled. He smiled. We kissed briefly as I dried his hair. He lifted his arms for me to dry underneath them. I worked my way down his body with the towel until he stepped out of the shower and wrapped the towel around his waist.

While he shaved and brushed his teeth, I got his clothes ready, making sure I laid out comfortable sweats and a T-shirt for the long ride ahead.

When he was done shaving, he came into our bedroom. Still, without words, I began to dress him. First his underwear. He stood and stepped into each side, one foot at a time and held onto my shoulders for balance.

Hunter came into the room and asked if he could watch cartoons. Wesley told him he could, so Hunter turned on the television in our bedroom and sat on the edge of the bed singing about the little explorer named Dora.

Hunter did not pay any attention to his dad and me. He was used to this daily routine. It had not occurred to him to question why Mommy dressed Daddy when even he did not need help getting dressed anymore. He just watched the television and immersed himself in the cartoon world as any four-year-old would. As it should be.

When I was done helping Wesley get his pants on, I got on my knees to put his socks on for him. He could put on his T-shirt himself.

He sat on the bed next to Hunter, holding his hand.

Wesley's feet were swollen from heart failure.

One foot at a time, I put each sock on his purple, oxygen-deprived feet. I wondered if his feet would ever look healthy and pink again, or if they ever had. I wondered if he would ever be able to shower himself and get dressed like any grown man would expect to be able to do. I wondered if he was right, and I might have to be the capable woman he believed in, raising our son alone. I thought about the many times he tried to shower and dress without my help when he first got sick. Then I considered what it must have been like for him when the time came to concede and accept my help.

As I put on his shoes that morning and heard his mom and Roger pull into the driveway of our home, I stood up to get in the shower myself. As I began to walk away, Wesley reached for my hand.

I looked at him and he looked at me, but we did not say a word.

The doorbell rang, and Hunter jumped up from the bed. "Nina and Papa are here!" he hollered as he ran to the front door.

Hunter opened the door and Donna and Roger came inside. Jimbo pulled in behind them in the driveway and joined us all in the house.

Two hours later, everything had been loaded into the rented trailer attached to the back of Jimbo's Suburban, and all the items on my list had been checked and double-checked. Donna and Roger were in their car and planned to follow behind us to Birmingham.

It was time to go, ready or not. I strapped Hunter into his car seat and went back inside the house for one last look around. Wesley stood in the family room of our home with me. We were both quiet. As we walked through the double doors that led to the driveway, Wesley and I were holding hands. He stopped and turned back toward the house. He took a long, hard look at our home.

The house had originally been Jimbo's. When Wesley and I were first married, we used to talk about living there. We had hoped that one day, when Wesley's sister Jenny left for college and Jimbo moved to the ranch full time, we could buy this house from him and make it our home. We did not know then I would get cancer, and everything in our lives would completely change in the years leading up to it, but ultimately Jenny did leave for college, Jimbo moved to the ranch full time, and we did buy the house. How we got there did not seem to matter once we had finally arrived.

We brought Hunter home from the hospital to this house after he was born. He had never lived anywhere else. This was all he knew. He had learned to crawl and walk and talk in this house. We became a family under this roof. As much as I wanted to stay and never leave the refuge of the place where we began, I knew we had to go, and so did Wesley.

"What do you need?" I asked him, not knowing what I could do to make this easier for both of us.

"I need to make it back home," he told me without hesitation.

"You'll be back," I tried to assure him.

"I hope so."

"I know so. I'm not coming home without you," I insisted, knowing returning here without him was something I could not begin to imagine doing.

We walked to the Suburban where Hunter and Jimbo were waiting for us. "Let's go, Daddy!" Hunter gleefully shouted.

"Let's go, Buddy."

And away we went.

CHAPTER EIGHT

Cowboy Up

Before we left, when I ordered everything we would need from the oxygen company for the trip, I told a big, fat lie and said our oxygen regulator broke. I knew on our long drive to Birmingham we would need two of the regulators that go on the tank to open it and regulate the flow of oxygen through the mask or nose cannula. From the start, they had only given us one, and I had a feeling they would not give us a second one. So I cut through the red tape to get another one, knowing we might run into trouble along the way and need the use of two tanks at one time. We would not have access to our plug-in unit during the two days it would take to reach our destination.

I was right. They did not want us to have a second regulator. They said they needed the broken one back, so I lied again and told them we did not know it could be fixed so we threw it away. They lectured me about the regulator being expensive and necessary—as if I did not understand how necessary the regulator was for Wesley's survival. If I had not already known it, our frightening and complicated pilgrimage to UAB would have shown me.

Our halfway stop was at a huge hotel casino in Biloxi, Mississippi. I stayed in the hotel room and put Hunter to bed after dinner while Wesley went with his mom, Roger and Jimbo to gamble. Before they left, I loaded up his wheelchair with two oxygen tanks and made sure he had everything else he might need. As Jimbo rolled him out of our hotel room, I had a bad feeling. I knew Wesley was going to cut loose and try to enjoy this opportunity to spend time with his parents before the trip's end, when he would have to hand himself over for a battery of tests that would lead to his transplant. I knew he was too sick to partake but also stubborn enough to ignore my plea. So I did not plead with him; I just let him go. I knew I would be there to help repair whatever damage was done that evening.

Wesley did have a good time, but the casino had no restrictions on indoor smoking. The smoky air, along with his ever-present heart failure and next to impossible ability to breathe even in the best environment, made him worse. By morning, when I was helping him shower, he was quickly using up the last oxygen tank in our hotel room. I ran down three flights of stairs to the crowded parking lot to try to find Jimbo's car to get a fresh tank and run it back to our room before he passed out, or even died, from lack of oxygen.

Just in case the first tank did not work, I grabbed two. While I ran back up the three flights of stairs—because the elevator was too slow and I no longer trusted elevators in an emergency—I was angry at Wesley. He had no business risking his precarious health just to enjoy the luxury of a good time. I was paying for his indulgence with this marathon effort to bring him oxygen. I was mad, but I knew he was paying for it even more, trying not to panic in the shower and trying not to let Hunter see his suffering.

A part of me wished I had stopped him from leaving our hotel room the night before, because it had set him so far backward in such a short time—and he did not have far to go to risk his life. But I knew Wesley had made up his mind he wanted to forget about his problems for the night; once his mind was made up, there was no changing it.

Wesley's choice to forget about his illness for just one night was irresponsible, but as a result he spent a night with his parents he cherished. I knew he desperately needed moments when he was able to forget about the agony of his plight, so perhaps the next day's consequences were worth it. If they were, then I was okay with whatever I had to do to help repair the damage. But I knew I could not let it happen again. I was not sure he could survive it.

By the end of the trip, Wesley's feet were more swollen and his breathing more labored than before we left home. Wesley's Aunt Rae had lived outside of Birmingham and had offered to let us store our belongings in her garage until our apartment was ready a few weeks later. When we arrived at his Aunt Rae's house to unload the trailer, Jimbo shouted to me from his car.

Wesley had been trying to back the trailer up to the house, but just the movement of turning his head and upper body right to left to check each side mirror as he backed up had made him lose his breath. He was having a hard time recovering.

"I need another tank!" Wesley yelled.

His shoulders were moving up and down quickly. His lips were purple. His faced showed panic.

I quickly unloaded our back-up tank, attached the second regulator to it and put the mask over his face. Even with the constant flow of 10-liters into his nose cannula, the 15-liter mask was becoming necessary more and more as each day passed. It was the second time in two days we had to use an extra tank fitted with the additional regulator I had lied to get. I felt no remorse for the lie.

I figured our insurance company could absorb the second regulator with more ease than Hunter and I could absorb losing Wesley simply because we did not have the necessary medical equipment.

In the days after the drive, Wesley continued to suffer from heart failure, agitation from the high-dose steroids he took daily, and saturations in the low seventies just trying to walk across a room. He was easily annoyed and difficult for us to tolerate—and he was not tolerating us very well either.

Although we could have stayed with his newly married Aunt Rae and her husband Mike, along with Donna and Roger, we moved directly into our temporary home, a one-bedroom hotel suite with a kitchen. It was not ideal, but Wesley did not want to impose on anyone. Daily care of Wesley was calculated and complicated. He did not like people to see how hard it was for him to function and perform daily tasks most people never even think about.

We would be in the hotel for at least ten days until the one-bedroom furnished apartment we had rented was vacated for our use. We settled in as best we could, experiencing moments of joy and laughter despite the tight space and uncertainty in which we were living. Wesley continued to read about transplant surgery. That week, there happened to be a special on television about transplants: one liver, one lung, and two kidneys. Only the kidney transplants were successful. The liver and lung patients on the show died within thirty days of surgery.

"That can't be good," Wesley said when the show ended.

"But that's not you, and that's not us," I told him. Then I went into the bathroom and tried not to cry.

After our initial meet-and-greet appointments with the lung transplant team, Jimbo had to return home. He left his car with us and flew, rather than drive. He wanted us to have OnStar in case of an emergency; the Jeep we had left in Houston did not have that option. He would use our car until we did not need the Suburban anymore, however long that would be.

When we dropped Jimbo off at the airport, I slipped him a note thanking him for all he was doing for us. He slipped me an envelope full of cash and told me, "You make sure you get the kid out of that hotel room and have some fun."

Donna and Roger planned to leave next because they were going on a cruise with Roger's family that had been scheduled months before. The plan had been for everyone to get us to Birmingham safely. The rest was really up to us. I was scared, Wesley was both scared and angry, and Hunter was in the middle of it all. Wesley was private in his suffering most of the time, at least when it came to revealing himself to anyone other than Hunter and me, but there were times when other people who were close to him would glimpse his agony and how it manifested itself in the harshest and most painful ways.

Before Donna and Roger left, they took us to lunch. We should have declined because Wesley did not have much of an appetite and even less energy. He felt worse than when we had arrived just three days before, and he was frustrated.

We had had our initial appointment with the lung doctors at UAB, and it was taking longer than we expected to schedule the tests needed just to enable Wesley to be considered for the transplant list. There was still no one at UAB with Wesley's rare blood type on the waiting list for lungs, but Wesley knew that did not matter if he was not on the list himself when a good match came.

It was a bad day from the start, and it soon became one of the worst. I do not even remember what was said or done to trigger Wesley's outburst, but he quickly became angry. In the restaurant and in front of Hunter, Donna, and Roger, Wesley started shouting at me, telling me I needed to go back home and leave him there to take care of himself. He told me he did not need my help and insisted I should just go back with his mom and Roger and leave him there.

I did not know what to say or do. I was stunned, and I was broken. There were no words. I got up from the table, held Hunter's hand and took him with me when I walked out to the car. Then I started the car and turned on the heater so it would be warm when Wesley got inside because he struggled even more to breathe when he was cold. No matter how much he hurt me, not taking care of him was not an option.

It took several minutes for Donna and Roger to pay for lunch and help Wesley out of the restaurant and into the car. I got out to help load his oxygen tank into the front seat while Roger folded up Wesley's wheelchair and put it into the back of the car.

When we were done, I did not know what to say to Donna and Roger.

"We'll meet you back at the hotel," Donna told me. She did not know what to say either.

All the way to the hotel all I could think about was how was I going to take care of Wesley, protect Hunter from his anger and frustration, and work out the logistics of appointments, all on my own. I was overwhelmed, and by the time we arrived at the hotel, I was fighting back tears.

After Hunter and Wesley were in the hotel room and Donna and Roger had said their goodbyes, I walked them out to their car. When we reached the parking lot, I could not hold back the tears any longer. Donna hugged me and told me she was so sorry for the way he had treated me. I just cried in her arms.

I knew Wesley was scared and did not want Hunter and me to watch him die if the transplant did not come soon enough, but this is why we had come to Birmingham: so that, no matter what, we knew we had done our best for our family. Reasoning this in my head after being hurt again was difficult, but I was devoted to Wesley and to his care and, most of all, to this family.

"I don't know how I am going to make all of this work," I confessed, terrified of the days and weeks ahead.

"I hate to leave you like this," Donna cried.

"Then don't," I pleaded silently in my own head but could not bring myself to say it out loud.

But she did leave. As I stood in the rain in that hotel parking lot, with Wesley and Hunter inside, she and Roger drove away. I felt frighteningly, hopelessly alone.

I wanted my own mom, but I knew she needed to take care of herself. For months she had been helping us with Hunter but neglecting her own health. She had recently been diagnosed with a rare blood disorder that could no longer go without treatment. Her first treatment was just days away, so asking her to come help again was not an option. My dad needed to be with her, helping her through her own health crisis.

As much as I loved Wesley and was committed to his care, I needed help. I felt there had to be somebody who could help me. Even though Rae and Mike were just miles away and more than happy to help, and even though having family nearby was part of the reason we had chosen to come to UAB for a transplant, Wesley consistently resisted help from anyone but me.

I did not know how to sort through everything that was going through my mind. I wanted to take some time away, to escape and have just a few hours to myself, but I couldn't. I wouldn't. I owed it to Wesley to love him through that moment and stay there. Right there. No matter what.

We did not speak the rest of the day. Then at dinner Hunter

sucked his spaghetti noodles into his mouth and got one noodle stuck on his nose. It made us both chuckle at the same time. Our eyes met, we smiled, and I could see his apology.

We put Hunter to bed soon after dinner on the sofabed in the living room. Hunter and I would be sleeping there so Wesley could have the bedroom to himself. He had trouble sleeping and if, by chance, he did manage to fall asleep, we wanted Hunter to have the freedom to utilize the rest of the hotel room without worrying about waking him.

I had just finished administering Wesley's Flolan and was sitting next to him at the foot of the bed.

"I'm so sorry for the way I have treated you and Hunter through this. I never meant to hurt you. I could not have survived any of this without you," he said. I knew it was difficult for him to say his was sorry, even though he was having to get good at apologizing.

"I know the steroids make it hard for you to be yourself. I don't know what it's like to be you right now," I replied cautiously, accepting his apology.

"I didn't mean what I said. I wouldn't make it here without you and Hunter. I wouldn't have a reason to fight anymore."

I could see his eyes welling up with tears.

Wesley laid his head in my lap and let himself need me for something other than his physical care. He did not want to need me. He wanted to be strong and save me from the fears that over-whelmed him, but, finally, after months of fighting the battle this disease had forced him to face, he showed his fear and his sorrow. Just as he probably always knew I would, I received his fear and I shared his sorrow. As the man I loved lay in the lap of the woman he loved, he showed me his heart, revealed, in that hotel room.

"I'm dying," he began.

"No, you're not," I interrupted.

"Just let me finish," he continued. "The three of us are here fighting for my life, but I am scared, and I don't want to die in this hotel room. If the lungs don't come soon, I won't make it out of here."

"The lungs will come." I tried to reassure him but my own optimism was waning.

"But what if they don't?" he questioned.

His fear and sorrow reminded me of my own when I had cancer—when nothing but the voice of this man telling me I would survive could get me through a fearful moment.

"They will, but we could be waiting a long time, and I don't want to spend the rest of the days leading up to it fighting you. I know who you are. I've always known who you are, but this time is all Hunter's four-year-old mind might remember," I reasoned. I needed to take what might be my final opportunity to get him to understand and help repair whatever damage was being done to Hunter in the wake of this horrible illness.

"I know," Wesley agreed, wiping tears from his cheeks.

"I don't know what it will be like for us if you don't survive. I can't imagine my life or Hunter's without you. I have no idea what to expect from that or how to even manage the possibility. Why would you want to make that any harder for Hunter and me than it would already be? Why would you choose to give me more damage to fix beyond just trying to face every day without you, let alone trying to make sure Hunter remembers you as the man you were when you were good and kind to us—not the man who yells at his mommy and makes every day a battle? Please, Wesley, somewhere inside of yourself, find a place that enables you to rise above the steroids and the fear and the relentless struggles you face every day to show up for Hunter and be the father he deserves to know, no matter how long you live. Please don't make him lose you before you are even gone."

Wesley broke down and began to sob.

Finally, after months of being the only man he knew how to be, determined and strong, he laid his fear in my lap. However briefly, he allowed me to save him the way he had saved me so many times before. Our marriage, our union, had been faced with such tragedy in the short decade we had shared. All we knew was as long as we were alive, we would be together—and as long as we were together, there was a fighting chance.

From that day on, Wesley stopped fighting me. He stopped carrying the anger he had felt since realizing we might not grow old together and he might not live to raise Hunter with me or have more children. He knew even with the most successful lung transplant, he would not be alive to meet our grandchildren. It did not mean he was not still difficult at times. The steroids made it almost impossible for him not to be, but somehow, knowing all the damage he was doing, he stopped fighting me and started being a positive, leading force in our family again, rather than feeling like its burden.

Before we left home to move near UAB, Wesley had let me read a passage he wrote about our plight in an email to Crislee, his friend since high school. In it, I recognized the honorable man I had fallen in love with more than a decade before, the man who would never let anything or anyone hurt me or our family. I read it again that week in the hotel room and any other time when I needed to be reminded of what he felt but could not always express. Whatever time we had left, he would fight with all of his might to love us through it, and that was something both of us could live with.

Wesley's email read:

I'm sure there will be a lot of reflection in the coming days and weeks, and I think it is good for the soul. It reminds me of how things can be, not as they are now. I am lucky to have such great friends, family and my wife. Lisa has gone above and beyond throughout this ordeal, and I can honestly say, I see how some couples don't make it through something like this. The good thing about us is I don't think we realize how hard it is, because as far as we are concerned, it was the hand we were dealt and we just cowboy up and do what we have to do. That, along with true love and a desire to never give up, is what will get us through this as a couple. A little luck from the Man above and my desire to not lose a fight is what will get me through the physical part. I'm ready. Squared up. Fists raised.

CHAPTER NINE

The Walk

The long road trip to UAB had proved to be more taxing on Wesley than we anticipated. He was not doing well and needed to go to the hospital, but he would not go, because he did not want Hunter to come with us, and he did not want to impose on Rae by leaving Hunter with her. Although Wesley's attitude had improved considerably since that night in the hotel room when he finally broke down, he still felt very uncomfortable asking anyone else for help. Hunter did not adapt well to people he was not around often, and Wesley did not want to leave Hunter with Rae and Mike, where he might not be comfortable.

I was already overwhelmed by concerns about how I would handle the logistics of our schedule, with the number of tests and doctor's appointments we were anticipating. Wesley's deterioration and need to go to the hospital, combined with trying to figure out what to do about Hunter, put me in crisis mode. Back home, I could arrange Wesley's appointments around Hunter's play dates and preschool. Even if Wesley had to be hospitalized, we always had family and friends willing to help us with Hunter when my mom could not be there. It was part of our routine, and Wesley was okay with it because Hunter was happy.

Wesley and I discussed our options and decided we had no choice but to ask Donna to consider coming back and giving up her cruise with Roger's family. I knew if we did not call her soon, she would not be available to come back for at least two weeks, and we needed her help desperately.

Wesley and I decided to call her, and when I told her Wesley was getting worse and needed to go to the hospital, she said she would fly out the next day and stay as long as we needed her. She and Roger had planned to return to Rae and Mike's after their vacation and stay until Wesley got a transplant and was cleared to go home. Instead, they gave up the vacation. She flew back the next day, and Roger arrived a few days later in their car. I was so relieved and grateful to know she was on her way, and I could see a huge burden had been lifted from Wesley.

I took Wesley to the hospital a few hours after she arrived. By then, fortunately, he was doing better. They bumped up his steroids and the water pills and sent him home without an overnight stay.

A few days later, we met with the team of transplant doctors to discuss the tests that were necessary in order for Wesley to be placed on the transplant list and what would be required of us in the immediate future. They did not go into detail about what we would be dealing with long term, after the transplant. They only told us what they thought we needed to know as we needed to know it and could absorb it—and we did not want to know more than they were sharing with us. We had done our research. We had made an informed decision. We were convinced, beyond any doubt, we had to do this to try to save and prolong Wesley's life. We were willing to do it no matter what the limitations of life after transplant might be.

We took Hunter and his coloring books with us to the appointment. We felt it was important the doctors meet him and understand our urgent need to get Wesley on the transplant list. Just showing up with health insurance and hope did not ensure Wesley would be added to the list. We brought Hunter to make sure the doctors knew the family they were fighting for—and that included Hunter.

Among the list of tests were extensive blood work for tissue typing and other markers; X-rays and CT scans to make sure he did not have any underlying disease and to size his lungs; a dental evaluation, because if Wesley had cavities, those teeth would need to be pulled to avoid dental work when on anti-rejection medication after the transplant; a psychological evaluation of both of us to ensure we had the mental and emotional capacity necessary to contend with the difficulties of a transplant; and a 600-foot walk in six minutes. They said he could use as much oxygen as he needed, but if he could not finish the walk in the required amount of time, he would not be listed.

"What happens if he cannot finish the walk?" I asked.

Dr. Young directed his answer at Wesley. "The transplant board feels it is cruel to put you through transplant surgery if you do not have the strength to survive it. The walk is the best way we have to determine your physical capabilities."

Because Wesley had severe pulmonary hypertension, even minimal exertion caused his oxygen levels to plummet. Many lung transplant patients are able to walk and build up strength, using extra oxygen, when preparing for a transplant, but Wesley was not capable of it because of his high pressures. I feared Wesley would not be able to finish the walk in the amount of time allowed, but he had several tests to undergo before we even had to consider the walk, so I put my fears aside.

"How long are you planning to stay?" Dr. Young asked.

"We moved here last week. We left our home in Houston and rented an apartment to live in until I get the transplant and am cleared to go home," Wesley answered, proving our commitment to being there and doing whatever it took to get the transplant.

Dr. Young looked surprised. He did not know we had already relocated.

"That's considerable effort for your family without even being on the list yet," he said.

"Dr. Young, I'm not getting any better. I brought my family to UAB because I know there is no one with my blood type waiting for a transplant here. I can't go home without a transplant," he told the doctor.

"We'll do all we can for you. There is no way to know how long it will take for lungs to come for you, but being here is the first step," he told us.

"The drive out here was hard on me. How do we handle the wait for the lungs?" Wesley asked, realizing he was getting worse by the day.

"We keep you alive until the lungs come; that's how we handle it."

"Then we came to the right place," Wesley responded, leaning toward Dr. Young from his wheelchair to shake his hand.

Before we left the pulmonary clinic, a nurse gave me a card with a phone number to call in the morning to start scheduling tests. We knew it might take days to even begin the simple tests, based on availability, but we were in this for the long haul.

As I walked through the lobby, I noticed several lung patients on oxygen. It was the first time we had been in a hospital where Wesley was not the only one. Not all the patients were waiting for lungs. There were also people there waiting for other organ transplants. One man we met while waiting for our appointment said he had had his kidney fifteen years and was only there for a routine check-up.

Another elderly woman in the lobby looked tired and weary. She was waiting for a lung transplant and had been waiting for eleven months. Meeting people like her scared me. I only wanted to meet people with successful transplants who were on the road to a full recovery, but, of course, that was not realistic.

Being at the hospital brought back memories of the time when I was undergoing treatment for Hodgkin's disease. I often had to go to the lab to have my blood drawn, and I got to know the people who worked there. Patients would frequently share their stories while waiting in the lobby. I met a woman during one of my visits who was incredibly sick with a blood disorder her doctors were not able to diagnose. They had done every test, tried every treatment, but she was not getting better, and they did not know why.

I felt sorry for her, although I was being treated for cancer. I knew even then I was fortunate to have something that was quickly diagnosed and had a protocol for treatment. The chemotherapy was grueling, and the idea of radiation therapy terrified me, but I knew what I had to do. I knew if I followed the treatment regimen we had worked with my doctors to choose, there was a very good chance I would survive and live a healthy life.

The girl I met at the lab knew nothing of her future or even of her present. She was bound by a disease that had no name and no treatment, and she was losing hope. Since Wesley had first started getting sick and the doctors could not tell us why, I had thought often of that girl with the rare blood disorder she knew was slowly killing her. I thought about what it must have been like for her and wondered if the doctors ever came up with a treatment to save her life. She and Wesley had found themselves in the same place: undiagnosed, untreatable, and slowly dying. Cancer is not the worst thing that can happen to a person, but it was the worst thing that had ever happened to us until Wesley's illness.

When we had arrived at the hotel the week before, the concierge told us there was another lung transplant patient living there. He told us she had received her transplant about six weeks before and was waiting for clearance to go home. He was not allowed to tell us what room she was in, but smiled and said if we hung out in the hallway long enough, we would run into her. Later that night, I saw a woman walking into her room across the hall from us. I greeted her, and she responded politely as she closed the door. That day in the clinic lobby, I saw her again and recognized her as she was leaving. I stopped her in the lobby and introduced myself.

"Hello, it's nice to meet you. I heard your family is living across the hall from me at the hotel," she said cheerfully. "Please stop by anytime."

She seemed short of breath. As she quickly walked away, Wesley looked at me with concern.

"She didn't look like she was breathing very well. Shouldn't she be better by now?" he asked me.

"Every patient is different. They told us that from the start," I reminded him. I tried not to show my fear, hoping his transplant would be different.

I had called the phone number on the card the nurse gave me the very next morning. When no one returned my call by the following morning, I called again. This time, a wonderful young woman named Deandra answered. She scheduled a few tests, but the first available times were for two weeks later. I was frustrated with the wait, but we understood and were prepared for the delay.

The next week Wesley was not doing well. We were going through more oxygen tanks than usual—at least thirty-five tanks a week. This was besides the plug-in oxygen machine Wesley used when at home. Much of the time he required both the plug-in oxygen and the mask. It varied from one day, or even one hour, to the next. There was no explanation for it. It was just a part of our everyday lives.

The men who delivered the oxygen to us twice a week were very kind. They could empathize with what we were going through even though they only saw us briefly during each delivery. But the company providing the oxygen started questioning our need for it. It was the office personnel on the phone who questioned me, although they did not have the right or the authority to do so. Our insurance was paying for every tank, and we were paying our deductible, not only for the oxygen tanks, but for Flolan and the numerous other medications Wesley was taking daily.

Wesley was having a difficult week and once again the woman on the phone questioned me when I called for an additional delivery of oxygen tanks. I decided I would put an end to this relentless questioning.

I asked to speak with her supervisor, who immediately came onto the phone.

"I don't know what your typical customer's oxygen use is in a week, but my husband isn't typical," I told her firmly. "He can barely walk across our small kitchen, and he had to stop reading our four-year-old son bedtime stories months ago, because even reading to our son made him too short of breath. We are here waiting for a double lung transplant. When I call to ask for additional oxygen tanks, it is because he is struggling more than usual. The last thing I want to do is explain myself to your employee, because all I am thinking about is how to keep him alive long enough for him to get the lungs he needs."

"I understand," the supervisor said. Again, here was someone telling me she understood, when she did not.

"Please don't say you understand, because you don't—and I don't expect you to understand. That's not what this phone call is about. It's about my need to be able to call for extra help—that, by the way, your company is profiting from—so my husband can stay alive and fight his way through another day," I stated.

"I will make sure you never have to explain yourself again. I apologize for any inconvenience this has caused you and your husband," she timidly replied.

I was never questioned again.

A few days later, we moved into our apartment. It was hard work getting settled and finding room for everything we had brought from home. At one point, after I had been unpacking and organizing our belongings for most of the day, I stopped to sit down. I looked around at all there was left to do, and my anguish and exhaustion must have shown on my face.

"Keep going, honey. You're doing great," Wesley said, encouraging me to get the job done.

"Okay," I said, then got up from the couch and kept going. We both knew if I stopped, I would have a hard time getting going again. Not knowing what our schedule would be like in the coming days, I wanted to get everything done while there was still time. I knew Wesley wanted to help me unpack, but he helped by appreciating I had to do it alone.

Since we had to wait for two weeks for Wesley's tests to begin, we decided to load up the wheelchair and several oxygen tanks into the car and explore Birmingham. We took Hunter to the park, browsed the nearby mall, ate lunch at an Italian restaurant, and ran a few errands. We needed to open a new personal bank account because our bank in Houston did not have a branch in Birmingham. Wesley had to go inside the bank with me, so I looked for handicap parking near the front entrance.

Just as I was about to pull into the handicap parking, the only parking spot left in the busy parking lot, a woman pulled into it, got out of her car and walked into the bank, seemingly without any handicap at all. I was furious!

Wesley turned to Hunter in the back seat and said, "Uh oh. Mommy's mad."

"Wait here, guys," I said to both of them as I got out of the car and stormed into the bank, looking for the woman who had just taken our parking spot and was illegally parked in handicap parking.

I quickly found her waiting in line for the bank teller.

"Excuse me. Is that your black sedan parked in front of the building?" I politely asked her.

"Uh, yes."

"I watched you walk in and, forgive me if I am wrong, you do not appear to be handicapped. I did not see any proof of you being handicapped on your license plate, nor did I see a handicapped parking permit hanging from your rear view mirror," I calmly stated.

"Yes, well, I am in a hurry. I'm on my lunch break, and the parking lot is full," she began with her excuses, not the least bit apologetic.

By now people in line were looking at us.

"Really? You're in a hurry?" I pressed.

"Yes. I'll only be a minute here, then I will move my car," she responded as she began to turn her back to me.

"You see my car out there?" I asked her, pointing to the Suburban which I had parked behind her car, wedging it in so she would be unable to move it. Wesley and Hunter could be seen through the window, so Wesley waved to her when she looked in their direction.

"I see it," she answered, folding her arms full of attitude.

"Well, that's my husband and our son in that car. My husband's on oxygen and can't walk ten feet without getting short of breath, so we need that parking spot, and we have a legal right to it. Surely you can see our handicap parking permit hanging on the rear view mirror."

Her arms still folded in anger, she nodded her head.

"Either you step out of line to move your car, or I'm not moving our car until a police officer has an opportunity to write you a ticket, which I am sure will not only make you late for work but will also cost you at least an hour's wages."

A gentleman in front of her in the line chimed in. "You know, my mom is handicapped and goes through the same thing all the time. People who aren't handicapped park in a handicap zone, without even considering the people who need it. You really should move your car, Ma'am."

"Your choice," I said, now folding my arms as well.

She huffed her way out of the bank, and I followed behind her so I could move out of her way and take the parking spot. She left the parking lot and did not go back into the bank.

"I can't believe you did that," Wesley laughed.

"You can't?" I chuckled, pulling into the parking spot that was rightfully ours.

"Well, I guess I can," he smiled.

Over the next few days, Wesley spent much of his time in bed. Any energy he had was spent on Hunter, playing with him in any capacity he could, which usually equated to watching Hunter play. By the third day, Wesley was coughing continually and having a hard time catching his breath.

The evening of the second day he spent in bed, he wanted to take a shower, so I helped him as I had been doing for months. As

I washed his shoulders and back, he sat on the shower bench and struggled to breathe through the steam building up in the bathroom, so I cracked open the bathroom door and turned on the overhead fan.

I began to study every inch of him. The man I had shared my life with for thirteen years, the man I thought I knew from head to toe, was unrecognizable to me now. As I studied him, something told me, "Remember every inch of him, because he is leaving the earth."

The words were not my own, and I tried to dismiss them. I did not want him to leave the earth, and I was doing everything I could to prevent it. But in that moment, my overwhelming reality was that he was leaving the earth, and I wanted to memorize every inch of him so I might remember in his absence every freckle, every muscle, every hair, everything about this physical being without whom I could not imagine living.

I was done rinsing his hair and body, so I handed the shower nozzle back to him, and he started to lean forward to turn off the water.

"Please stay," I asked him as I put both of my palms on his shoulders. "Just stay."

Wesley paused for a moment, but he did not look at me. He just leaned back on the bench, into my open hands, and closed his eyes. I rubbed his shoulders and tried not to cry. As the water splashed my hands and face, I stood in the brief moment we shared at the end of that shower. I rested my chin on the top of his head and was silent. The bathroom was full of steam, my hair and clothes were wet by now, but I just stood next to him and held onto him, taking him in.

The longer we stayed in the bathroom, the harder it was for Wesley to breathe because of the humidity in the room. I did not want him to struggle, so I kissed him on the back of his head, let go of his shoulders, and stepped away from the shower.

As Wesley reached forward to turn off the water and stood for me to dry him off, I said again, to myself this time, "Please stay." I did not want him to leave the earth.

Wesley's ability to breathe was getting worse, so I decided to call Deandra again the next morning. I explained to her Wesley was struggling more than usual and wondered if we could at least get squeezed in for some simple blood tests or the chest X-ray, so he could feel like something was being done. I told her it might raise his spirits if he knew the process was under way to become listed so he could begin the wait for a transplant.

She agreed to do her best. When she called back an hour later, she had scheduled three tests for the following week: blood work, a chest X-ray, and the psychological evaluation. She said each department had a cancellation, so she grabbed the appointments while she could. I was elated, and Wesley seemed relieved. This meant Wesley's tests would begin a week earlier than planned, and he might be listed sooner. We could not ask for much more than that.

By the time we went to the clinic for his tests, he was doing a little better, but we had to load several oxygen tanks in the car to take with us. We never knew what kind of traffic we might face on the freeway or how long the wait would be for each appointment. We still had Jimbo's car, which was equipped with OnStar in case of an emergency, but I hoped we would never need to use it.

Hunter stayed with Donna and Roger while Wesley and I went to his appointments. Going anywhere was a challenge, but we had developed a system. Wesley would get in his wheelchair. I would load one tank into the tank holder I had assembled on the wheelchair, lean one tank on each side of his legs, then place two more in a large duffle bag we had bought to strap onto the back of the wheelchair. We parked the car in handicap parking so it was always close to the nearest exit in case I needed to get more tanks; having five tanks with us gave us enough time to anticipate needing more.

It was not easy pushing Wesley in the wheelchair with the additional weight of the tanks, but I built up strength and even learned how to maneuver elevators, sharp corners, and people who walked freely without considering the load I was pushing, often cutting me off without even realizing it.

Somehow, we always managed to arrive everywhere on time, despite the obstacles we faced in getting to any destination. In hospitals that usually meant we ended up waiting, and that was true this day as well. Wesley went through one oxygen tank just waiting for the nurse to draw blood.

We did not know what to expect during our psychological evaluation. We planned to be honest and try not to anticipate the doctor's questions or manipulate our answers. We figured we had what it took to get through what we had endured thus far, and we would do whatever it took to learn to thrive after the transplant. We just needed to get on the list.

The doctor's line of questioning was almost predictable. It did not seem like an evaluation at all by the time we were halfway through it. I think she must have figured us out early on and knew the rest was just a technicality.

"Do you have a supportive family back home?"

Wesley answered. "Yes, my parents are living here while we wait for my transplant. My stepdad has already been here once and will return often. Lisa's parents have been instrumental in caring for our son, especially in the months before getting here. Her mom stayed with us a lot to look after Hunter when I was in the hospital throughout the past year."

"Have you two had to deal with significant stress in your marriage before?"

"Yes, I was diagnosed with cancer two years after we were married," I told her. "I underwent chemotherapy and radiation. Wesley went to every appointment with me and was my strength throughout it. I've been well for nine years now."

"How much do you think your son understands, and what are your plans for helping him cope with your new life after the transplant?"

"Hunter is a very bright kid and has been adaptable throughout my illness. We've raised him to rely on us. He trusts us, so we know as we learn to cope with transplant life, he will follow our lead," Wesley said as he conveyed to the doctor what our family was all about.

"What scares you most about a transplant?" she asked Wesley.

"Not getting one," Wesley answered.

That concluded our evaluation and led to a relaxed, additional ten-minute conversation about our lives in general. When we were done, she told us she had never met two stronger candidates, from her point of view.

She watched as I switched Wesley's oxygen tank because the one he was using during our appointment was running low. She saw us struggle to get Wesley out the door in his wheelchair.

"Have you done the walk yet?" she asked.

"That's next week," I answered, knowing what was on her mind. I am sure she, too, wondered how Wesley could possibly do it successfully in his condition.

The next day I called Deandra to find out what other tests had been scheduled. She had managed to get every remaining test scheduled for the following week. I could not believe it. I thanked her and told Wesley the good news.

The final test of the following week was the 600-foot walk in six minutes. There was no way to physically prepare for it, so we just told ourselves Wesley would do his best and make it through.

The night before the walking test, we went to rent a few movies. Wesley had stopped going into the store with us during errands but often came with us in the car just to get out of the house. As Hunter and I were walking out of the video store, a severely obese woman was walking in. When I got back into the car, Wesley looked troubled as he stared out the window.

"What's the matter?" I asked, wondering what had caused him to look so upset.

"I just have a hard time watching something like that. That incredibly obese woman who has a choice about her health and quality of life is abusing her body, but she can still manage to walk into the video store—and I have to wait in the car because the walk is too difficult for me."

I did not know how to respond to his comment. I just held his hand.

The morning of the walk, I made a healthy breakfast for us and made sure Wesley was able to sleep in and get as much rest as possible. I knew he would not eat much, as he rarely did these days, but I wanted to make sure he had the option for optimum nutrition.

Hunter stayed with Donna and Roger, while Wesley and I headed for the hospital with eight oxygen tanks. We would be meeting with Scott, Wesley's physical therapist, for the walk. We had met with him a few times before, but because of Wesley's pulmonary pressure, he could not do much to help him prepare for surgery.

When we arrived, Scott had a portable oxygen machine and heart monitor ready. He said he would carry everything and push Wesley's additional oxygen tank for him during the walk, so Wesley could just concentrate on walking.

We sat on the chairs lining the wall of the physical therapy room. There were no other patients there, just Wesley. Scott explained to us Wesley would walk the circle of the room three times and he would be timed. He had to complete the walk within six minutes to pass the test and have any chance of getting listed for a transplant.

I could not see the entire path of the walk because there were offices in the center of the room the walkway circled. Scott asked me if I wanted to walk with them, but I declined. I did not want to interfere. I was not wearing a watch, and I did not look for a clock in the room. I did not want to know if he passed until it was over.

Wesley stood up and was ready to begin the walk.

"This is it," Wesley said to us.

He looked calm and as prepared as he could be. I was a nervous wreck but managed to hide it from Wesley.

"You can do it," I assured him.

"You ready to get started?" Scott asked him.

"Yep. Let's do it."

As the two of them walked away from me, I immediately began to pray for Wesley to have the strength to pass the test and finish the walk in time. When he turned the bend and was out of my sight, I held back the tears, trying to remain positive for him, knowing he would turn the corner soon and see me. I could not show him my fear.

When he came back into sight and smiled at me, I did not say a word. I just smiled back. I did not want him to exert any energy trying to respond to my comments.

Wesley and Scott rounded the next corner and were out of sight again. This time it took them longer to turn the bend. I was getting worried about Wesley's ability to finish in time. If his pace slowed with each circuit, he would not finish the walk in six minutes.

This time, he did not look at me; he just concentrated on walking.

I started to cry when he rounded the corner again and could not see me. It felt like an eternity as I waited for him to turn the final corner. I waited and waited. There was no sign of him. Each second felt like minutes.

What was happening? Had he stopped? Had he gotten into trouble and fainted, or worse, during the last lap?

Still, there was no sign of him. I could not hold back the tears. "It's over," I thought to myself. After all we had done to get here, it was over. No matter how solid or capable or insured we were, it would all come down to this walk.

My mind began to race. I could not stop thinking about starting over at a new transplant hospital with more tests. I knew Wesley might not survive that. I thought about what to say to him if he failed. This walk was everything to us. Our family, as we knew it, depended on Wesley rounding that last corner in time. If he did not, he would surely die.

"I'm done," Wesley said, as the two of them appeared, finishing the last stretch of the last lap.

"You want to stop right here and catch your breath?" Scott asked him.

I was silent. It felt like more than six minutes, but I could not be sure. I waited for one of them to say something, anything.

Wesley nodded and stopped, just a few feet away from where I was still sitting, still waiting. Scott was holding the heart rate monitor and the portable oxygen tanks.

"Congratulation, Wes," Scott said.

I jumped out of my chair and into Wesley's arms. He had done it! He had finished the walk in time! Somehow the man who, on a daily basis, could not get from one room to the next without struggling to breathe, had managed to find it in himself to finish the walk in six minutes.

This 600-foot walk represented everything to me about our journey thus far: the fear of taking it on, the difficulty of being a spectator, and the joy in finding hope where it was least expected. I was never more proud of Wesley than I was that day. Other than our son Hunter, there was nothing more important to both of us than his finishing that walk and getting on the transplant list. How long he would have to wait, if the lungs would come in time, what the outcome would be—none of that was in our control. The walk, he could do, and he did it.

Until he had finished and was resting in the chair next to me, I had been so distracted I had not noticed he was wearing the baseball cap I had given him for Father's Day two years before. I had had "Hunter's Pride" embroidered on the front of the hat because that was how I could best describe him and what he meant to Hunter.

"You wore the hat," I said to Wesley, pointing to his head.

"Yeah," he gasped, still trying to catch his breath.

We got the call the next day that Wesley was on the lung transplant list. The transplant board voted unanimously in his favor. It was a Wednesday. The waiting had begun.

CHAPTER TEN

Three-Day Wait

"If you see a light, run away," I told Wesley as the nurses prepped him for surgery.

"Okay," he said with a chuckle.

"No, really," I told him. "If you see something I cannot see about your life, and you don't come back to me, I'll know it's the only way, and I'll accept it. I'll know you were better off and that's the only reason you did not come back to us."

There we were, in the middle of the miracle we had prayed for, ever aware of the gift a complete stranger had given us. It was the answer to our prayers, but we also knew, with life after transplant, we would be trading one set of complications for another. I needed him to know if God showed him something I could not see from where I stood—conscious and on this side of life waiting for his surgery to end—I would understand; I knew the only thing that would keep Wesley from returning to us was if he saw a life he could not live or did not want our family to endure.

When Dr. Young told us Wesley was being listed for transplant and explained the process to us, we were faced with the realization that sometime soon someone was going to die—and Wesley might live because of it. Our tragedy would end as someone else's began. There was no way to reconcile that in our minds. The one thing that gave us both peace was that we knew Wesley would have done the same for someone else. Even before Wesley got sick, he was adamant about being a registered organ donor; he had a heart symbol on his driver's license to prove it. We realized he was not asking anything from a transplant donor or the donor's loved ones he would not have been willing to give himself, and that allowed us to move forward. We were fully committed to our decision and had no doubts.

Shortly after midnight, just three days after Wesley was listed for his transplant, we received the call. It was exactly one year from the day he had cleaned out the old cabinet in our garage the year before and first became sick. Hunter and I had gone to bed, but Wesley could not sleep. I was in charge of keeping our cell phone with me in case we got the call. We had asked our friends and family not to call us past 9 p.m.; when the phone rang at that late hour, I knew before I answered it there was a match. Wesley heard the phone ring from the living room where he was watching television. He also knew what the call was about.

We did not expect to get the call so soon. A three-day wait for a transplant was unheard of, and to our knowledge had never happened at this hospital. But it was Trina, our transplant coordinator, on the phone. She told me there was a match for Wesley; he would be on standby for surgery through the night. She said she would keep us posted, and if everything continued as planned, we would need to be at the hospital by 5:30 a.m. that morning.

The first thing we did was say a silent prayer for the family who had just lost their loved one and for the donor who had lost his or her life. We promised to never forget or take for granted the gracious gift given to us by a stranger.

Trina told us to try to get some rest, but neither one of us could sleep, so we began calling family and friends. We had given my friend Kelli a list of family and friends' email addresses before we left Houston, so she could email everyone and keep them informed when we got the call for the transplant. She quickly emailed everyone on the list. Our phone began ringing and continued to ring throughout the night with calls from our loved ones, overwhelmed by the news.

I tried not to worry about the actual surgery because a lung transplant was the only option Wesley had left for survival. I had to believe getting the call so soon after Wesley was added to the transplant list was a good sign we had made the right decision.

Donna and Roger made plans to be at our apartment at 5:00 a.m. Donna and I would take Wesley to the hospital while Roger stayed with Hunter. The plan was for Roger to care for Hunter while I was at the hospital off and on during the two weeks the doctors told us it would take for Wesley to recover from the surgery if everything went well.

There was so much to do to prepare. I made a list of Hunter's needs and comforts, hoping to make it easier for Roger. I also hoped to make Hunter more comfortable in our absence by writing down his schedule. I cleaned the apartment and in between I sat with Wesley, making sure he was coping well with the sudden news and the reality of the surgery he would undergo in just a few hours. Hunter was fast asleep and completely unaware of what was happening.

Just the day before, we had explained to Hunter we hoped his daddy would be having surgery that might help him get well. We told him we did not know when it would be. We read him a book the hospital had recommended written to help children understand when a loved one was receiving an organ transplant. We feared the questions Hunter might ask. We knew he would understand someone would have to die for his daddy to live. To our amazement, the book had just enough explanation for him. He was satisfied to know we were doing our best to keep his daddy here with us.

At one point, as I was busy preparing our apartment for our expected absence, it occurred to me I should stop what I was doing and just sit with Wesley. It was possible the surgery would go badly, and if it did, this could be our last night together, our last hours to talk and to say what needed to be said at a time like this. Although the truth was, there was nothing left unsaid. We were committed to our choice for transplant, and this was part of that choice. We knew it was our only hope, and we also knew if he did not have the surgery soon, he might not live much longer. We could not ask for this gift, then question it. We were steadfast.

Nevertheless, I stopped cleaning and sat at the foot of Wesley's chair. We talked for a little while about all that was running through our racing minds. Then Wesley said, "Keep going. We have to make sure things are ready for Hunter."

Trina called again just before 5:00 a.m. and said, so far, the surgery was still scheduled. We had been warned of false alarms—a last minute unexpected problem with the donor lungs, an unanticipated complication with the match, any number of reasons to cancel the surgery and begin the wait all over again. We had even heard of patients being wheeled into the operating room and then wheeled out again at the last possible moment, the surgery canceled for an unforeseen reason, so when we got the call from Trina to go ahead and leave for the hospital, we were relieved everything was going ahead as scheduled.

"Are the lungs a good match for Wesley?" I asked her. "Are they the perfect match?"

"There couldn't be a better match for him, and the lungs are very healthy," she reassured me.

We followed her directions to the wing of the hospital where Wesley would be prepped for surgery. As he was being prepped, a nurse named Kim removed the end of his oxygen hose from the tank we had brought with us and started looking for a wall unit to attach it to. She wanted to save the use of our tank, not realizing we had two more in the duffle bag attached to his wheelchair and four more in the car, in case the surgery was called off and he needed the oxygen to get home.

The longer it took for the nurse to find a place to attach the oxygen tube, the more concerned Wesley and I became. His lips were turning blue and his breathing was labored after just seconds without oxygen.

"Please plug him back in until you find a wall unit to use," I told Kim, walking to Wesley's bedside to reattach the oxygen tube to the tank we had brought with us.

She had not looked at him since removing his tube from the tank. When she did, she was shaken and amazed.

"Wow. You are really struggling," Kim said as she handed me the tube and I reattached it to the tank. "I'm so sorry. Your saturations dropped to the low seventies in a matter of seconds."

Wesley was struggling to recover from the short amount of time he went without oxygen.

"That's why we're here," I said with a meek smile. "We are more afraid of what will happen if he doesn't get this transplant than if he does, because at least with the transplant we have a chance."

"We call you a 'lunger,'" Kim told Wesley. "Every lunger has a person who they keep close in case they get into trouble. You're the one he counts on, Lisa. You're his person."

By now, Wesley was breathing better and responded, "Yeah,

Lisa's my person."

He smiled and winked at me. I knew what he meant, and I smiled back.

Dr. Wille was examining Wesley and taking notes. I had met him the first day we came to the transplant hospital. He was very approachable.

"Will you be reversing Wesley's blood thinners with plasma?" I asked him.

"We will," he answered.

"He doesn't tolerate the cold plasma well. He's crashes if it goes in too quickly. Can you please put a note in his chart to titrate the plasma slowly?" I asked.

"Yeah, I will make sure I make a note of it," he assured me.

"Will you be in the operating room?"

"No, Dr. Zorn will be performing surgery."

"Would you please tell him yourself as well as adding it to your notes?" I pressed him. "Wesley doesn't have far to fall, and I've seen how quickly he declines when compromised."

"I'll be sure to let Dr. Zorn know," Dr. Wille reassured me.

The nurses struggled to shave Wesley's goatee. No one had told us he needed to be clean shaven before surgery, or he would have done it himself that morning.

Soon, Wesley was wheeled out of the room and on his way to another wing of the hospital for surgery. The nurses explained where they would be taking him and where Donna and I could wait during the long surgery.

It was time to part ways in the hallway around the corner from the elevator. I would not see him again until after the surgery. I was scared. He must have been scared, too, but he did not show it. He just gave me a kiss and told me he loved me. I kissed him back and told him I loved him. Then he was gone.

Within a few seconds, I knew he would be on the elevator and I would not be able to talk to him again for hours, so I called to him, without seeing him, "I love you!"

Wesley called back, "I love you!"

Donna and I walked to the surgery waiting room and settled in, knowing it would be many hours before the surgery was over.

As I gazed at the blooming pear trees in front of me through the large picture window of the waiting room, I thought about Wesley upstairs, the bad lungs being replaced with the good. I thought about our son Hunter and how he would wake up in the morning and we would not be there. We had prepared him as we had prepared ourselves—but is anyone ever truly prepared?

The pear trees, the operating table upstairs, the scalpel, the doctors, the nurses—a brief picture of each flashed momentarily in my head, one after another. There was so much the staff here did not know about Wesley and me. They did not know we had met when we were kids and I still remember what he was wearing the day we met: reddish-brown corduroy pants and a red, orange, and white striped shirt. He had long, blond hair and freckles.

They did not know how close our families were; his father was like my own; my father was like his own. They did not know we married fourteen years after meeting that day in my front yard, or that two years after we married I was diagnosed with cancer.

They did not know the pillar of strength he was to me when I was sick or how he saved me every day as I feared for my life and our future together. They did not know he was at every doctor's appointment and on the other side of the door during every grueling procedure I endured, including two bone marrow biopsies.

They did not know we had our son three years later, despite the risk of infertility from my cancer treatments. They did not know Wesley had stayed awake until 3:00 a.m. on Christmas Eve, just two months before, and I woke to find him in our kitchen putting the last of four casserole dishes he had prepared into the refrigerator for Christmas dinner later that afternoon. His legs were blue and the oxygen tubes attached to him were not helping him enough, but the lack of oxygen would not stop him. They did not know he did these things because he wanted to do them, not because he had to do them.

This was Wesley. The months before this day had been turbulent while Wesley was on high doses of steroids and suffering from extreme oxygen deprivation. He had endured countless medications, months of oxygen machines that still did not help him get across a room without struggle, and more hospital stays in one year than most people experience in a lifetime. But he was here for the transplant, to do all he could to live even a little while longer. He was fighting for another Little League season with Hunter, another anniversary with me, another day on the water enjoying the outdoors—these are the things he lived for.

All they knew at that very moment was Wesley was prepared to have his lungs removed from his body and replaced by a stranger's, and it was their job to make sure he survived it. But that was all they needed to know.

As I stared at the pear trees, I considered Wesley's grit and tenacity—the fight that had always been in him, even when it was not necessary. As he was upstairs fighting for his life, and I waited in front of the picture window, I realized every part of him was necessary. It would be what got him through the next hours of his life. It would be what got him to the other side of the barricade of pain and released him to the mountain of hope that awaited us.

By now, we had been married for more than ten years. We had put each other first and worked through the issues in our marriage that could have ended us but never would. We were solid, and we genuinely wanted to be exactly where we were. Whatever it was I felt when I met him—a whisper from God or a schoolgirl crush—it stayed with me all my life, and it was with me in that waiting room.

It had only been an hour since they finished prepping him for surgery and wheeled him to the operating room. It was just after 7:00 a.m.

Suddenly, I had a bad feeling, a feeling something was going wrong upstairs and Wesley was in danger. I could not shake it. Just then, a voice came over the loudspeaker telling some of the other family members in the waiting room to go to the fifth floor waiting area to speak with the surgeons for an update. Wesley's surgeon was not announced, but I took the elevator to the fifth floor anyway. I figured I could at least have someone make sure he was okay. Someone could reassure me of his safety and make the sick feeling deep inside of me go away.

When the elevator doors opened, several people were there, waiting for updates. I stood in front of two large, swinging wood doors. "DO NOT ENTER" the sign clearly read. To the right of the sign was a red button that could be used to call a nurse to the door, but I was told to wait as the surgeons would be out shortly.

After a few minutes, the large wood doors swung open. I could see inside. I could see the patients in recovery. One of the surgeons I had met the week before was talking on a telephone in the middle of the room. He said, "Yes, I'm on my way!"

Then he hung up the phone and ran in the opposite direction of the waiting families. The doors closed and immediately reopened. A nurse talked to one family privately, then told the rest of us to wait downstairs; we would be updated shortly.

I got on the elevator with the one family that had been briefed by the nurse.

"Dr. McGiffin had to go assist a surgery. A lung transplant patient coded," the older gentleman said.

"What does coded mean?" the younger man next to him asked.

"His heart stopped," he answered out loud as I answered simultaneously in my head.

When the elevator doors opened and closed, I went back up to the fifth floor. I pressed the red button and was soon greeted by a different nurse than before.

"My husband is in surgery. He's having a double lung transplant. I heard another family talking about a lung transplant patient coding. Is it my husband? His name is Wesley. Is he all right?"

"Wait here. I'll see what I can find out," the nurse told me.

The doors closed again.

My body became cold. I began to shiver. I always shiver and my teeth chatter when I am nervous. My heart was racing. It was more than fear. It was a glimpse into the other side, my first glimpse with such immediacy. In the months since Wesley had gotten sick, I feared the reality I would grow old without him. I feared what might happen if he did not get better and then, when he did not get better, I feared the transplant and what would happen if a donor did not come in time. There was so much to consider, but this was different. This was now. Right now. If he died, it was over. I was terrified.

My mind raced and the bad feeling intensified. No tears. No words. There was just overwhelming fear. Silent fear. I did not have a single continuous thought. Just one thought and then another before the first could be completed. I thought about Hunter, awake by now and told by his Papa we were at the hospital. His daddy was getting new lungs, and we hoped he would be better soon. He was waiting for us, as I was waiting for Wesley.

We had not made Hunter any promises, even though we wished

we could. We wished we could promise our four-year-old son his dad would be there to watch him grow up. We wanted that for him more than we wanted anything else, but Hunter trusted us and we could not lie to him. The most we could do was tell him we would do our best for him and for our family. That had to be enough.

As the fear of Wesley being the patient coding in the operating room mounted inside of me, I wanted to tell him I was not ready. I was not ready to raise Hunter by myself. I was not ready to live my life without him.

"Code. Code. Code," I said it repeatedly in my head.

I asked how this could happen. How had we come so far? We had moved to another state because the wait for lungs with Wesley's blood type was shortest here. We had lived in a hotel, the three of us, because the apartment Wesley found was not ready when we arrived. We had come here together, as a family, the three of us against the world. It was never a question. We were here to save his life and the only life I could imagine living. Our life together, like everything about Wesley, was necessary.

The two wood doors opened and the nurse from before was standing in front of me.

"Your husband is fine. His surgery hasn't started yet," he told me, then quickly shut the door.

I was soon in front of the pear trees again, hope restored, but the sick feeling did not go away on its own. I had to force it away because I knew I had to clear my head of any negative thoughts. The clock on the wall was no longer taunting me. The eight hours they had told us to expect turned into nine and a half hours in surgery, but I knew he was alive, and that was all that mattered to me. I knew if they could keep him alive, Wesley would do the rest.

Finally, I heard our last name called over the loudspeaker. The elevator ride to the fifth floor seemed endless. Dr. Zorn was waiting for us when Donna and I stepped off. The rest of Wesley's family was on their way from Texas but would not arrive for two more hours.

"The lungs are a good match. A good set," Dr. Zorn told us.

"Did everything go well?" I asked.

"He tried to check out on us in the beginning. His heart stopped," he told me.

The nurse had lied to me earlier when he told me Wesley was okay and his surgery had not started yet. When Dr. McGiffin had been called to help, it was Wesley who had coded. I knew it. The sick feeling happening inside of me, my gut feeling, had been true, but I did not mention it.

"How did you bring him back?" I asked.

"I massaged his heart," he said, reenacting the motion in front of us with his hands. "He could have died at home any day without the transplant."

"And now?" I asked.

"Now he has a good set of lungs and a good chance," he answered.

A good chance. It was more than we had gone to sleep with the night before. The call came at 12:32 a.m. and it was the beginning of this day—a new day of hope. It was the day of the gift of lungs from a stranger, the picture window, the pear trees, and our son waking up with the news his daddy had a chance to be okay. That was enough. A good chance was enough.

I was able to see Wesley, even though he had not awakened from surgery yet. He was still in recovery and on life support—he was not breathing on his own. This was expected. It would take a few hours for him to wake up.

When I approached his bedside, I instantly noticed the color in his face was much better than before his surgery. I lifted the sheet and blanket from his lower body and was overjoyed to see his legs and feet were no longer pale purple but were now a perfect shade of creamy pink. It was absolutely incredible to see the difference throughout his entire body. I believed he could hear me, even though he was asleep.

"You did great, Wesley. You've got your new lungs and they are the perfect match for you. No rejection. No infection," I assured him. "You just rest, and we'll be out of here before you know it. You're going to walk Hunter to his first day of kindergarten in September without any oxygen tubes attached to you, just like you hoped."

Several hours passed. All we could do was wait. But the hours that elapsed without him waking up from surgery meant more than I realized. By then, the rest of the family had arrived, including Jimbo. It was the next morning after his surgery and Wesley still was not awake. I needed answers. This time, Jimbo took the elevator ride to the fifth floor with me.

I pressed the red button and asked for Dr. Zorn. He soon appeared.

He explained to us when Wesley's heart stopped, his blood pressure never fully recovered and his brain was deprived of oxygen. He told us Wesley might not be waking up because he had suffered brain damage. We could not know what damage was done, but the longer it took for him to wake up, the less likely it was he would wake up at all.

"So are you telling me if he wakes up then he did not suffer brain damage and he could still be himself? He could still be Wesley?" I asked him, trying to find something good in what he had just said to me.

"I am telling you he has suffered brain damage. We just don't know how much," he answered.

"But it's possible he could wake up and still be Wesley?" I pressed further.

"There's no way to know right now," he told us.

As we entered the elevator, I began to cry tears of rage. Anger filled every part of me.

"All he wanted was to be himself. The rest he can do, but he has to be Wesley! Damn! Damn! Damn!" I yelled.

For the first time since we had left Houston for the hope of returning one day with more life and breath inside of us, I slid to the floor in tears of despair. Jimbo tried to hold me up, but the weight of my heart was too heavy. After the extraordinary gift of Wesley receiving lungs in three days when they warned we might wait for months, how could this be? Where had the hope gone?

I had talked to my sister Bev several times since we received the call about the donor lungs. She kept offering to fly in, but I had told her I could handle it. Bev did not want me to be alone, but Wesley's family was my family, too, and they were there. I had told her I could cope without her, but when Dr. Zorn told me about the likelihood of brain damage, I immediately called and asked her to come.

"Somebody needs to get on a plane right now and get out here. I don't care who. Just get somebody here now!" I told her when she answered the phone. I was crying uncontrollably.

"Okay, Lisa. I'll get on a plane. I'll get there as soon as I can. Are you all right?" She had to ask.

"I'm not all right. Nothing is right. Wesley was very clear he wants to come through this and still be himself, or he doesn't want to come through it at all," I cried.

"He's strong, Lisa, and he loves you and Hunter. You mean the world to him, and he will get through this for you." She tried to reassure me.

Her flight would arrive at 9:30 the next morning, the Monday after his surgery.

I went to see Wesley again. He was still sleeping. We both knew his thirty-five-year-old lungs would not have lasted until his thirty-sixth birthday. The undiagnosed illness he had suffered was relentless. This surgery was, after all, our only hope.

I sat at his side and held his hand. I told him I loved him, and I told him I would wait as long as it took for him to wake up.

"I'm in charge of you. Nothing happens to you without my permission, and I will wait as long as you need. You just find your way back to us," I whispered to him.

In the weeks before his transplant, Wesley read everything he could about transplant patients. He had read about a man who had a heart transplant that did not go well. The man was in a coma for almost a week after surgery and could hear all of his family talking to and about him. He could even hear the doctors trying to prepare them for the possibility he might not wake up, but he just could not respond. When the man finally woke up, he was able to recall small bits of what had transpired during his coma.

"You have to give me enough time to wake up," Wesley told me after he read that story. "I want six months, no matter what they tell you. I want six months to come out of it. After that, you do what you think is best, but you have to give me a chance."

"Six months. I promise," I assured him.

The day dragged on and on. I visited him every hour and spoke to him quietly, each time telling him we loved him and reminding him I would wait as long as it took for him to wake up.

Later that day, almost twenty-four hours after his surgery, one of his doctors told me Wesley was having small seizures and they were not sure what was causing them, other than complications from the surgery.

Worry filled me. All I could do was enter the room and go to his side every hour, continuing to assure him nothing would happen to him while I was looking out for him.

A night without his voice and his arms, even without the noise of his oxygen machine, was long and lonely. I wanted to go to Hunter, but I could not leave Wesley. I had to stay and wait for him to wake up.

Wesley was still in the recovery room. They would not move him to the ICU until he woke up and was stable. When Donna and I entered the room during the 1:00 a.m. visit, nearly thirty-six hours after his surgery had ended, the night nurse greeted us before we got to Wesley's bed.

"We've got something to show you," he told us.

Donna went to Wesley's bedside on his left, where his head was leaning. He was still on life support and nowhere near breathing on his own. I walked to his right side. The nurse stood behind Donna.

"Your wife and your mom are here. Let's show them what you showed me," the nurse told him.

I had no idea what to expect, but before I could imagine what was coming, Wesley opened his eyes and looked at his mom.

"Can you hold up one finger for us, Wes?" the nurse prompted him.

This was it—a gifted moment in my life. This was a moment I could tell Hunter about. This is what we came for. We came to save his daddy's life, and his daddy fought the good fight to come back to us. The many nights without his daddy while he was in the hospital in the months before were worth this very moment. The times Hunter visited him in the hospital and was not afraid of the tubes and machines because all he cared about was seeing his daddy were also worth it. The vows we had taken to love each other in sickness and in health and for better and for worse were upheld. This was the moment when the restoration of what love can conquer and what hope can bring, even in the face of enormous tragedy, came shining through. This was about Wesley and the journey I knew he had taken.

I knew with all of my heart he had left during the surgery when his heart stopped yet God had brought him back to us. As if in slow motion, with perfection and clear intent, Wesley lifted his left hand slightly off the bed and held up his pointer finger.

I was overcome.

"You worked hard today, didn't you, son?" his mom said to him as she held his finger in her hand. He nodded slightly.

"I love you, Wesley," I said.

He instantly tried to turn toward my voice but could not.

"Do you want me to switch places with Lisa so you can see her?" his mom graciously asked.

He nodded again.

As I walked around the bed to the other side, his face was filled with questions, but was met by the pure emotion I gave to him, from the deepest part of myself. Hope was what I had to give.

I held his hand and stared deep into his stunning green eyes. He could not speak because he was still on a ventilator, but he did not need to speak. There were no words needed to be said. Everything I needed to know was already there. I knew I had been gifted one of the many lessons we can all hope to learn while on earth: unconditional love. I loved this man unconditionally. As I held his face in my hands and kissed his forehead, I thought about the years we had spent together—the good times and the turbulent times. I thought about the stubbornness in him that used to make a hard day harder and a big fight bigger. I thought about this man who had been my friend for more than two decades and my lover for more than half those years. Wesley had been a good father to our son and felt like the only other person I needed to know on the planet because he was the only man to lead this family.

As I held his face in my hands, I considered how fortunate I was to know this love. I did not know what Wesley had endured to find his way back to me, but I had no doubt he had been to the light we talked about; he would return from it again and again to save our family from a life without him.

"You found your way back," I whispered to him.

He nodded.

Wesley was never the kind of man to raise the white flag. I knew what our family meant to him, and he would never surrender to this without a fight. Everything about him—good and bad, difficult and easy, subtle and brash—had led us to this fight, to this chance. I realized then no matter what was to come, Wesley would try with all his might to stay with us. That would always be enough, and that would always matter most.

CHAPTER ELEVEN

OnStar

Knowing Wesley was upstairs and awake, or even partly awake, gave me peace. It restored my hope we would make it through and go home to Texas to continue with the plans we had for our life together. Wesley would coach Hunter's Little League team and be at every school event, just as he was before he got sick. All of it was coming back to us, and I was grateful for this second chance. In my restored hope I believed Wesley could be the exception as a lung transplant patient and be one of the fortunate recipients who lived long, full, and active lives after transplant.

So many people had been calling in the two days since the surgery; I finally stopped answering the phone unless it was my parents, my friend Kelli, my brother Vance, or my sister Bev. Almost as soon as we got the call for Wesley's transplant, Kelli had begun emailing everyone on our list, and her email communication with our family was already making a difference in how quickly and thoroughly they received updates. Kelli was extraordinary. Her medical background and her willingness to update our family and friends was an enormous help. Nothing I told her was lost in translation.

She provided a much-needed bridge between us and the people who loved us, who wanted to know what was happening as it was happening. I found it nearly impossible to communicate with anyone beyond Kelli and my immediate family, because there was so much happening at once, and repeating myself was exhausting.

Wesley's family members lived closer than mine and were able to drive or take a short flight to reach us. My family lived much farther away, on the West Coast. My parents were struggling with not being there with us, but I understood my mom's treatment was equally important, and my dad was needed at her side.

I called my parents after I left Wesley's bedside.

"Mom, he held up his finger when the nurse asked him to, and he cried when I talked to him!" I exclaimed tearfully, overcome by the progress he had made.

My mom and dad were staying with Wesley's Aunt Lavaun and Uncle Mike in California while she was undergoing treatment. All four of them were still awake, knowing I would be visiting Wesley at 1 a.m. and waiting for any news about him.

My mom started to cry.

"He held up his finger and he cried," she repeated to them.

I could hear all of them through the phone, cheering and crying, thanking God.

I was reluctant to leave the hospital, but I had not been back to our apartment since Wesley's surgery, so I decided to go home to Hunter after calling my parents and be there when he woke up in the morning. It was strange to sleep in the apartment without Wesley there. The silence was almost too much to bear without the humming of his oxygen machine in the corner of the room. Hunter woke up during the night crying for his dad and had a hard time getting back to sleep until I turned the machine on. No matter how debilitating Wesley's need for the oxygen machine had

been or the horrible truth it represented, the sound of it was familiar to us both and helped Hunter drift back to sleep.

It had only been two days and one night, but it felt as if I had
been away from Hunter for days and days. So much had happened
since we got the phone call for Wesley's transplant.

"When can I see Daddy?" Hunter begged me when he woke up
in the morning.

He always wanted to see his daddy, no matter what, but I felt
I should stick to our rule that Hunter not see Wesley in the ICU.
Even though Hunter was used to seeing Wesley with his oxygen
tube and Flolan catheter, during Wesley's numerous stays in the
ICU at the hospital in Houston, there were often other patients
even more critical than he was. Frequently, there were family members suffering the loss of a loved one, and the emotional turmoil
was heartbreaking to witness. We decided it was best to shield our
young son from seeing such things. Hunter would have to wait
until Wesley was in a regular room. From recovery, they would
move him to the ICU and, if everything went well, he would be in
a regular room within a few days. I knew I could hold Hunter off
until then, or at least I had to try.

"You'll see Daddy as soon as he can see you. Right now he's
still sleeping a lot. He's resting up so he can come home to us," I
assured him.

The beauty of our son has always been his trust and faith in us.
He knows we always have done our best for him. He makes our
world go round despite everything and because of everything; he was
why we were here. He was what made the future worth fighting for,
no matter how insurmountable the odds might seem at times.

Hunter cried at the door when I left the apartment that morning to pick up Bev at the airport. His Papa Roger tried to comfort
him, but it did not work. I hated to leave him, but I knew where

I was needed most. Hunter was safe, even if unhappy. I had to be with Wesley now, and I knew Hunter would understand one day.

Bev was waiting by the curb when I arrived at the airport. It was such a relief to have my family with me. She makes everything better just by being around. My parents took Bev in as their foster daughter when she was a teenager, and I was only six year years old. I was thrilled to have a big sister and, even though she only lived with us a short time, we have remained very close. When I was being treated for cancer, she took care of things for me I did not even know were needed. She can fill a gap—and there had never been a bigger gap to fill than now.

"He already looks so much better. I am just amazed. He's still in and out of it, but they say it looks like the damage to his brain was likely minimal, and we may not even notice a difference in him, it may be subtle," I told Bev, so grateful to have her with me.

"You sounded terrible on the phone yesterday. I was really scared for you. For all of you," Bev confessed.

"I know. I'm sorry. I don't usually let myself fall apart like that, but it was just too much," I apologized, feeling hopeful the worst was behind us.

"I was coming whether you asked me to or not. I knew it was time," she said.

"Well, it looks like everything is going to be okay now. I cannot tell you how relieved I am," I told her, holding one hand against my chest and the other on the steering wheel as I drove us to the hospital to see Wesley.

My phone was ringing. It was Donna.

"Hey, I'm on my way back from the airport now," I told her.

"You need to get here right away! He's going!" Donna cried. There was extreme panic in her voice.

"What? What do you mean, he's going?" I shouted.

"They think he has a blood clot in his lungs! His heart stopped again! They said you need to get here now! He's not going to make it!"

I hung up the phone as I entered the freeway. The hospital was at least ten minutes away, even without Monday morning traffic. My heart raced and my body felt cold again. I was shivering and driving and trying to call Jimbo at his hotel.

"Do you want me to drive?" Bev asked, fearing I was in no condition to be driving.

"No! You don't know where you're going! Please just call Jimbo!" I cried as I tossed her my phone.

I knew I had to get there fast. I turned on my hazard lights and immediately pressed the OnStar button. The operator answered.

"My husband is at UAB in the ICU, and they just called to tell me I have to get there as soon as possible. His heart stopped!" I tried explaining to her.

"Is your husband in the vehicle with you now?" she asked, sounding confused.

"No! He's in the ICU. He had a lung transplant, and I have to get to him. I am driving there now and need you to send a police car to escort me. I have to get there fast! Please! Can you send someone? Or can you at least tell them not to pull me over if they see a black Suburban on the highway?" I begged her.

I did not really know what I needed her to do, I just knew I was not going to slow down, and I was not going to stop if a police officer tried to stop me.

By the time she figured out what I was asking, I was driving down the shoulder of the freeway to avoid traffic and could see the hospital exit.

"Ma'am, there is a police car at the off-ramp, and he will escort you through town to the hospital. Just stay behind him," she told me. "I hope your husband makes it."

I thanked her. I could see the police car ahead. I followed him and his sirens through the busy streets. When we arrived near the enormous hospital complex, he pulled over in front of the wrong building. I gave up following him, put the Suburban in park in the middle of the street and got out of the car to run the three blocks to the building Wesley was in.

"Park the car and ask someone to take you to the transplant ICU waiting area!" I yelled to Bev as I ran down the street.

I had never been more scared in my life. I was so confused by the false hope the day before had brought. Now we were worse off than before.

"He can't die. Please don't let him die. Save him like you saved me. Save us. This family isn't a family without him," I prayed as I ran through the glass doors that led to the fifth floor elevator.

Though it took only seconds, the ride up in the elevator seemed to last minutes. When the doors finally opened, I saw Donna and Heather, Wesley's stepsister, sitting on the floor in front of the two swinging wood doors. I stood in front of them, crying and trying to breathe. I could not get words to come out of my mouth, and they were not saying anything. Donna had a blank, tormented look on her face and could not speak.

I looked at Heather and asked her with my eyes what I could not express with words.

"He's still alive," Heather quickly said.

"Then there's a chance. He's still alive!" I cried, falling to the floor in front of them.

I do not know why my immediate response was to be hopeful. I just knew he was still on the other side of those doors, and as long as he was alive, then I was supposed to fight for him. I had promised him.

"Dr. Zorn thought he had a blood clot to his lung, but now

they are not sure. They are working on him," Donna said quietly. "We just have to wait here for someone to tell us something more."

I could not sit still, so I paced back and forth. I did not know what to do. By then, Wesley's brother Wayne, his cousin Casey and his wife Jessica, his sister Jenny, his stepdad Jimbo, and my sister Bev were all standing outside the swinging wood doors with us. A nurse came and escorted us to a room a few doors down, telling me Dr. Wille would be in to talk with us when he could.

I sat in a chair and shook and prayed while we waited. I prayed for God to keep him alive. I prayed for the doctors to be his vehicle for a miracle. We waited.

Finally, Dr. Wille entered and scanned the full room for me. Our eyes met as he sat in front of me and started to explain what seemed impossible to hear and even more difficult to believe.

"The surgery was very hard on your husband. His heart has suffered a lot of damage and right now we are having a hard time keeping a pulse. We are giving him medications to aid his heart and blood pressure, and the nurses are suctioning fluids from his lungs constantly, but it just doesn't look good. I honestly don't think he is going to make it through the day," he explained.

"You mean you think he's going to die today?" I asked him, devastated by what I was hearing.

"I don't see how we can turn it around at this point," he said to me.

Other family members asked a few questions, and he took his time answering them, but I could not speak for a moment. I could not even listen. I had to just be. I struggled to find the words that would help Dr. Wille understand.

"When we came here, we were willing to do anything to give Wesley more time with us. You told us the statistics for long-term survival after a double-lung transplant were not optimum. We knew that coming in, and we signed up anyway. I know what Wesley is capable of," I told him with conviction. "I am telling you if there is more medication you can give him or even one more thing you can do to get him through this day alive, then he will do the rest."

"We'll do all we can for him. He has been incredibly strong to make it this far, but we just can't know the outcome right now." He tried to convey to me the likelihood Wesley would not survive.

"We read that 90 percent of lung transplant patients survive the first thirty days. Right now, I have to believe he can make it through this second day and the days after. You just have to keep him alive today," I reiterated.

He left to take care of Wesley and told us we could all go in to see him. I thought it was generous of him. I did not realize that is what they do for families when their loved one is not expected to survive. Visiting hours no longer apply.

It was already two days after his surgery, and Wesley had not even made it out of the recovery room yet. I was the one he counted on to take care of him. I could not do that if I lost hope.

We took turns at the sink, washing our hands before we could see him. I was the first to finish washing and begin walking in the direction of Wesley's bed. After just a few steps from the sink, I stopped and turned to our family behind me.

"No tears. If you can't handle being in there without crying, then don't go near him. If he hears your fear, it'll scare him," I said to our family standing near me.

As I walked toward Wesley's bedside, I was overwhelmed by what I saw. His eyes were swollen, and he looked full of sorrow. I cannot explain the sorrow. I just felt as if he knew much of what had happened to him, and he wanted it to stop.

"I'm here, Wesley. I'm here with you," I told him as I held his hand tightly.

By then our family was crowded around his bed. As Bev

approached, I had a sudden memory of the times I would stand on the wood stump next to my house, so I could see over the fence into our backyard and watch Wesley play football with my brother and their friends.

"Wes, it's me Beverly. We're all here for you, buddy. You have to hang in there for Lisa and Hunter. She's loved you her whole life. I remember when she used to peek over the fence at you in her backyard playing football."

"I was just thinking of that! Just this very second, I was thinking of that," I smiled at Bev.

More than ever, I was glad to have her at my side. Many people knew the stories of Wesley and me when we were kids, but Bev actually had lived some of them with us.

"Hey Catfish, it's Jimbo. You gotta get out of here so we can do some fishin' with Hunter."

"We love you, son," Donna said.

I considered everyone speaking to Wesley might scare him because he would think everyone would only show up like this if something was going really, really wrong.

"You know me, I got them to break the rules and let everyone in at once. I thought it was better than visitors coming one by one," I told him, trying to reassure him in any way I could.

We stood around him for a few more minutes. No movement, no tears. There was nothing from Wesley to show us he was aware of our presence. Our words were acts of faith. Faith he could hear us even if he could not respond. Just like the man he had read about.

After a few more minutes, everyone else left the recovery area to let Wesley rest. I approached Dr. Wille and asked if I could speak with him privately. We sat in a nearby hallway.

"Dr. Wille, you've met our son." I said to him.

"I have," he responded.

"I don't know of a man who wants to be a father more than Wesley. I really don't. He reads all of my parenting magazines. He takes him to movies. He teaches him how to work in the yard with him. His life's work is what he can contribute to Hunter's life. He didn't grow up in a family that stayed together, and all he has ever wanted is what we have now. We wanted to be married for fifty years. We know now we won't grow old together—transplant life won't let us. But we came here for as much more time as we could borrow. I just need you to know how strong and stubborn Wesley is. I need you to know he would want you to do everything you possibly can to keep him alive. He will truly do the rest, but you must do everything you know to do to keep him alive."

"He's very fortunate to have you looking out for him," Dr. Wille said.

"This is what we do, Dr. Wille. When I had cancer, he fought for me when I was too frightened to fight for myself. We fight the good fight."

The look on Dr. Wille's face when I informed him about the cancer was telling. It showed me this all made sense to him. We had been here before, and we knew what was possible on either side of life.

"I'll let you get back to work. Can I come back in an hour?" I asked him.

"You can come back as often as you like," he answered, encouraging me to spend time with Wesley no matter how sick he was.

Our family was spread around the hospital, but Jimbo was staying close to me. He wanted me to go for a walk and get some fresh air, but I would not leave the building.

"Then, let's just walk," he said, as we paced the length of the waiting room hallway.

I was worried about Hunter. I had told him his daddy would be home soon, but now I did not have any idea when—or even if—he would be coming home. Meanwhile, our son was miserable without us, and I worried about the toll our absence was taking on him. Wesley's cousin Amy had offered to come from Texas and help with Hunter, but at the time she had offered, I did not think it would be necessary. I could not have anticipated such complications after Wesley's surgery.

Amy had called me the day of his surgery to tell me she and her husband John wanted to help us with Hunter. She said John would drive her and their two daughters, Cameron and Avery, to Birmingham, then he would fly home. Amy said she could stay for two weeks with Hunter and her daughters, then John would fly back to Birmingham and help her drive home. When she called to offer their help, Wesley was doing better. Now that he had taken a turn for the worse, this seemed like the perfect solution. Amy being willing and able to stay a few weeks would hopefully be enough time to get Wesley on the mend and out of the hospital.

"Amy offered to take care of Hunter," I told Jimbo.

"Yeah. And what do you think of that?" he asked.

"I don't see any other way. She offered to come here, but I think it would be better to take Hunter to her first. I could spend more time at the hospital with Wesley, and Hunter could be with his friends for a week before coming back with Amy. Bev said she would fly Hunter to Texas on her way back to California tomorrow. Her plane has a connection in Dallas. But he's never been away from us for that long, and it would mean he would be in Houston for his fifth birthday, without us. If I do it, I can't let Wesley know I sent Hunter away or he'll panic. He knows I would never let Hunter go unless something went terribly wrong."

"So what are you going to do?" He was letting me talk.

"I don't know. What do you think I should do?" I asked him.

Jimbo has always been a man of few words. When he says something, anything at all, I know he means it.

"I think you should get the kid the hell out of here," he answered bluntly.

Within an hour he had bought Hunter a ticket to fly with Bev the next day. My dear friend Peggy would pick Hunter up in Dallas and drive him back to Houston to stay for a week. She would have a birthday party for him. Then at the end of the week, Amy would bring him back here. She would stay here with her daughters for two weeks and care for Hunter.

When a family rallies, it is a wonderful thing.

Although I was afraid to leave the hospital, I did. I took Bev to the apartment and spent some time with Hunter. When I told him about the plans we had made, he was excited about staying with Peggy and her children, Natalie and Grant. He loved being at Peggy's house and would be comfortable and well cared for with her. His preschool was even going to let him return for the week he was in Houston. It was the best possible plan. All I could hope for was he would return in a week to a much better scenario. It would be difficult to let Hunter leave Birmingham without us, but I was doing what I had to do and what I hoped was best for everyone. I needed to focus on Wesley, and Hunter needed to focus on being a four-year-old little boy with a birthday party coming up, not the reality his daddy's life was hanging in the balance.

I continued to check on Wesley every hour for the rest of the day and night. He had made it through the long and grueling day, and every hour he was alive brought hope he would live another hour. Dr. Wille and the nurses were at his side the entire day. Everyone was working hard for Wesley. His heart required several medications to maintain even the minimal level of progress he had managed. A test that afternoon showed his heart was only working at 10 percent of normal capacity. He was barely hanging on, but he was still alive, and I was so very thankful for that.

By morning, Wesley was starting to show signs of waking again. I could see on his face he was in pain.

"Has he been given pain medication lately?" I asked the nurse. "He looks like he is in pain."

Dr. Zorn was standing next to Wesley, so she asked Dr. Zorn if it was okay to give him more pain medication. He said it was, so she prepared to give it to him.

"Wesley, they are giving you medicine for the pain. She's getting it now. I'll make sure they take care of it," I told him. I knew he could hear me. I could see it in his face. "Don't be scared. You're okay."

I told Dr. Zorn he was showing signs of knowing I was there. He was trying to wake up. He was doing better.

"But he's still very, very sick," he told me, as if I did not already know.

This frustrated me. I could see he was sick, but yesterday I had been told he would not make it through the day—and he was still alive today. This reminded me of the things the doctors and nurses could not possibly know about us yet, but would soon learn.

"I'm a glass half-full girl," I told Dr. Zorn.

My comment was greeted with little reaction or emotion, but I accepted that about Dr. Zorn the first day I met him. His job was to perform a miracle. His hands were meant to remove the decaying lungs from Wesley's body and replace them with the perfect match this hospital had found for him in record time. Dr. Zorn's work was done. Dr. Wille would take it from here. I already knew that.

As I was getting ready to leave and return in an hour, I glanced at Wesley one more time. The medication had kicked in. No more pain showed on his face. He was sleeping again.

By midnight, when Donna and I approached Wesley's bed for our hourly visit, I thanked God Wesley was still alive. The doctors said he would not survive, but he had.

There he was, his eyes open, his heart somehow mending. I knew when I saw him during that 1 a.m. visit he was out the woods again. I knew I would be able to send Hunter to Texas in the morning and be there for Wesley all day, every day. I would not feel torn about where I should be when I could not be with both my boys at the same time.

"I heard he had a scary day today. He almost didn't make it," his night nurse said to me.

I held my pointer finger in front of my lips and motioned him to be quiet.

"But he did make it," I told the nurse, making it clear I did not want negative comments made in Wesley's presence.

The nurse smiled and left me with Wesley while he sat in a nearby chair and wrote in Wesley's chart.

I was standing next to Wesley's bed, looking over the machines and reviewing the numbers. I had come to learn what each number meant, and I could see he had improved from my previous visit. Progress.

When I looked down at Wesley, his eyes were closed, but he did not seem to be sleeping. There was a tear falling from his left eye and down the side of his face, dropping into his ear.

"Have you given him anything for his eyes? Did you add moisture to his eyes in any form?" I asked his nurse.

"No. That's him," he told me.

"Is he crying?" I asked.

"I believe he is."

I leaned next to him and wiped the single tear from his face. He leaned just slightly into my hand.

In the tenderness of this quiet moment after a long and frightening day, I could think of only one thing to say to Wesley.

"Hunter's pride," I whispered to him.

CHAPTER TWELVE

Slip on Shoes & My Best Friend

"How long has he been here?" Wesley's respiratory therapist asked, as he administered medication through Wesley's breathing tube.

"Just a few days," I lied to him.

Donna looked at me questioningly. It had actually been almost two weeks. When Jake left, Donna asked if she could talk to me in the hallway outside of Wesley's room. Wesley was sleeping.

"Why did you lie to him?" she asked me. She was confused.

"Because Wesley may be able to hear us, and he doesn't need to know how long it has been. Let him lose track of time and think things are better than they are," I told her.

After that horrible day the doctors had said he would not survive, Wesley had been slowly recovering and had been moved to the transplant ICU. The doctors were amazed by his progress, and as I passed them in the hospital, every nurse who had worked on Wesley that day and into the night told me he was a miracle. And he was. But he still did not need to know how bad things had been. He did not need to know his kidneys were failing or he was still on a ventilator because the doctors were having a hard time weaning him off it. He did not need to know the longer he was on the venti- lator the less likely it was he would ever get off it. He especially did not need to know he had missed Hunter's birthday or that I had missed it, too, because I sent him back to Houston without us. He just needed to know of his improvements and, unfortunately, there were not many that were lasting without interruptions of further complications.

Wesley was having long periods of consciousness and was becom- ing more aware of his surroundings. The doctors had removed the tube threaded from his mouth down his throat and instead given him a tracheotomy, surgically placing a tube from the outside into his neck. It allowed him to breathe, although he still needed the assistance of the ventilator. They hoped this would be a bridge to recovery for him.

Another week passed slowly. Wesley had endured more than three weeks of complications since his surgery.

Heather, Wesley's stepsister and my good friend, came from Houston for a few days. I was surprised when Donna and Roger told me she was coming because I knew she had to work.

"I came for you," she told me when she arrived at the hospital. "There's no one here just for you."

It was good to spend time with her at the hospital, and it was hard to see her go when the time came for her to leave.

As planned, Amy had been here for two weeks to care for Hunter, but it was time for her to go home. With Wesley still not making much progress, I had arranged to have my best friend Tami fly in from Los Angeles to help. If it were not for the dedication of others to my son's well-being, I do not know how I could have balanced taking care of both Wesley and Hunter.

Wesley was still on dialysis, but for the first time in weeks his body was making urine and it looked like his kidneys were rebounding. The doctors explained when Wesley coded during surgery, his kidneys took a hit; now they were recovering. I finally understood why Dr. Patel had told us more than once that Wesley's youth was in his favor because his other organs had never suffered damage. His healthy, young organs were able to manage the relentless threats against them.

Every hour of every day brought change, sometimes for the better, other times not, but Wesley was becoming more himself—which also meant he was getting frustrated. By the time he was completely coherent, he was downright grumpy. He was not aware of all he had been through to get to where he was.

Dr. Young had been out of town for a few days and was eager to see Wesley on his return. I knew he and his team would be making rounds that morning, and I had heard they did not put up with any negativity from patients or their families.

"Dr. Young will be here soon, so you are going to need to cheer up," I lectured him.

He nodded but did not look at me. He was depressed. I could see it. He wanted to get out of the hospital and go home. He knew nothing of the brush he had had with death. All he knew from his fog of survival was he should have been better by now.

"This is the part the psychologist talked about. This is the part when you have to push through and be stronger than you think you can be. When Dr. Young comes in here, you need to smile and show gratitude for all they have done for us. Don't let them see this side of you." I clearly told him my expectations and what I assumed would be theirs.

The doctors soon entered the room and were in a celebratory mood.

"You're a champ. How does it feel to be a champ?" Dr. Young asked Wesley.

Donna was there with us, standing behind the doctors when they entered the room. She clasped her hands together, bent her elbows and motioned to either side in a winner's gesture. Wesley saw her, smiled and imitated her.

"You were down to 10 percent function on the left side of your heart, my friend. It doesn't get much worse than that," Dr. Young informed Wesley. It was the first he had heard of just how bad things had gotten for him, for all of us.

Wesley looked at me with a question in his eyes.

"Scared me," I said to him quietly.

"But look at you now. You're doing great. We should be able to start weaning you from the ventilator soon. Just need to give you a little more time to recover," Dr. Young said.

Their visit was brief. It was the beginning of several days of small steps in the right direction.

After our visit with Dr. Young, I called Deandra, the young woman who had scheduled the tests needed to get Wesley on the transplant list. If she had not been so kind and done her job so well by fitting Wesley in for appointments sooner than planned, he would not have received these lungs in record time because he would not even have been listed when they became available. I thanked her for making a difference in our lives and for giving us this chance to save Wesley.

Tami arrived a couple days later. She brought her three-year-old son Mason with her, and they planned to stay two weeks. She has been my best friend since junior high. Having her there made all the difference to Hunter and me.

It had been twenty-three days since Wesley's surgery, and Hunter still had not seen his dad. It was obvious Wesley was not going to be out of the ICU any time soon, and I could not bear to keep Hunter away any longer. He had been asking for his dad since the day after the surgery. He had cried for him during my daily phone calls when he was in Houston. Every part of Hunter's life was unrecognizable to him and to us. He needed to be with his dad, even with all the tubes attached. I suggested to Wesley we break our rule of never letting Hunter see him in the ICU and let him visit.

"I'll take a picture of you and show it to him, so he can see the tubes and how you look, then let him decide," I suggested.

Wesley nodded. Nearly three weeks after surgery, he was still on a ventilator and unable to speak.

The photograph was pathetic. Even though he tried to smile, Wesley looked tired and sad, with a dozen tubes attached to him, including a feeding tube through his nose. But Hunter took one look at the picture on the digital camera screen and cheerfully exclaimed, "Yep, take me to my daddy!"

I went in ahead and covered the dialysis machine attached to Wesley so the blood running through the tubes would not frighten Hunter. No one could enter Wesley's room without a gown, mask, and gloves. Hunter thought it was fun to put them all on. He dashed into his dad's room, and I could see his smile through the mask. I fought back tears as my two boys held hands and watched cartoons. The night shift nurses looked in the room and smiled at me as they passed by the wide-open sliding glass doors.

I observed our son and his excitement at seeing his father. He paid absolutely no attention to the tubes or the machines that were keeping his daddy alive. He asked no questions. He just smiled at his dad and talked and talked about all he had been doing. He told him about his new Spider-Man toy that shot out spiderwebs and said he liked to play at the playground of our apartment building. Wesley could not speak, but he smiled, nodded his head, and did his best to respond and to keep up with our enthusiastic son.

I stood aside and let the two of them have their time. I just marveled at my boys doing what they had done so many times before, watching cartoons and laughing at the simplest things Hunter said with his usual charm and articulation.

When the cartoon ended, Wesley motioned me to take Hunter out of the room and looked at the ice packs under his arms. He had been growing uncomfortable from the cold but did not want Hunter to see his discomfort.

"I'll be back, Daddy!" Hunter cheered as he blew Wesley a kiss and skipped out of the room with me, still smiling.

"My daddy has new lungs!" Hunter shouted with joy to the nurses as we walked toward the ICU waiting room where Tami and Mason were waiting.

"Yes, he does. It's a gift, isn't it, Buddy?" I cheerfully replied.

"The best gift ever, Mommy!"

Wesley's nurse had placed the ice packs under his armpits in an effort to reduce his fever, which had slowly started to rise since earlier that afternoon. A fever is never a good sign after transplant.

"Please take Hunter home. Wesley has a fever. I can't come home tonight," I told Tami without Hunter hearing.

My fear of yet another complication showed on my face.

She hugged me and left with the boys.

By morning, Wesley's fever was complicating his condition, and it put a complete stop to his progress. When I walked by the nurses' station later that day, Dr. Young was sitting at the computer.

"I saw him earlier. The fever is a problem, isn't it?" I fearfully asked Dr. Young.

"He isn't doing well. I'm ordering him Propofal right now," he answered without looking up at me from the computer screen.

Propofal is a quick-acting medication that would put him into a medically induced coma. Wesley had been on it in the hours after he first crashed following his surgery. It meant he would be unconscious for hours, maybe even days. I missed him again already.

I entered Wesley's room and could immediately see his breathing was labored.

"You'll be asleep again soon. You'll feel better with rest," I reassured him. He did not respond. He was barely conscious. "I'll be waiting for you when you wake up."

The nurse came in a few minutes later and started the Propofal. Within less than five seconds, he was completely unconscious, his breathing less labored, his face more peaceful. I spoke to him quietly, hoping to get in his head as he drifted off to a different state of being, leaving me in the shadow of the dark clouds of despair that had become all too familiar to me.

"Please, stay away from the light. Stay right here. I'll be waiting for you to wake up," I promised as I held his hand and rubbed his sweaty forehead, knowing the next few days would be difficult for both of us—only he would be asleep, and I would be wide awake.

My parents called daily. My mom had been feeling sick from her treatment but was doing better now. My dad offered to come help me, but with Tami visiting, I did not need him yet, so I held him off.

Over the next several days, I spent most of my time in the ICU waiting room with my new friends Leeandra and her family. I had met them a few days after we arrived. Leeandra's mother Cathy was a lung transplant patient who had received her lungs nearly twelve years before. She had been admitted to the hospital the week after we arrived for a surgery unrelated to her transplant, but she had suffered numerous complications and was still unconscious, not waking up after surgery. After years of living with a transplant, her body was tired, but her family was fighting for her. They had set up camp in the ICU, just as I had done with Donna and Roger.

Leeandra's family made day-to-day life bearable in the ICU. We shared fear and sadness, as well as indefinite hope. What we all wanted more than anything was for both Wesley and Cathy to get better and for all of us to go home—but nothing was going our way.

Leeandra and her family were some of the kindest, funniest, most loving people I had ever met. Their empathy was limitless and their support endless. People who have never hung in limbo as we were doing, literally spending hours and hours for days and days in a small room where despair was abundant and hope limited, are nearly incapable of understanding what it is like. Visitors come and go, but the people who stay take on a new existence. What used to be normal, like a simple meal, is accompanied by stress and anxiety, especially when trying to leave the hospital to eat. Will something happen while I am gone? What if there is an emergency? What if he asks for me, and I am not near?

How many times have you walked into a hospital ICU waiting room and seen a half-completed jigsaw puzzle on a table? It is what people in ICU waiting rooms do because it helps pass the time. Concentrating on that one puzzle piece that should fit but does not seems to help redirect the mind from the turmoil of critical illness or injury. No one minds when a stranger sits down and goes to work on the puzzle because the puzzle belongs to no particular person. It is there for everyone, gentle therapy for people who are breaking apart inside but trying to keep themselves together.

I was spending every night at the hospital and only going home for a few hours a day to spend time with Hunter. Keeping my balance was nearly impossible, but it was a bit easier when Wesley was assigned nurses I trusted and preferred. By then, I had learned if I had a good reason to do so, I could remove any particular nurse from Wesley's rotation, so I did.

"Can we talk, Lisa?" Dr. Young asked me when I was in Wesley's room during visiting hours. Wesley was still in the medically induced coma, fighting an infection whose origin they could not determine, with a high white cell count of 90,000 instead of the normal 10,000. He was in bad shape, with no improvement in sight.

"Sure," I answered and followed him to an empty room two doors down from Wesley's.

I sat down in a chair across from Dr. Young and had a feeling this had nothing to do with Wesley's current condition. I felt as if I had been called into the principal's office.

"I understand you asked that Daniel not be assigned to Wesley again. You had him removed from rotation?" he questioned me, seeming irritated with my actions.

"I did. I was told I could," I answered him with conviction. I knew I had done the right thing and was not concerned with being confronted about it.

"Why did you remove him?" he asked me, as he rested his eyeglasses on the top of his head.

I firmly stated my case. "You run an amazing clinic and this hospital saves lives every day, but Daniel doesn't believe in Wesley's survival, and I can't allow anyone who doesn't believe in my husband's survival to take care of him," I explained.

"How do you know he doesn't believe in Wesley's survival?" Dr. Young asked, assuming I was making assumptions of my own.

"Because he told me," I quickly replied. "The last time Daniel took care of Wesley, he told me Wesley probably would not survive because he was too dependent on the vent and would never get off of it."

Dr. Young did not respond. I guessed he needed more, so I gave it to him.

"What if Wesley crashes again and there is one more thing that can be done to get him through it but Daniel is his shift nurse and doesn't go that extra step because he doesn't think Wesley will survive it anyway? That's unthinkable to me as Wesley's wife and as Hunter's mother."

There was another moment of silence. I stood my ground and waited for Dr. Young to speak.

"I understand. Daniel shouldn't have said any such thing to you," Dr. Young said, somewhat apologizing.

"I'm actually glad he did tell me, so I could know how he felt and take him off the rotation," I told him.

The conversation was over, and I returned to Wesley's side. Two days later, when a young nurse who was studying to become a physician's assistant was assigned to Wesley for the second time and brought his books to study while he worked, I asked him directly not to be assigned to Wesley in the future. He respectfully agreed. That was the last time I had to call off a nurse from Wesley's care.

I felt no guilt or regret about my decision to be selective about Wesley's nurses. I respected their work and their unique abilities, but just as with any profession, there are people who fall short. Wesley's life was at stake. There was no room for people who did not believe in him, and there certainly was no time to study while on the job. Not on my watch.

*

The days were dragging on. By day three of Wesley's fever, every number that meant something positive about the progress he had made since his surgery had either plummeted or skyrocketed, whichever direction indicated he was getting worse.

Wesley was septic, which meant his body was riddled with infection, and his organs were slowly beginning to shut down. If things did not turn around, he could die within hours. It was exhausting to endure the constant roller coaster of events. Even though at no point did I feel like giving up, I often wondered how much more he and I could take.

It had been several days since we had interacted and, by now, it had been four weeks since I had even heard his voice. As worried as I was and as much as I was trying to get the three of us through it, I missed my husband. I wanted nothing more than to crawl into his lap and tell him about what was going wrong. I knew it was selfish, but I wanted him to comfort me and tell me everything was going to be all right. I wanted him to kiss my lips so I might remember a time when he was not sick and all we had was love and passion, free of worry and strife. This is the time when I needed him most, but he was so far from me and the life we had shared.

I wanted to tell him what a hero he was and how much I loved him for fighting for us. I wanted him to know Hunter had turned five—he would be proud of how well our son was handling our absence. I wanted him to hear me say I would sleep in the ICU waiting room for as long as it took, I would never give up on him, and our family would not work without him.

I wanted to say all of these things, but I did not say them aloud. Wesley had enough to think about without having to worry about me. All I could do was wait for him.

The infection was raging inside of him and so far, nothing had stopped it. Dr. Wille wanted to try an aggressive medication that could turn it around.

"We can start it today but we only have twenty-four to ninety-six hours to turn this around," Dr. Wille told me. I could not tell whether he thought it would actually work or not. I was just relieved there was one more thing we could try in order to save Wesley. I understood it could only be administered for a specific period of time; it had to show signs of working within twenty-four hours to hold any hope for Wesley to pull through.

"Please do it," I instructed him, unsure myself, but willing to try.

"If the guy could just catch a break." Dr. Wille sighed in disbelief at the relentless complications Wesley was continuing to endure. "I've never had one patient go through so much in such a short period of time."

About a month before we had moved to Alabama to get on the transplant list, Wesley, my mom, Hunter, and I were in our car as I was driving down the freeway just a few exits from our home. A man in the lane next to us cut me off, and I had to swerve out of the way to avoid him hitting our car as he sped past us.

Wesley was absolutely livid and told me to catch up to the driver. I refused, but we ended up next to his car anyway because of the flow of the traffic.

"Pull over! Pull over!" Wesley was yelling from the passenger's front seat, across me and out my window to the driver on my left. "I'm going to kick his ass!"

I thought it was ridiculous, as I watched Wesley get alarmingly upset and try to instigate a fight he could not possibly finish. The driver seemed equally disturbed by Wesley's rage as he could see Wesley's oxygen tube resting on his ears and into his nose. His fury, steroid induced or not, was absurd.

While this was going on, my mom tried to distract Hunter in the back seat by singing him a nursery rhyme that required hand movements and interaction.

The driver sped ahead of us, and we soon turned off at the exit leading to our house. I stayed in the car with Wesley then waited for my mom to help Hunter out of his car seat and take him inside the house.

"You're in no condition to start a fight you can't finish. What exactly were you planning to do if he and I had pulled over?" I lectured him as I got out of the car and helped him unload his oxygen tank.

"I'd have a good minute and a half in me," he said quietly, knowing he had reacted foolishly to a situation that would have otherwise made him mad but not enraged.

That day on the freeway instantly came to my mind twenty-four hours into the last-chance medication when Dr. Wille told me Wesley's status. To everyone's amazement, the medication was working. Wesley's blood work indicated the infection was relenting.

I had known Wesley most of my life. When I first fell in love with him, I was mesmerized by how complicated he was and the way he thought about everything to the point that sometimes his thoughts kept him awake at night. I loved that I felt safe with him because he was strong in will and would fight to his death to protect me. When I was sick and going through chemo, struggling with the fear cancer forced me to face, Wesley was my rock and my touchstone. He managed to balance the strength to be firm and advocate for me while remaining sensitive to my need to be reassured and coddled in my darkest moments of fear.

Years later, when I was in labor with Hunter, Wesley again maintained the balance I needed to get through our natural birthing plan. He helped me breath and push and was there with strong hands to hold our son when Hunter was naturally delivered from my tired, overwhelmed body and entered our wonderful new world.

That day, when he had yelled at me to pull the car to the side of the freeway and was screaming at the man in the car next to us to do the same, I felt sorry for him. Not because he did not realize his limitations, but because he did.

The capable man I had loved for years, who had seen me through cancer and had been a wonderful, devoted father to our only son, was lost in a weakness he did not recognize nor want to befriend. His greatest enemy was not the man on the freeway or even his tired, diseased lungs. His greatest enemy was himself, the sick version of himself he refused to accept or even spend time getting to know. Wesley wanted no part of the weakness rearing its head at nearly every turn. Even though almost everything relating to his loss of strength in the physical sense was completely out of his control, he could not bear to succumb even slightly to becoming anyone other than the man he knew and believed himself to be.

When the infection receded, I thought of that man on the freeway driving ahead of us, seeming afraid of this fragile, oxygen-deprived man. I liked to think of the infection in the same way; it tried to stand up to Wesley but pulled away in fear as he confronted it with the same rage he had shown to the man who carelessly endangered his family. It was such moments of realization that made me grateful for the stubborn, complicated, and often difficult man Wesley was, even if he was sometimes a complete pain in the ass. If I were an infection trying to lay the groundwork for death in a man like Wesley, I, too, would withdraw to find a different, weaker body to attack, where I might have a chance to win. A battle in Wesley's body was uncertain, shaky terrain for even the most determined infection.

Over the next few days, the nurses gradually reduced Wesley's Propofal medication. In anticipation of his awakening, I visited the hair salon adjacent the surgical waiting room on the bottom floor of the hospital. The hairdresser was kind enough to let me use her curling iron and hair supplies. After weeks of barely even being able to shower due to my accommodations at the hospital and brief visits to Hunter at our apartment, I wanted to at least try to look attractive when Wesley woke up from his most recent coma.

By the fifth day after receiving the anti-infection medication, he was completely awake again. Although he still was on the respirator and could not speak, it felt good to talk with him and communicate. I knew him well enough to know what he was trying to tell me. We spent a few days together that revived my hope.

Wesley was on the mend again, so I went home for most of the day to spend time with Hunter and visit with Tami before she returned home at the end of the week. We had fun that day, watching the kids play and catching up with one another. I had not been able to spend much time with her since she arrived, but she understood. She knew her stay was about Hunter, not about the two of us. As we talked and laughed, I felt relaxed and hopeful.

I was grateful to her and for the gift she had given Hunter with her presence. Simply by engaging him in fun activities, he was able to enjoy what this new city had to offer. She took the boys to the museum, to nearby parks, and even to pajama night at the local library. Every time I talked with Hunter on the phone while Tami was there, he was happy and asked less often when I would be able to come home. My gratitude for her care of our son was immeasurable.

That evening, Hunter visited his dad for the second time since the surgery. Wesley was in and out, sleeping much of the time Hunter was there, but Hunter did not mind. He understood his dad needed rest to try to get better. Hunter sat next to Wesley's bed and held his hand while he watched a movie on television. I sat at the nurse's station and talked with Kim, Wesley's nurse for the night—the same nurse who was with us the morning of his surgery.

Wesley was stable and resting but had spiked a fever again the day before and had developed secretions in his lungs that needed to be washed out. Dr. Wille did a bronchoscopy (inserting a tube directly into the bronchial tubes and lungs) to remedy the secretions and his compromised breathing. It seemed to help, but we still were not sure what was causing the setback.

I had planned to go home with Hunter for the night, but I was reluctant to do so, considering the most recent developments. Kim assured me Wesley would be fine for the night. He did look peaceful and comfortable when it was time for us to leave, so I decided to go home with Hunter and spend an evening with Tami and our boys.

Hunter had written a note to Wesley. Hunter said he had written Wesley a letter in cursive writing, but he did not actually know how to write yet, so it was really just a small piece of notebook paper with squiggly lines on it. As we quietly left his daddy's room, trying not to wake him, Hunter slipped the note between Wesley's fingers.

"You don't have to read it right now, Daddy. You can read it in the morning when you wake up," Hunter whispered to him.

Then we left the room and the hospital, heading for an evening together at our apartment.

It was a good night at the apartment with Hunter. I needed to be with him, even if Wesley could not be there, too. The simple bedtime ritual of a bath and a bedtime story gave me comfort. As I read to Hunter, I thought about how Wesley could not do it, even before the transplant because he was so oxygen deprived. I hoped one day soon he would be home from the hospital and able to enjoy a simple bedtime story with Hunter again. That night, at bedtime, we said our prayers and asked God to make Hunter's daddy all better.

I held Hunter's hand as he fell asleep and noticed he was still biting his fingernails. He had been biting them and his cuticles until they were raw and sometimes bleeding. Gayle, his preschool teacher back home, had told me it was a common stress reaction in children. Not knowing the damage Wesley's illness might be doing to him, I had taken Hunter to see a counselor months before, when he first started biting his nails. After the counselor evaluated him, she told me he seemed to be coping in his own way and whatever we were doing to get him through it was working. She said we should watch for any changes in his behavior, as well as any changes in his sleep patterns or appetite. None of these changed, so we just kept trying to love him through it the best we could.

After Hunter fell asleep, I caught up on some work related to my business. Christi had continued to do an amazing job handling the day-to-day business operations, but some things still needed my attention. Magazine features in *Parents* and *InStyle* magazines would be hitting the stands soon, driving more traffic to the website than we were used to having, so I worked with Melody, the web developer, to make sure everything on the website was in place to ensure easy online product ordering. The editors I had been working with at both magazines had no idea what was happening in my personal life. They just knew the *Friends* television series was ending in May, and our product needed to be featured in their magazines before the show's finale in order for the story to be timely. As much as I yearned to shut the business down—as I had throughout Wesley's illness and particularly since the transplant—Wesley had made me promise a long time ago I wouldn't. I kept my promise, but it wasn't easy.

✳

Morning came and everyone in the house was still sound asleep when the phone rang.

"Lisa, it's Claire. You need to get here right away; he's crashing," Wesley's nurse told me in a calm, level voice.

Not again! This could not be happening again! He had been doing so well. The infection was gone. He was conscious. His kidneys were beginning to function properly. There was talk of him being off the ventilator by the end of the week.

Tami had heard the phone ring and came to the living room, hearing only my side of the conversation.

"What do you mean? What is happening!" I panicked but tried to keep my voice down to not wake Hunter.

"He doesn't have a pulse," Claire told me, still trying to remain calm.

I hung up the phone and quickly scoured the messy apartment for the few items I had brought home with me the night before. I gathered what I could as Tami stood in the middle of the room not knowing what to do for me.

"He doesn't have a pulse," I cried without even looking up at her. "I can't find my shoes."

I quickly grabbed my car keys and my purse, hoping Hunter would not wake up and see me leave.

I was in such shock from the words Claire had just said to me I did not realize I still was not wearing shoes when I ran to the back door of the apartment to leave.

Just before I opened the door, Tami quietly dropped her slip-on leather shoes in front of my feet. Without looking up or saying a word, I slipped on her shoes and ran from the apartment to my car.

I would not see Tami again before she left and my dad arrived.

CHAPTER THIRTEEN

Move Something

As I ran toward the hallway near Wesley's room, I could hear the ventilator and the heart monitor alarms blaring. I stood outside his room waiting for someone to let me know what was going on. Despite my panic, I knew he was still alive and that gave me hope.

"Somebody tell me what is happening!" I shouted from the hallway, afraid to approach his room.

Nurses and doctors were rushing in and out. The sliding glass doors were wide open from both sides, giving complete access to his room. I could see gloves on the floor and the back end of a crash cart. I knew we were in trouble.

"We are doing everything we can for him, but he has been down a long time," Claire told me as she walked me toward an empty room a few doors down from Wesley's.

"How long?" I was afraid to ask.

"His heart stopped for about forty minutes. He just has a faint pulse now."

She asked me to stay in the room she had led me to until Dr. Wille could come talk to me.

On the way to the hospital, I had called Donna, Jimbo, and my parents. Jimbo was leaving Texas immediately and would be with us in Alabama by the evening. My dad was scheduled to fly in the next day. Donna and Roger were in the room with me, waiting for Dr. Wille.

I fell to my knees in front of Roger and began to sob. I did not think it could get worse for Wesley than it had the Monday after his surgery, but this was worse. I knew his body had already suffered and it might be impossible for him to recover from another setback, and this was worse than a setback. He did not have a pulse. He had been clinically dead for forty minutes.

I did not know where Wesley was. I knew he was physically down the hall in his hospital bed, still attached to machines and barely alive, but I did not know where his spirit was or where it had been. I felt certain he had transcended to a place we only hear about from people who are declared dead, yet return to tell of light and love and loved ones who have died and are now in the presence of God. If it was true people can go to the light and come back from it, nearly dying or returning from death, I was certain he had been there.

As I sat on the floor and cried, I pushed away the thought Wesley would not return to me. I forced myself to believe Hunter's visit to him the night before in the ICU was not the last time he would ever see his father. I crumbled at the memory of Hunter's big smile under the sterile hospital mask.

I knew that was not the way Wesley would want their last moments together to be. He would want to hold Hunter in his arms and tell him how much he loved him. He would want to tell him he was sorry he had to go and encourage him to find a way to have a long and happy life without the lingering sadness of his daddy dying when he was only five years old. He would want to tell Hunter he would be okay and Mommy would take good care of him. If he had to leave Hunter, I think those are the things he would want to share with him before dying.

Or maybe he would not want to say anything at all. Maybe he would want to play catch with him in our front yard or take him to his Papa Jimbo's ranch to fish off the pond bank one more time. Maybe he would take Hunter on a boat and let him steer it while sitting in his daddy's lap so one day, when Hunter was old enough to drive one by himself, he might remember how to do it. Maybe Wesley would give him all of his favorite music, the artists who meant something to him, so Hunter could share the soundtrack of his daddy's life.

I did not know exactly what Wesley would want, but I knew he would not want this.

The wait for Dr. Wille felt like hours, but it was just a short time before he entered the room and shut the door behind him. Alyson, my favorite nurse, was standing next to him.

I got up from the floor and stood before him.

"I have to start by saying we don't know how this happened. Claire said one minute he was fine, and the next he did not have a pulse," Dr. Wille began. "She was at his bedside when it happened, so she was able to start compressions right away. We worked on him for about forty minutes before he had even a faint pulse again."

"How is he now?" I cried.

"He's very critical. We have the ventilator back up to its maximum capacity, and he's barely holding on. He's on a number of heart-supporting medications keeping him alive. His blood pressure is still very low," he continued.

"Will he recover from this?" I was searching for hope in Dr. Wille's response.

"Lisa, I'm sorry, but I don't know that he will. We really don't expect him to make it through the day," Dr. Wille told me. He looked at me with sympathy.

Immediately, I began reaching, looking for hope.

"But we've been through this before, the day after the surgery. He made it when no one expected him to make it through the day," I reminded him.

"You're right, and I certainly don't want you to give up hope, but that was four weeks ago. His body has been through a tremendous amount of stress. Many of his vital organs were taxed by the sepsis and will suffer further from him coding today."

I knew he was right, but I could not give up. I could not begin to imagine this was Wesley's last day.

"What do we do now?" I asked sadly, holding back my tears long enough to listen to Dr. Wille's plan of action.

"We wait. There are a few settings I am going to try on the ventilator, but beyond that, we are doing all we can," he said.

"What are we looking for, to see improvement?" I persisted, searching for a way to prove even the slightest progress.

"Right now, his oxygenation is about 45, which you know is critically low. It was at 95 before this with much less ventilator support. His blood pressure is stable with medication but is also low. That needs to come up. We'll be watching his kidneys and looking for indicators his condition is stabilizing. There are many factors here to consider. We'll check his blood gases hourly and hope his oxygenation improves. It's not optimum for his oxygenation to remain so low for a long period of time, but he's been dealing with low oxygenation for a long time, so it's not like you or I trying to recover with those numbers," Dr. Wille told me.

He asked us if we had any more questions, but we did not. We were leveled again, back to the beginning of the nightmare that kept playing over and over.

"Can I see him?" I asked reluctantly, feeling afraid of what I would find when I saw Wesley.

"Of course," he answered.

I approached his hospital room nervously, trying to prepare myself for what I might see, but I could not possibly have been prepared.

The crash cart, with the defibrillator and various medical devices, was in the middle of the room. On the cart next to the other side of Wesley's bed, I saw packaging for a large needle, although I did not see the needle itself. There were latex gloves on the floor, the sheets were hanging from the bed, and nurses were still in his room monitoring and adjusting any number of IVs and machines attached to Wesley.

It looked like pictures I have seen of the aftermath of combat, only there was no blood.

As bad as the room looked, and as obvious as it was he had just been in the fight of his life and was nowhere near the safety of his corner of the ring, Wesley looked even worse than anything in the room indicated.

His hospital bed was tipped backward, with his head resting low on the bed and his feet tilted up high, almost to my shoulders. His eyes were covered with a clear, cold rubber compress and he was still bagged, with a nurse standing over him with one knee on his bed, forcing short spurts of air directly into his lungs through the tracheotomy tube still in his throat.

I immediately went to his side and held his face in my hands. The nurse standing near his head removed the compress covering his eyes. I could barely recognize his swollen face. His eyelids were swollen shut, and he was completely unconscious.

At first, I could not speak. I just held his face in my hands and held back my tears as best I could. If he could hear me, I needed him to know I could handle this.

When I found the words, I kneeled down next to Wesley's left ear and whispered to him, hoping he would somehow hear and return to me.

"Where are you?" I whispered.

I leaned my face against his, my lips still near his ear.

"Please stay. I'm not ready," I quietly pleaded. "Please stay."

As much as I wanted to believe he was with me and he could hear my pleas, I was afraid he was in a place from which he might never return. In that moment of utter disconnect, between the world where I was living—in a tormented hell, watching him die and knowing he might leave behind our precious child, our enduring marriage, and the life we had worked so hard to build—and his world of unconsciousness, where I knew God was cradling him in the throes of what would be the end of this life and the beginning of the next, I struggled to find peace. Hope was beginning to leave me.

"Please stay," I begged him again. "Please stay."

I repeated those two words over and over again, hoping Wesley could hear me, and if he could not, then perhaps God would change His plan and bring Wesley back to me. If ever there was a time when a person could be between heaven and earth, watching from a place I could barely comprehend, this was it. If Wesley was watching me, I wanted him to know I was waiting for him to return, and if God could bring him back, I would wait right there by Wesley's side until He did.

Wesley was going away, and I wanted God to change it back.

Throughout the weeks we had endured camping out in the ICU waiting room, the kind hospital chaplain, Chaplain Davis, had urged me to pray for God's will, but I had refused. It was not because I was angry with God or defiant. It was simply because, deep down in my heart, I knew Wesley was dying and I never wanted God to think I accepted that part of His plan. It was not part of my plan or what I thought our family could possibly endure, so I refused to say out loud to God I was praying for His will to be done. His will was not my own, and if it meant Wesley was leaving the planet, then I wanted nothing to do with His will.

On this day, I felt more strongly than ever God and Wesley were working it out. Before his surgery, I had told Wesley if he saw a light he should run away from it and return to me. I also told him if he did not return, I would know he could see something about his life I could not see. I told him I knew that was the only reason he would not return, and so I would accept his departure.

My words seemed prophetic now, and I felt the meaning in them more than ever before.

Again, I whispered to Wesley, "Please stay."

I stood up and looked around the room at the monitors. I knew what each of them meant. I knew every medication and its purpose, and every porthole into Wesley's body through a tube or an IV, thirteen in all. Some connected to the catheter in his chest, where the Flolan used to flow before his surgery. Other lines of medications were in his arms, each of them necessary for his survival, much as the Flolan used to be. Every tube in the room led to Wesley's ravaged body.

By now, Dr. Wille was making his adjustments to the ventilator. The nurse stopped forcing air through the bag as they reattached the tracheotomy tube to the ventilator. Wesley's oxygen level decreased slightly, which Dr. Wille said was to be expected, then returned to the mid forties.

I stepped away from his bed and finally let go of his face. I knew it was time to let him rest.

Before I left the room, I kissed his forehead and whispered in his ear, "I'm not ready."

I soon found myself standing in a corner in the hallway, my nose pressed against the wall. I was completely overwhelmed. As sick as Wesley was and as much as Dr. Wille was trying to warn me he would likely not make it through the day, I was not capable of giving up on him.

My head hurt from crying, and the pounding in my head was growing more intense, so I walked into the nearby bathroom to wash my face with hot water and try to regroup.

As I stood over the sink, I felt like Wesley looked: broken and weak. I was discouraged by the terrible hand we were being dealt on a daily basis. I felt the stillness of that moment, hearing the hot water flow steadily from the faucet, watching the mirror above as it was covered with a thin layer of condensation until I had to wipe it clean of wet mist to see myself.

I turned the water off, looked deep into the mirror, and stared at my reflection. I spoke out loud, asking myself, "How much can one person take?"

I locked my eyes on the mirror. I studied my face, the tears still running down my cheeks, not a bit of makeup, just me in the raw- ness of the moment. I felt completely present, aware of every single thing happening outside the bathroom door and down the hall in Wesley's room. I knew he was fighting for every breath and, if the doctors were right, he would take his last assisted breath and die attached to a ventilator before sunset that very evening.

"No, really. How much can one person take?" I asked again, louder, nearly shouting.

I felt a rage of anger at what I feared was coming and did not know how to stop. I asked a third time, screaming the words. "How much can one person take?"

In a rage of tears, I sobbed out loud and fell to my knees, unable to stop the pounding in my head or the tears rapidly running from my cheeks to my lap below. I was angry. I was in a shouting match with myself. I was furious I could not stop Wesley from going to God. I feared by nightfall the two of them would greet each other in the light and the promise of an afterlife, and I would be left on earth to pick up the shattered pieces of my broken heart. And worst of all, our beautiful son would lose the man who loved him most.

Twenty minutes later, I peeled myself off the bathroom floor and unlocked the door. I knew I had to find a way to bring Wesley back. God could not have him yet. I had to stop it. I just had no idea where to begin. Again.

✳

The rest of the day, I visited Wesley's room every hour to check his vitals and find out the results of his blood gases, hoping against hope for even minor improvements that would prove he was fighting his way back.

Jimbo arrived late in the afternoon. He offered to take me to a nearby restaurant to eat dinner, but I would not leave Wesley, who was still hanging on. Kim, Wesley's night nurse, said I could come back every hour to check on him through the night, despite breaking hospital rules about ICU visiting hours. Kim had been the nurse with us the morning Wesley was prepped for surgery. She knew I was "his person," as she had called me at the time.

Donna and Roger slept on the couches downstairs in the surgical waiting room, where we had been camping out for weeks now, but I spent the night in the ICU waiting room just outside the ICU doors. Staying in the ICU waiting room overnight was also against the rules, but no one tried to stop me.

Jimbo stayed there with me. I did not sleep. The night passed slowly, one hour at a time, one test at a time. It was an excruciating wait. One hour Wesley's oxygen levels seemed to improve; the next time I checked on him, his number would plummet. Starting with oxygen in the low forties, he did not have far to go to be in more danger.

By morning, his oxygen level had managed to inch its way to the low fifties, but his kidneys were failing again, so he was put on dialysis again.

Claire was his nurse again for the day shift. When I pointed out to her his oxygen was rising, she did not seem optimistic. I asked her what the next step was.

"We can keep doing what we are doing for now," she quietly told me.

"What do you mean for now? What else would we possibly do but wait for him?" I asked frantically.

"His pupils are fixed and dilated. He isn't responding to simple commands," she stated as she checked his chart.

"But his oxygen levels are improving. We have to give him time. You used an epi pen to his heart when he coded—that could explain his pupils being fixed and dilated, couldn't it?"

I was reaching for anything to assure me she was not telling me Wesley might never wake up. It was becoming abundantly clear Wesley's minor improvement in oxygenation meant nothing if he was brain dead.

"I think you should talk with Dr. Wille," Claire advised me, and she walked away to find him.

Within minutes, Dr. Wille was standing in front of Wesley's hospital room, which still had its doors wide open, offering easy access for those who were caring for him around the clock. He started to speak, but I asked him if we could first step away from Wesley's room in case he could hear us.

"This is about Wesley not waking up, isn't it?" I pressed.

"It is, Lisa. Wesley went without a pulse for several minutes. Although we were forcing oxygen while we tried to revive him, it's not likely he'll recover from such an extended code," Dr. Wille broke the news to me.

"But you said you didn't think he would make it through the day, and he did. Doesn't that mean something?" I pleaded.

"It means his heart and other organs are stable for now, but it doesn't have anything to do with his brain function," he told me.

"I am not capable of doing anything but waiting for him to wake up. It's barely been twenty-four hours. He needs more time," I insisted.

"Let's see what the day brings, and we'll go from there," Dr. Wille negotiated.

"I need you to understand, Dr. Wille. I promised Wesley I would give him all the time he needs to come back from something like this. He was very clear he wanted six months in this hospital to pull through if he ended up in this situation. I made him a promise," I cried.

"Let's just wait and see," Dr. Wille said again, as he placed his hand softly on my shoulder and then walked away, leaving me with my hope and my husband, both barely recognizable to me.

In that instant, I made up my mind my promise to Wesley meant more to me than any medical opinion. I had to believe there was a reason for Wesley still being here, even though the day before I had been told for the second time since his transplant he probably would not survive the day.

I had to wait it out, just as I had promised Wesley I would. When we decided on a transplant, I told him I was in charge of him, and no one would do anything without my permission. I still had hope. Even if it was just hope Wesley would do his best for us.

We were capable adults. We had health insurance, and we

could afford to try even harder. It occurred to me everyone who was taking care of Wesley was hired by us to do so. We had the right to make informed decisions and, at this point, I needed more information. But the information I needed, Wesley's ability to pull through, could only come from Wesley.

I felt sorry for my dad when he arrived in Birmingham and came to visit Wesley that afternoon. It was not as if those of us who had remained at the hospital were used to seeing Wesley looking so terrible, but it was worse for my dad because he had never even seen him in a hospital. The last time he had seen Wesley was when they had waved goodbye to each other in our driveway in January. To see him then, even though he was very sick, was nothing like seeing him now. My dad tried to hold back his tears when he saw his condition, trying not to show me he feared the worst, but I could see it. Anyone who saw Wesley in the hours after his heart stopped for forty minutes was seeing a side of Wesley and life's frailty that surpass all understanding.

My dad tried to get me to leave the hospital to eat lunch and get some fresh air, but Roger quickly told him not to bother.

"She won't leave him, Mick," Roger told my dad, and he believed him.

I continued to check on Wesley throughout the day. I was certain he was showing signs of gaining consciousness. His eyes had remained half open while he was in a comatose state, and I thought he made eye contact with me twice when I stood on a stool to look directly into his eyes. Roger had thought Wesley had squeezed his hand slightly, but he had not moved or mastered even the slightest progress when prompted by the nurses or Dr. Wille to try to move any part of his body.

"He won't have the fine motor skills to move his finger before he is able to look into my eyes," I insisted to Claire, but she still was not optimistic.

"Would you like to be alone with your husband?" Claire kindly asked me.

I had not been alone with Wesley since the night before his surgery when we were getting ready to go to the hospital. There had always been a doctor or nurse nearby with Wesley's door open. It had not even occurred to me I could be alone with him.

"Is that an option?" I questioned.

"It is. It's time, don't you think?" answered Claire, smiling as she finished noting his chart and began to leave Wesley's hospital room.

I stood up as she walked toward the sliding glass doors and quietly said, "Thank you."

"I will stay close to the door, close the curtains, and not let anyone in. Take as much time as you need."

We were alone, and I did what I knew I had to do.

His oxygen had progressed to the low seventies and his blood pressure was holding with medication. I had to believe he could hear me, just as the man he had read about before surgery. That man was the reason he wanted at least six months to recover from an episode like this.

"We are alone, Wesley. Claire is letting us have some time alone," I began, assuring him he was safe with me.

I held his hand, hoping I would feel him, hoping he could somehow show me he knew I was there, but he did not.

I let go of his hand and moved the small stool I had asked for in his room next to his bed, so I could stand directly above him where our eyes could meet. Still, he did not focus on me. He showed no signs of being inside of the shell I was clinging to with my hands and my heart.

"Wesley, the doctors have been trying to get you to show signs of recovery. You took a really bad hit this time. Your heart stopped, but you came back, so now I need you to let me know where you are. I need you to know I am waiting for you. I need you to know Hunter is waiting for you," I spoke to him in a loving but strong voice.

"You've been here for a while, and I don't know if you know that. I don't know how much you are aware of, but what I need from you now, more than anything else, is for you to move something. I am not leaving this room until you move something."

The alarm bells on his ventilator started ringing, as he was beginning to overbreathe it. He had done it many times before; this time I hoped it meant he could hear me and was responding, but I knew I had to balance his anxiety, so he did not become unstable.

"I know you can hear me, but you have to remain calm because they won't let me stay in here with you if you don't. Just try to stay calm and listen to me," I pleaded with him.

I stepped down from the stool and got out the hand-held recorder I had carried with me two days before when Hunter and I were on a walk near our apartment. I had brought it with me so Wesley could hear Hunter's voice.

"Hunter isn't here right now, but he recorded a message for you," I told him as I pushed play on the recorder and placed it next to his ear.

Hunter: Hey, Daddy, I'm walking with Mommy behind our apartment. You should see it back here, Daddy. It has a lot of trees and you can see the street. Maybe you can come here when you get better because you have new lungs now and you don't need your wheelchair anymore. Okay, Daddy?

Me: Tell Daddy about all of the fun things you have been doing. Tell him about library night and wearing your pajamas to story time.

Hunter: Oh, Daddy. We listened to story time in our pajamas. Isn't that silly, Daddy? Oh, and Daddy, I got a new toothbrush. It's got He-Man on it, Daddy. It helps me get rid of all my sugar bugs.

And Daddy, I have been playing at the park at our apartment, and I have made some friends. I get to play outside and have to wear a coat because it's cold outside, Daddy.

Me: *What else can you tell Daddy?*

Hunter: *Ummmmm, I think that's all.*

Me: *Okay, Buddy. I'm sure he will love to hear about your new toothbrush and the library.*

Hunter: *Oh, wait, Mommy. I have something else to tell Daddy.*

Hey, Daddy. When you get to start eating again you have to eat vegetables so you can get big and strong again. Okay, Daddy? Eat vegetables so you can be big and strong like me.

Okay, Daddy, that's all. Love you, Daddy. And I miss you, Daddy.

As soon as Hunter's voice could be heard on the recorder, Wesley's ventilator went back to normal and the alarm was silenced. Twice while the recording was playing, I thought Wesley leaned his head slightly toward Hunter's voice, but I was not sure.

"Hunter misses you, Wesley, but we will all wait as long as we have to for you to wake up and get better. I promise, no one is going to get in the way of you having more time to get better. I promised you I would give you six months, but they are trying to tell me you may not be yourself anymore after what you just went through. You said you didn't want to come back if you weren't going to be you. You said you didn't want to be a burden if you lost yourself, so I need to know where you are. I am going to fight for you no matter what, but I really need to know you are still alive in there. Wherever you are, I need you to come back and show me you are here. I am not leaving this room until you move something," I insisted to him again, making sure he knew he had to somehow muster the strength to show me he wanted to live—that he was still Wesley and not just the shell of his body.

More time went by, and I continued to talk to him. I remained firm, repeating again and again I needed him to move something before I would let him rest.

I waited.

Nothing.

It had been fifteen minutes, and he had not moved anything, but I could not give up. I still had to try to bring him back to us.

"Do you remember two nights before Hunter was born? We thought I was in labor, but we weren't sure, so I called the hospital and told the nurse about my contractions. She told me to go to bed, and if I fell asleep, I was not in labor. Do you remember that night?" I asked him, not expecting a reply.

"I remember that night so clearly. We knew Hunter was coming soon, and we couldn't wait to meet him, but we also realized it would be the end of just the two of us after five years of being married without a child. I remember when I got off the phone, I walked over to your side of the bed and told you what the nurse said. You lifted up the blankets and asked me to lie down beside you. You said, 'Let's lie here, just the three of us, and Hunter will come when he's ready.'"

As I spoke to Wesley and reminded him of this story, I knew it was one he would remember.

"The way you held onto my belly and made me feel safe under the blankets with you—that was one of the sweetest moments of my life," I whispered to him, touching his arm with one hand and his face with my other.

"Wesley, I'm not leaving this room until you move something," I quietly whispered to him, then sat down next to his bed and watched his chest as he struggled for each breath, even with the help of the ventilator.

For a moment, I wondered if I was asking too much of him. I wondered if it was impossible for him to show me what I needed to see, but I could not give up. I told him to move something, but I could not be sure I truly expected he would.

Wesley's body lay limp. There was no movement, no indication what the doctors were telling me about the possibility of him being brain dead was not true. I studied every inch of him, hoping to see a sign of life I could hold onto, anything indicating my husband was still there.

One more time, I said it.

"I'm not leaving this room until you move something. You have to move something." I pleaded with him, holding back my tears, my frustration, and my greatest fear.

Just then, Wesley gave me life.

With every amount of effort his tired body could muster, he slowly and methodically lifted his weak and trembling wrist off the bed, his right hand remaining limp at his side.

I could barely speak; I was so overcome with knowing he could hear me, and he still wanted me to fight for him. I knew him. I knew if he was ready to give up, he would have stayed still, keeping my hope captive.

"I knew you were in there, Wesley. I love you," I cried, as I stood to kiss his lips that could not yet respond to mine.

I sobbed as I wrapped my arms around his frail body, knowing I would not feel his physical embrace in return. I did not need his arms to hold me or his words to comfort me. In that beautiful moment, another beautiful moment of my life, I had all I needed from him: his will to live. I knew no matter what happened to him in the days to come, no matter how hard he had to work to come all the way back from where he had been, he wanted to come back. If the fight was still in him, then the fight was still in me.

"You have six months; I promise. I'm in charge of you," I assured him as I held onto his wrist and buried my head in his chest and continued to sob.

I cried for the hope he had given me and for the strength it took him to actually grant my request to move any part of himself in order to show he was still alive in the way he needed to be to carry on. I cried imagining what it was like for him to hear Hunter's voice and want to be with him. I cried because even after forty minutes without a pulse the day before, Wesley was still there. He had worked it out with God and come back to me. I had been gifted one more chance to fight for him, and I would. With everything inside of me, I would meet him where he was and bring him back to life.

God had changed it back.

CHAPTER FOURTEEN

Good Bye To a Stranger

My head was moist and my pillow was cold from the sweat on my face and in my hair. I had not yet opened my eyes, but I felt certain I had been sleeping. At least I hoped I had been sleeping.

I could hear people around me talking, and the familiar sounds of the surgery waiting room: people laughing as they played games and shared stories to pass the time; another family speaking quietly in the distance; a woman crying as someone tried to calm her. I knew where I was, but I could not wake up from where I had been. The image was still blazing in my mind, etching a place in my conscious thoughts. I wanted to throw it away, as a quarterback would throw a football with seconds to go before he knew he would be tackled and pummeled into the ground. I wanted to escape the image, but I could not. I felt forced to absorb it, to remember it, to know it as a truth that would somehow come to fruition, no matter what I tried to do to stop it.

In the dream, Hunter was standing next to me, though I could not see his face. I knew it was him, but I could not tell how old he was. I only knew he was very young because I was holding his hand as I had always done when crossing a street or walking him into his preschool class.

All I could see were his clothing and his small hand still holding mine. He was wearing black shoes, grey slacks, a white dress shirt, a blue blazer, and a green tie. Hunter had never worn a blazer. He did not even have one. As I peered deeper into the vision of him in grown-up clothes, I noticed his hand again. His fingers were small, the tips of his fingers were red, his fingernails were short, and one had a Band-aid where he had chewed his finger until it bled.

We were walking down a hallway that did not have much detail or color, just tan carpet and tan walls. I noticed nothing but Hunter in his blazer and his small hand holding mine. There were people around us. They seemed to want to be near us, but I did not welcome them, so they remained a few steps behind.

As Hunter and I approached two large, oak doors, I heard laughter to the right of us, but when I looked, I saw two people crying, not laughing. I was confused and did not know where the laughter was coming from, although I heard it clearly. Everyone looked sad and no one was talking. Through the large, wood doors, I heard the faint sound of music playing, but I could not make out the song.

I heard the laughter again, this time louder. Instantly, the hallway where I had been walking with Hunter evaporated as I began to wake up.

I finally opened my eyes and could see where I was. I was back in the surgery waiting room. A woman in the corner of the room laughed as she played with a young child.

"Are you okay?" Donna asked me, concerned by the confused and questioning look on my face. It took me a moment to collect myself.

"I think so," I hesitated, barely awake. "I'm fine."

"You slept for a while," she said, then went back to her puzzle on the floor.

I did not tell her the truth. I was not fine.

I wiped the sweat from my face and pulled my damp hair into a ponytail. I slowly sat up and rested my feet on the floor, looking for my shoes under the bench.

I held back tears as I put on my shoes.

"I'm going to check on him," I told Donna as I stood up and walked away.

It was not until I entered the elevator alone I let myself cry as I leaned against the cold, wood paneling of the elevator wall.

I knew what I had seen. It was Wesley's funeral. The vision was clear, but I was too terrified to admit it. I told no one and pushed it from my mind.

✳

Within twenty-four hours, Wesley had made such enormous strides doctors from throughout the hospital were coming to see him. Nurses were amazed by his progress, and the mood lightened in the coming hours. He had moments of complete coherence followed by hours of sleep. The doctors told us he had again beaten the odds and was capable of a full recovery.

By now, Alyson, my favorite nurse on the floor, was requesting Wesley during every shift she worked. It made such a difference, not only for him, but also for me. It gave me the freedom to leave his side with confidence he was in the most capable hands. Alyson always told me there was hope as long as he was still alive, and I believed her.

Jimbo had to return to Houston, but he was having a hard time leaving Wesley. He came to say goodbye just before he departed for home.

Wesley was struggling with the ventilator and kept trying to turn toward Jimbo's voice.

"It's okay, Wes. I'll be back. You just keep getting better," Jimbo assured him, trying not to cry.

Wesley did not want him to leave.

"You're going to be fine here, and I will be back before you know it," Jimbo said as he forced himself to go, unable to say anything more.

Two days after Wesley had moved his wrist for me, I went to the cafeteria with my dad for lunch. That morning Alyson had told me seeing Wesley's rapid progress—from being in a coma to being awake for long periods of time—she was going to push him to further improvement today and test his limits.

When my dad and I returned from lunch, Donna and Roger were in the room with Wesley. The rule was no more than two visitors in the room at a time, but somehow we were all there and no one told us to leave.

I walked in and Alyson was standing in front of Wesley, so I could not see him.

"You're back. Wait till you see this," she proclaimed as she stepped to her right, allowing me to see Wesley.

I could not believe my eyes! He was actually sitting up, eating ice chips.

We all started to cry and cheer for him. Wesley looked at us like we were crazy. He had no idea how far he had come.

"Dr. Wille will probably sleep at home tonight," Alyson said to me as we walked out of Wesley's room. "But he'll be fine here with me, and Kim is his night nurse again."

I already knew who Wesley's nurses were because I checked every day, but I was confused by what she said about Dr. Wille.

"What do you mean? Where else would Dr. Wille sleep?" I asked her.

"He's spent the last two nights down the hall. I don't think he wanted to leave Wesley," she said, telling me of his dedication to Wesley's critical continuous care.

I had never doubted Wesley's care in Dr. Wille's hands, but I was grateful to know he, too, stayed close by when Wesley was in the most danger.

While things were turning around for us, Leeandra and her family were struggling more than ever. Her mother Cathy was getting worse, and her organs were beginning to shut down one by one. The doctors had tried everything they could to turn it around for her, but there was nothing more they could do. They gave the family as much time as they needed, but it had been weeks with no response from her and the sepsis could not be reversed. She had been living with a lung transplant for more than a decade. Her body was tired. They suggested turning off life support and letting her die peacefully without tubes or medications prolonging her life.

It was a difficult decision for them to make, but they decided it was best for their mother. Her transplant had given her 10 extra years and the opportunity to see her children grow into adults, marry, and have children of their own. She was a wife, a mother, and a grandmother. She was loved, and even though I only saw her from afar, in her room a few doors down from Wesley, I knew her spirit and the joy she brought to everyone who loved her. I had watched them suffer as they saw her to the end of her wonderful life.

I sat with Leeandra and her grandmother, whom I had started calling Ma-Mah, just as her family did. We waited for all of their family to arrive, and I tried to stay strong for them, but it was a struggle. Part of me felt guilty because Wesley had managed to pull through sepsis, something Cathy was not capable of surviving. But having heard from them of Cathy's years of medical complications since her lung transplant, another part of me felt complete and utter fear for what loomed ahead for Wesley and our family after he recovered from the transplant surgery.

I had met many transplant patients over the weeks we had spent at UAB, and what I knew for sure was lungs were complicated organs to transplant. With every breath we take, we are exposed to the elements of our environment. Because of the immune suppressive drugs that must be taken to avoid organ rejection, a simple common cold can send even the healthiest transplant patient to the hospital.

Lungs are not like livers, kidneys, or even hearts, tucked safely in unexposed cavities of the body. And the other organs do not seem to need as many anti-rejection medications. I had been told of many patients starting out on a few dozen pills per day who eventually required ten or fewer to maintain the balance between rejection prevention and quality of life.

None of this had deterred us from accepting the choice we made to have the transplant. We knew enough about medical research and progress to know the longer Wesley was alive, the better chance we had of being part of lung transplant progress. We also knew the more lung transplants that were done, the more opportunity there was for learning.

When told their only hope for survival is a transplant, many people go forward and choose the transplant, no matter what the risks. It is part of how humans are made. We want to survive, and we will do just about anything to live. When I was told I had cancer with about an 89 percent chance of surviving and going on to live a healthy life after being cured, I was still afraid I might not be one of the people on the survival side of the statistic. I was told I had a very treatable form of cancer, but that did not mean I would be any less dead if I were one of the 11 percent who did not survive. But, of course, I signed up for the treatment. It was proven to work for many, and it offered me a chance to live a long life.

A lung transplant was much different. Wesley might walk away from the hospital with new lungs, but we knew even if all went well, we would return many times. The risks were too high, the medications too complicated, and it would always be an expensive, taxing, and emotional effort to keep Wesley alive. We made the choice to do it regardless: it was what we had to do to survive.

I left Leeandra and her family in the ICU waiting room with Dr. Wille and walked to Wesley's room, where I found him watching television. It was not visiting hours, but I did not care. I wanted to be with him, knowing Leeandra and her family would soon say goodbye to Cathy as Dr. Wille turned off the machines, not knowing how long it would take for her to die. Dr. Wille hoped she would go quickly, but he could not be sure.

I sat next to Wesley. He noticed me watching Leeandra and her family as they walked past his room, but he did not know what was happening, and I did not tell him. By now he knew who they were because I had told him about how wonderful they had been to us and how close we had all become. Each of them would wave to Wesley when he was awake as they walked past his room on the way to Cathy's.

Wesley nodded his head at me. He was still on the ventilator and unable to speak, but I understood him. He saw them crying and was asking what was going on.

"Cathy is having a hard day, but she'll be fine," I quietly told him as I reached for his hand, looking away from him and back at the television.

He did not want to know more, and there was nothing more I

wanted to tell him. I had not lied to him. In a few moments, she would be fine. She would be with God.

In each ICU room of the transplant unit there is a monitor above the bed, allowing the nurses to monitor other patients in case of an emergency. For privacy reasons, the monitor does not identify patients, but I knew which line on the monitor represented Cathy. I knew when Dr. Wille turned off her ventilator and her heart stopped, the alarm would sound on the monitor in Wesley's room as she flatlined. Quietly, without him noticing, I turned down the volume.

For several minutes I sat with Wesley, trying not to look at the monitor. I did not want to invade their privacy, but I also wanted to send the family my prayers and strength as they were letting her go. It was a difficult day on the unit because many of the nurses and doctors had known Cathy for more than a decade. While it was their job to remain professional and support the family's loss, they were suffering a loss of their own.

The third time I looked up at the screen, I saw Cathy's line on the monitor slowly change from a jagged, active line that represented her living, beating heart to a motionless flatline that represented her death.

I could not visibly react to what I had just seen because I did not want Wesley to know.

"I'm not supposed to be in here right now," I whispered to Wesley.

He nodded and pointed to the sign I had made and placed by the clock. I had posted the visiting hours so he would know when I would be in to see him.

"You know," I smiled.

He nodded and squeezed my hand, then nodded his head toward the door, telling me it was okay to go.

"I'll be back in two hours."

I leaned my forehead near Wesley's face, and he kissed me good-bye. Without him noticing, I turned the volume back up on his monitor before I left the room.

In the ICU waiting room, Leeandra and her family were already gathering up their belongings and beginning to leave. Ma-Mah was sobbing and could not be consoled, although everyone tried to comfort her. She kept calling out her daughter's name, "Cathy! Oh, my Cathy!"

"We're going to get her in the car and out of this place," Leeandra whispered to me as she reached to hug me.

As I hugged every member of her family and said goodbye for what I knew would be the final time in the transplant ICU waiting room, I could not speak. Then Ma-Mah called my name.

I walked toward her and tried not to cry.

"Lisa. Lisa, honey. You stay strong for your husband, honey. And for your little boy," she cried as she held her arms out to me.

I was amazed by the kindness of this wonderful woman. In the midst of the most tragic moment of her life, she had words of encouragement for me.

As I hugged her and held on tight, still without saying a word, I noticed Jerry, Cathy's husband, over Ma-Mah's shoulder.

"I'm so sorry," I mouthed the words to him as I hugged Ma-Mah.

"I know," he said, managing a smile through his tears.

Soon, all of them were gone, and I was alone in the waiting room. It was one of the loneliest nights of my life. I called Kelli and cried over the phone for an hour. She talked me through it, but when I hung up, the silence in the room was almost unbearable.

Finally, two hours passed, and I could visit Wesley again.

I stood at the sink, washed my hands, put on a gown and mask and walked into his room. He was still watching one of his favorite

197

channels, The Food Network. *Rachael Ray's 30-Minute Meals* was on. He was a fan of Rachael Ray and had been known to download her 30-minute recipes, print them, and leave them on my desk at home. It was his not-so-subtle way of trying to get me to cook more and try new recipes. He knew any recipe with more than five ingredients overwhelmed me. I had my talents, but cooking was not one of them. I had accepted this over the years, even if he had not.

I sat down on the chair next to him, casually propping my feet up on the edge of his bed. As sad as I was Cathy had died, I wanted to honor Ma-Mah and do what she had asked of me. I wanted to be strong for my husband and our little boy.

I was just so glad Wesley was alive, and I could do the simplest thing with him, like watch a cooking show on The Food Network. I knew I could not grieve the loss of Cathy and still be present for Wesley. I made myself let go of thoughts of her and just be there with him.

"So, honey, what's Rachael cooking up for dinner tonight?"

CHAPTER FIFTEEN

24/7

I could hear Wesley's ventilator alarm ringing from outside his door where I was washing my hands. Now that his infection had been treated, we were no longer required to wear a gown, mask, and gloves when entering his room.

"Just try to relax, you're doing so well, but you are overbreathing the vent," urged Kari, Wesley's nurse for the day.

I went to his bedside. He was looking at me to fix it, but only he could do that.

"There's talk of beginning to get you off the vent this week, but you are overworking yourself by overbreathing it. Just try to relax," I said in a calm, direct voice.

I held his hand with both of mine and kissed his forehead.

"Just relax," I said.

Slowly, the alarm was silenced by his slow, steady breaths.

He nodded at me—his way of letting me know he was listening to me.

"Can we see about getting the vent adjusted?" I asked Kari. "He's off to a good start today, and he shouldn't have to work so hard not to breathe on his own."

"I'll talk with Dr. Wille," she agreed. "Wes sure does calm down when you're around."

"I'm his person." I smiled at Wesley.

Later that morning, Dr. Wille turned off the ventilator for five minutes while Donna and I were in the room. He wanted to see how Wesley would do breathing on his own. Although his breathing was labored, it was amazing to watch him take each breath, using the lungs of a stranger, his own lungs long since removed from his body. His face looked determined and focused, a calculated effort to do what most of us never even have to think about.

He was tired when the five minutes was up, but he did well enough Dr. Wille changed the ventilator settings to force Wesley to breathe on his own with fewer assisted breaths per minute. It was a step in the right direction and allowed us to believe Wesley would eventually get off the ventilator for good.

"You're in good hands with Kari," I assured him. "I think I'll go home to Hunter for a while today, if you are okay with it."

He nodded several times and waved his hand toward the door for me to go. He knew Hunter needed to be able to spend time with at least one of us.

I soon left him there, feeling confident it would be a good day. He had a good nurse assigned to him, Alyson was on the floor, and Donna and Roger were at the hospital.

When I arrived at the apartment, Hunter was playing with his action figures near the back door where I entered. My dad was in the kitchen.

"Mommy!" Hunter cheered as he wrapped his arms around me.

We embraced for a good, long, much-needed hug.

"You surprised me, Mommy!" Hunter said. He had not known he would see me that day.

"Daddy is doing well today, so I wanted to come home and hang out with you."

Hunter immediately started showing me all the projects he had been working on in my absence—every picture he had drawn, every watercolor he had painted, every action figure he had assembled. For hours we played on the floor in the apartment, took a walk along the nearby trails, and had lunch at the Mexican restaurant across the street from our temporary home. My dad played with us but also gave us time together alone.

It felt good to have a little break from the hospital to catch up with normal life. Besides seeing Hunter, I needed to do some work on my neglected business and tend to Wesley's and my finances.

Bill collectors were starting to call for the first time in my life. We had always paid our bills on time, even during the difficult months before moving to Birmingham, but we had been falling behind. I had been camping out at the hospital for weeks because my priorities were Wesley and Hunter, not money.

I had recently sold the rights to my pillow designs to a company in Europe and was being paid in quarterly installments for one year, which made it easier to maintain two households. In fact, I had not yet filled out the paperwork for the insurance to reimburse us for the apartment, so I took the time to do that while Hunter played with my dad.

It is true Wesley's illness was a financial burden, and I knew it would get worse as time went on, with costly anti-rejection medications and continuing care—particularly because we would have to return to UAB for routine checkups and to treat any complications that might arise. But so far we were doing okay financially. We would worry about the rest later. We were also very fortunate Wesley's parents, Donna, Roger, and Jimbo, were able and willing to help us if we needed it and had been generous in the past, particularly when I was sick years before. We knew how fortunate we were—not everyone has that kind of resource and support in their family. We still tried to do everything on our own, but knowing help was available definitely reduced our stress level.

That afternoon, I called one of the banks that had been pursuing me, even calling me at the hospital, to collect the money we owed. The amount was less than $200 and was not yet thirty days late. Even so, the man was extremely rude and unconcerned with our circumstances. It was unbelievable to me a financial institution whose records showed we had never before been late making a payment could be so unfeeling in a time like this to dependable clients like us.

The other bill collector I called was very polite, however, and noted our circumstances on our account. That day I set up automatic banks drafts for most of our bills so I would not have to worry about writing checks and mailing bills from the hospital or taking time to pay bills when I could leave the hospital. What little time I had at the apartment I wanted to spend with Hunter.

I also checked in with Christi. She had been very patient with me and worked extra hard in my absence. A feature article I had been working on before leaving for Birmingham with *Blue Suit Mom* magazine was about to go to print and would be released in less than a week. Orders were still up from the feature a few months before in *Better Homes & Gardens Kids' Room*.

Ironically, the work Wesley had insisted I stick with throughout his illness was beginning to pay off in a big way—but it could not have been farther from my thoughts. Even when *The Oprah Winfrey Show* and *Good Morning America* considered me for both shows, each featuring stories about entrepreneurial moms, I had no interest in being on national television if it meant leaving Wesley's side. I knew there was no way I could manage the growth either show would bring to my business after appearing on the show. I was keeping it going, as I had promised, but I was content to leave the handling of daily operations to Christi and grateful she was so capable.

My part in the business had always been marketing and promotion, but I had lost my motivation. I started the company to better our family and have a creative outlet, but for now, all my energy was directed toward helping Wesley. I had written a book that was published five years before about my experiences with cancer. Many of the nurses at UAB were reading it while Wesley was in the ICU. They kept asking if I was going to write a new book about our experiences with Wesley's illness when he got better, but I told them I would not. All I wanted was to take my husband home and live with our family in our little corner of the world. I was no longer driven by the possibilities for my own life if I could not share those possibilities with Wesley. After weeks of not even being able to hear his voice, I struggled to celebrate the growth the company was experiencing in his physical absence.

Wesley always fully supported whatever I set out to do. I often commented he was the kind of man who would throw himself in front of a bus to save me—and he also would be proud to see my name on the side of the bus. During one of my first visits to spend time with him when we were adults, I brought some of the things I was working on at the time—songs I was writing, articles I was pitching, a script idea I had. All of these were dreams I wanted to fulfill, and at age twenty there was nothing stopping me. I remember Wesley standing in his kitchen reading every word and making me promise no matter what, I would always keep writing.

I started to fall in love with him that day in his kitchen. I knew he understood me, and as he shared with me the dreams he had for his own life, I felt excited about the possibility of sharing my life with someone who wanted what I wanted. I saw our future as a volley of giving and supporting, creating the life we had both wanted even before we considered being together. Now that we were coming together, it seemed anything was possible. I was completely willing to pack up and move to Texas to find out—so that is what I did. I have never regretted that choice. It is one of the decisions that most impacted my life. Even as Wesley was fighting for his life now, I felt blessed to be at his side instead of hearing about it from his family. When Wesley told me just before his surgery I was meant to be there with him through this, he was right.

I hurried through paying bills and catching up on my work so I could make dinner and spend as much time as possible with Hunter. My dad had been doing his best to care for him, and the two of them were enjoying each other. Although he had heard regular reports from my mom on what was happening in Texas when she stayed with us to help with Hunter before the transplant, when he arrived in Birmingham, my dad was unaware of what Wesley and I had been experiencing on a daily basis. Hearing about it was not the same as being there or living through it.

Just as we sat down to the table to eat dinner, the hospital called, which was never a good sign.

"Lisa, everything is okay," Alyson assured me.

"Okay," I paused, suspicious of a phone call from the hospital for any reason.

"Well, it appears Wesley has developed shingles. A virus…"

"I know what it is. It's like chicken pox, but it usually develops in older people," I interrupted her.

"And in people with a compromised immune system. The sores can be painful, but Wesley seems to be tolerating it well," she continued. "The sores have just begun to appear. Kari noticed them when giving him a sponge bath a little while ago."

"I'm just curious. Why is it you who are calling me, rather than the nurse assigned to him today?" I politely inquired.

"Because they thought it would be best coming from me," she explained. And she was right. Alyson was still the nurse I counted on most, especially when things were going wrong.

"So what does this mean for him?"

"Well, it does complicate things a bit, because we will need to move him into isolation to prevent the spread of the virus to other patients," she explained cautiously.

"Does that mean I won't be allowed to see him if he's in isolation? Because that's just not possible," I told her. I could not allow the option of my not seeing Wesley.

"No, not at all. You'll just need to go back to wearing a gown, gloves, and mask to protect yourself. And Hunter won't be able to see him again for a few days if he hasn't had chicken pox, because Hunter could end up with chicken pox from this virus."

I had planned to take Hunter to see Wesley that evening, He had not seen him since the day he left the squiggly note in Wesley's hand, but I knew we could not risk exposing Hunter to the virus.

"Okay. I understand, but what aren't you telling me?" I asked Alyson, sensing there was more to her phone call.

"Well, I don't think you are going to be happy with the room we have available that offers the isolation components necessary for Wesley," she continued.

"What's wrong with the room?" I pressed.

"Are you coming back tonight?" she asked.

"I am."

"Come find me when you get here, and we'll get it worked out."

I reluctantly hung up the phone, wanting to ask more questions but knowing this was something I needed to be at the hospital to address.

I sat back down at the table and finished dinner with my dad and Hunter. Then I gave Hunter a bath. Even though it was still light outside, I read him a bedtime story, since I would not be there later to do it.

Then, when I had stayed with Hunter as long as I could, I left him again and headed for the place I dreaded most but needed more, the hospital where Wesley remained fighting for his life every minute of every single day.

When Alyson told me about the shingles, I had very little reaction to the news. At that point, it just seemed par for the course. I believe in the power of our thoughts. Negative things can come to us if we think them possible, so I would never say I was expecting something to go wrong when things were going so well. But on the drive to the hospital, I started laughing out loud at the absurdity of Wesley developing shingles. I did not think it was funny, just cruel and ironic. In the privacy of the car, I responded as anyone would when hearing news that could push them over the edge and force them to consider giving up and losing their mind.

What a ridiculous and grueling turn of events! I just could not believe how incredibly arduous this experience was turning out to be. I was enraged. Wasn't it enough Wesley had endured a yearlong illness and his only hope to survive even a few more years was a double lung transplant? Wasn't it enough for him to endure a surgery in which the surgeon removed his own lungs and replaced them with a stranger's, all the while hanging on for dear life when his heart stopped during his surgery and his blood pressure never fully recovered? And after the second time in four weeks that doctors said Wesley would not survive the day, when his heart stopped for nearly forty minutes, didn't the fact he had survived and come back from it as the Wesley I have always known make a difference in how this all turned out? At some point, didn't this part of the journey get easier? Things had become so bad at times I was afraid to even go to his room during visiting hours. I would ask Roger to go ahead of me and come out to say he was okay. Every day was uncertain. At some point, didn't we get to take Wesley home to Houston and at least have the opportunity to learn how to live as a lung transplant family?

Somewhere out there, a family lost someone they loved and were generous enough to donate his or her lungs to us. Donating organs is not something doctors can do without family permission. Someone had to be asked and agree to this gift in order for us to even try to keep Wesley alive with new lungs. Wasn't it only fair the gift we had received just three days after being listed should be a blessing to Wesley and a bridge to his new life?

These questions ran through my head as I drove the familiar route to the hospital from our apartment—the apartment Wesley had found for us. He had spent hours researching a place for us to live close enough to the hospital for our convenience to down-town but far enough away from downtown crime for our safety. He made phone calls to the insurance company. He asked all the right questions and took notes as each person gave him the answers he was seeking. He did all he could and when he needed my help, I helped him. I once spent four consecutive hours on the phone making sure everything was arranged for us when we arrived at the transplant clinic as we were not in their records yet. Moving to Birmingham was an act of faith; we arrived there without Wesley even having been evaluated or listed for transplant.

The endless logistics of the past several months were screaming in my head. All I could think of at the end of my dance with rage was the pain Wesley would be in when the shingles reached their peak—and how could I protect him from a room Alyson was sure I would not like?

I found Alyson when I arrived at UAB. She took me to the room they planned to transfer Wesley to by the end of the day.

It was just three doors down from Wesley's current room, but it was very different. Instead of glass, it had a large wood door that would have to remain shut as long as Wesley was quarantined, and a small window near the hospital bed with broken blinds that could not be opened.

"This is unacceptable. How will anyone be able to hear his alarm sounding through the closed wood door?" I questioned Alyson, unhappy with the option being presented to me. "And the blinds won't even open."

"We can get maintenance up here to fix the blinds or even replace them," she offered.

"That doesn't change no one will be able to hear him if he gets in trouble. No. There's no way this room can work for him," I insisted. "You know he is too critical for this. His condition changes without warning."

"Let me see what I can do." Alyson assured me this would all work out and left to discuss it with the rest of the team to make a decision.

She returned within minutes to say they were going to hold a meeting to discuss my concerns and consider our options, keeping both Wesley's safety and that of the other patients in mind. I certainly did not want to risk infecting other transplant patients with compromised immune systems, but I also was not willing to leave Wesley in a dark room with little supervision.

Within an hour, Kari came to the waiting room with good news. Alyson was tending to another patient.

"We met about your concerns, which are certainly valid, and we have decided to bend the rules for Wesley's sake," she explained. "I told them what happened this morning—that Wesley was overbreathing the vent and seemed agitated, but when you walked in the room and started talking him through it, he immediately settled down. He does better when his family is with him, so, this is what we've decided. We are going to extend Wesley's visiting hours beyond normal hours. You can be with him 24/7, if you want to and are able, and you can spend the night with him in his new room."

"Spend the night?" I asked, elated at the idea of sleeping in the same room with him again for the first time in over a month, no matter the circumstances.

"Yes, you can spend the night. We decided if we are really considering what is best for the patient, then the rules we have in place are meant to be bent to ensure we are taking the best care of Wesley and considering his peace of mind."

"Oh, thank you so much! He definitely wouldn't want to be in that room alone," I said, still overcome with joy about their accommodations.

Then, a bit of reality set in.

"But wait. He's still critical and still needs rest. Can we say his visiting hours are still the normal hours with the exception of one of us being in there with him outside of visiting hours? Our family frequently comes to visit, and I don't want people in his room all day. He needs his rest," I told her, after considering exactly what she had offered us.

"Of course. We'll keep regular visiting hours for everyone but you," she readily agreed.

"And his parents?" I assumed.

"Yes, of course. You and his parents."

"And can we work out amongst us who spends the night with him?" I further requested.

"Sure. We'll limit it to you and his parents and leave the rest up to you about who spends the night with him on any given night," she answered, still completely accommodating my wishes.

"Thank you. Thank you so much!" I said, holding her hands in mine.

"You're welcome. I think this will be good for all of you."

This was good news. Not that shingles was good news, but getting to be with him 24/7 was a blessing for us. I did not like the idea of Hunter not being able to see his dad because of the shingles, especially since Wesley was doing so much better and could actually begin to interact with him again, but I knew Hunter was happy to be with my dad. My mom would be arriving Saturday, just a few days away. I also knew Hunter getting chicken pox right now was not an option in our already very complicated lives.

It took a few nurses and Dr. Wille to move Wesley to his new room. They even brought a cot for me or whomever would be spending the night with him.

Wesley was lightly sedated to combat the pain, allow him to rest, and prevent a setback due to shingles. His breathing was labored and his blood pressure was dipping, likely due to the fever he had developed that day, which the doctors hoped and assumed was from shingles—but none of these things were of great concern to them. There was an enormous sense of relief among the doctors, nurses, and our family after watching and waiting as every conceivable complication beat us down one by one.

I spent the first night with him, then went home the second night to be with Hunter while Donna slept in the room with Wesley. She and Roger had still been living in the surgical ICU waiting room. Unbelievably, we had adapted to our environment. We had some routine in our day and had accepted that sometimes clean clothes and a shower were impossible. Our priority was Wesley and being nearby in case he needed us at anytime for any reason.

Donna called me from the hospital the next morning.

"I think something is not quite right with Wes," she told me, concerned about some of the things he had been communicating to her.

"What do you mean?" I pressed further.

"Well, he's asking for his dad."

Wesley's dad had been dead for more than ten years. Wesley was trying to write but was still too weak. She said he was mouthing the words clearly, but seemed confused about his dad.

I called Dr. Wille and he assured me he was not overly concerned. He said Wesley was likely suffering from ICU psychosis, which was common in patients who had been in the hospital for so long. He said patients lose total track of time and even confuse their days and nights. Wesley was also still on dialysis, but was finally producing enough urine to get off it within the next day or two. Dr. Wille said once his kidneys were fully functioning, he would do better because the built-up medications and toxins would flush out of his system.

Later, when I returned to the hospital for the night, I talked to Wesley about his dad.

"Your mom said you have been asking for your dad," I cautiously asked him.

He nodded and lifted both of his hands, as if to say, "Why?"

I tried not to lead him with my questions, but I already knew the answer.

"Do you feel like you were with him?"

Wesley calmly nodded, as if Donna and I were finally understanding what he had been trying to tell us.

I did not say anything more at the time, but I truly believed when his heart had stopped a few days before, he was with his dad. Donna and I both believed Alton, Wesley's dad, had been with him when we could not be.

Later that day, when we were alone, I talked to Wesley again about his dad. For the first time since his transplant, I leveled with him about how sick he had been and how close he had come to dying. I wanted him to know he was still here for a reason and understand he had been all the way to heaven and back. That was why his dad felt so real to him again. As we talked, I knew he understood.

I did not tell Wesley, but I feared much of what he had endured would be lost from his memory after he recovered. I knew there was much he would never remember but I would never forget. I knew when he got well and we returned to Houston to rebuild our lives, I would need to be patient with him as he adapted to the limitations his new body would force him to accept. I believed he was capable of having a normal life, but I also knew it would have to be a new kind of normal for him.

A few weeks before, while Wesley had been struggling in the ICU after his surgery, there had been a group meeting for transplant patients and their caregivers led by a transplant coordinator. Wesley was too ill to attend, but Alyson suggested I go so I would know what to expect when he recovered, and we were sent home with new responsibilities as a transplant family.

I must admit, I was overwhelmed by all of the information given to us that day. As I sat listening to the coordinator, I absorbed all that was being shared and asked questions of my own. It became clear to me why this kind of meeting was not scheduled to take place until after transplant. I think it takes the experience of actually waiting for and then receiving the organ to fully appreciate the gift that has been given. That way, when sitting in a meeting hearing about all the potential challenges of living with a transplant, all one can really feel is grateful. Being overwhelmed is just a minor emotion compared to the gratitude one feels for the gift of a second chance at life.

During the meeting with transplant patients and their caregivers, they told us patients should not eat steak unless it was fully cooked, gardening without gloves was dangerous because of the contaminants in the soil, and alcohol interfered with the immune suppressive medications. The list went on and on. I knew there would be times when Wesley would choose to buck the rules and do what he wanted to do, and I just had to hope it would not be too costly. A simple cut from a fishing hook could send him to the hospital with a raging infection. These are the things I feared for Wesley but tried not to think about yet.

With all I was learning in the weeks I spent at UAB, I still believed in transplant. I believed in its progress and knew the more transplants that could be done, the more the doctors could learn, not only from the actual surgery but also from the medications required to keep patients from rejecting the organ once it was transplanted. I also knew many patients learned to adapt and manage their care while living long lives surrounded by gratitude, family, and friends. I prayed that would be true for us.

Even with the expenses, the responsibility, and the uncertainty, I knew we had made the right decision. I was willing to do whatever it took to keep Wesley alive, and so was the rest of our family.

Nighttime came, and I let Wesley rest while I lay down on the cot with a magazine. I fell asleep for a few hours and when I woke up, Wesley was awake, just staring at the ceiling.

I watched him for just a few minutes before getting up. I watched him scratch his nose and yawn. I noticed every time he blinked and how his long eyelashes overlapped and stuck together in places, just as they always had. As I stared at him, I felt sorry he had been lying there in silence with nothing to do but stare at the ceiling. I knew he wanted out of that bed and hoped he would be soon.

I got up slowly from my makeshift bed next to his and approached him with a smile.

He greeted me with the same.

"You aren't tired?" I asked him.

I was tired. I was exhausted, but I did not want to give up this time with him. It was rare for us to be alone and for him to be conscious enough to know it.

He shook his head and mouthed the words, "Are you?"

"No, I'm fine," I lied as I pulled a chair next to his bed and sat down beside him.

He reached for my hand. I was wearing gloves, but he did not seem to mind. He had asked his mom earlier that day where his wedding ring was. I had been wearing it since his surgery, and I showed it to him now.

"You gave it to me before your surgery, and I haven't taken it off since. I taped the bottom of it so it wouldn't fall off."

He motioned to me to put it on his finger, but I could not because of the gloves and because his fingers were still swollen from an overload of fluids in his body.

"It's okay; I can hold onto it for you," I smiled.

"Okay," he mouthed.

We sat quietly talking for a long time before his nurse walked in to check on him.

"What are you two doing up so late?" she whispered.

"We're on a date," I joked.

The three of us shared a smile and the nurse left the room, leaving us alone on our date.

For several minutes, we just sat holding hands. I talked, he nodded. A few times he would mouth words I could understand, but mostly we just sat together quietly, not needing words.

I will never forget the time I spent with Wesley that night. It was time together I needed and we had lacked for so many weeks of nights spent apart. Most of the time, Wesley was completely unaware of the distance between us—him in the ICU, me sleeping on a bench two elevators and a long corridor away from him. The hours we shared that night in his room restored the clarity I needed and renewed my hope we could return to each other even stronger than before the transplant. This interaction with him, after weeks of barely being able to look into his eyes for hours and days at a time, was a much-needed respite from the crisis mode we had been in, not only since the day of his surgery but also in the months after he first got sick. In eight years time, we had been through cancer and a transplant. I wanted the tragic madness to stop.

As I sat with him in the dark, quiet room, the only light coming from the monitors and machines beside and above us, I thought about how much this man loved Hunter and me. I looked at the healing wound from the surgical incision across his entire chest, now beginning to scar, and let the magnitude of what he had endured for us sink into my mind. Showing little fear and absolutely no hesitation while knowing all the risks, Wesley had entered the operating room. Think about that. The lungs that began to form in Donna's womb as she carried him to birth, the only two he was given when being created, were being taken from him to save him. And he was willing to endure all of it so he could have more time on this earth with us.

"I love you," I told him, squeezing his hand.

"I love you," he mouthed back to me.

I lowered the side rail of his hospital bed so I could get closer to him. Then I rested my head on his lap until we both fell asleep. How long we slept, I do not recall, I just remember waking up next to him for the first time in a very long time and feeling like the little bit of time we had managed to share that night would get me through the days ahead until he could get out of that bed.

If anyone had the capability and strength it was going to take to recover, it was Wesley. Together, we would find our way out of this place and return home where we all belonged. We would make the long drive home to Houston, only this time there would be no oxygen tanks and Flolan packs. This time it would be us on the open highway, stopping along the way to see what we had missed the first time. How I longed for the day when, in the not-so-distant future, Wesley could be Wesley again.

CHAPTER SIXTEEN

Easter Sunday

"Look at what the guys from work sent to you." I showed Wesley the picture his coworkers had emailed me. It was a sign they had made that read, "GET WELL SOON. WE MISS YOU!"

Wesley smiled and shook his head.

If you knew these guys, you would know how incredible it was for them to come up with such a gesture. They were good guys—just not the "hey, let's make a sign, take a picture, and send it to Wesley" kind of guys.

Wesley had worked for Jimbo in the oil and steel industry for many years. He loved the work he did and could not wait to return to it.

There were several doctors in and out of Wesley's room that day. Many were coming to meet the miracle patient who had managed to fight his way back again. Others were there with an agenda. His feet had terrible bed sores and some flesh wounds had developed from the medication that forces blood flow to the heart to maintain blood pressure, sometimes at the expense of extremities. A plastic surgeon visited and decided his feet did not need grafting, thankfully, because I had heard it was a painful procedure. He just prescribed a washing fluid that Alyson started using on Wesley's feet right away. By the middle of the afternoon, they already looked better.

The infectious disease doctor also stopped by to say there was no new infection. Wesley's white count was on a downward trend, nearing twenty thousand. In the weeks since he had developed an infection, Wesley's white count had been as high as ninety thousand and had been hovering above forty thousand for the past few days.

The kidney doctor also checked in. Wesley was producing urine like a champ. They were going to do a twenty-four-hour analysis to make sure it was safe to remove him from dialysis. The doctor expected he would be off dialysis the next day, which was Saturday. This meant Wesley could be out of bed and into a cardiac chair by Easter Sunday for the first time in exactly six weeks.

Wesley had lost a great deal of weight, his muscles were suffering atrophy from disuse, he still could not eat and had a feeding tube through his nose, but none of these things was critical. We were facing weeks of rehabilitation—the doctors said it might take some time before he could even walk again—but I felt confident Wesley could endure it. I knew when Wesley became frustrated during the weeks of recovery that lay ahead, I would remind him of how far he had come; God had brought him back for a reason. If that did not work, I would show him the photographs I took of him after his surgery.

He had asked me before the surgery to take pictures so he could see them later. I did not think I would want to be reminded of how sick he had been, but after that critical Monday following his surgery, when he miraculously recovered after having coded so many times, I brought the camera a few days later and took pictures. I knew the road ahead would be difficult as he struggled to rebuild his physical and emotional strength; I hoped the photographs would be a reminder to him of what he was capable of overcoming.

Wesley's recovery was finally heading in the right direction. My mom had finished her treatment and received the go-ahead from her doctor to travel. She would be able to stay as long as we needed her. My dad had been able to take some time off work, so he could stay to help with Hunter. Having the three of them together would give me instant relief from the guilt I felt being away from Hunter and the constant feeling of being torn between the needs of my husband and of our son.

"My mom is coming tomorrow," I reminded Wesley.

He nodded and smiled.

"So you know Hunter will be in good hands for the duration of your stay here. He's almost as happy with my mom and dad as he is with us." I wanted to make sure he knew he did not have to worry about Hunter, so he could concentrate on getting well and getting out of the hospital.

"Hunter here?" Wesley mouthed, wanting to know when Hunter would be coming to visit.

"The doctor said maybe by Monday or Tuesday. Your shingles are already drying up, but we want to be sure Hunter doesn't get chicken pox," I explained.

He nodded.

Brian, one of my favorite nurses, was assigned to Wesley that day. Alyson was also working on the floor. The patients on the transplant floor were doing well, most just in for minor complications, and no new surgeries had been performed in over a week. The mood was light as people talked about their plans for Easter that coming Sunday and what to bring to the potluck they were having on the transplant floor for those who had to work on the holiday.

Dr. Wille stopped in a few times that day and let me know he would be gone for the weekend. He had been tireless in his care of Wesley. I was relieved to know he was confident enough in Wesley's progress to be away from the hospital for a few days.

"He's got a will to live I have rarely witnessed. His strength is amazing," Dr. Wille said as he and I stood talking outside of Wesley's room.

"He's still a little foggy about some things. He's still not quite right," I told Dr. Wille, concerned about any brain damage Wesley might have suffered.

"I think all of that will resolve as he gets off dialysis and begins to move and talk and interact. He's already made such progress. Overall, does he seem like himself?" Dr. Wille asked.

Other than the morning Wesley was being prepped for surgery, most of the doctors and nurses had had little or no interaction with the Wesley I knew. They had not even heard him speak, so they did not really know him as he had been before the surgery.

"Definitely. His overall personality is the same," I answered with certainty.

"Then just give it time. He took a very big hit with the last code. Truly, I don't know how he survived. I hope all of it is behind him because after all Wesley has been through, there comes a time when we have to ask ourselves if taking such extraordinary measures is what is best for him."

"But it was worth it. He made it through, and he's still here. He's still Wesley," I said, trying to remind Dr. Wille this time it had worked out for the best.

"Oh, I agree with you. I'm thrilled with the outcome. Don't get me wrong. I just want you to know there could come a time when it will be up to you to decide how far we go to bring him back, and if that is what will really be best for him," he explained.

I knew Dr. Wille was pleased about his decision to take extraordinary life-saving measures with Wesley the morning he had coded just a few days before and through every other complication Wesley had suffered. But I also knew he was right. Wesley was doing wonderfully now, but we had seen things turn quickly for him too many times to think he was completely out of the woods.

"I understand," I told him, and I did.

I called my dad to tell him about the great day Wesley was having. The ventilator had been turned off several times, allowing him to breathe on his own, and he was still producing enough urine to get off dialysis the next day.

I told my dad I planned to come home to our apartment for the night while Roger stayed with Wesley. My mother was arriving the next day, and I wanted to clean the apartment before she came. Roger would spend the night in Wesley's room, as Donna had left the hospital the day before to stay at Rae's because she was getting sick and could not risk passing anything on to Wesley.

As I was talking to my dad quietly in the corner of Wesley's room while Wesley slept, his ventilator alarm began to sound. It often happened momentarily when he yawned, so I looked at him but was not concerned.

When it did not stop sounding, I looked over at him again.

"Dad! I have to go! I have to go! Wesley is having a seizure!" I exclaimed in a panic as I hung up the phone without waiting for my dad's response.

Wesley's whole body was shaking and his eyes were open. I threw open the door and called for help. Brian was not nearby but Alyson was. She ran to the medication room and came out quickly with a syringe.

I stood by the doorway waiting as she ran past me into the room. By the time she got there—less than a minute of my calling for her—the seizure was over. I let the door shut behind her and stood outside of Wesley's room, keeping out of the way of the other nurses who were running to help her. Honestly, I could not watch.

A few minutes later, I opened the door and looked inside at Wesley. His eyes were fixed and lifeless and his head tilted oddly to the right. He was not moving. He looked like a hollow shell, unnatural. I had never witnessed a seizure before with its violent uncontrollable thrashing, and I was terrified of the damage it would do to his already grossly assaulted body, particularly to his brain.

"This is normal after a seizure," Alyson tried to calm me. "He'll come out of it. Just give him a little time."

Time. I was beginning to feel like time was running out. All I could think about was what did this new problem mean for him now? Was this what Dr. Wille had warned me about just a few hours before?

Just then, Dr. Wille appeared. He touched my shoulder as he approached Wesley's bedside. By then, Wesley was starting to come around. He looked at me as if to say, "Why is everyone in here?"

No one said anything to him. If he did not remember it, Wesley did not need to know he had just had a seizure.

I stepped outside with Dr. Wille, and he told me an antiviral medication Wesley was on from his previous infection had been known to cause seizures. They did not believe it posed a risk because he had not seized at all since the day after his surgery.

"How bad is it?" I questioned.

"We'll keep an eye on him, stop the antiviral medication, and give him medication to reduce potential risk of additional seizures, but he's already coming around from it. He'll probably be very tired and sleep for quite a while. I will not sedate him. He can recover on his own from this."

I walked back into the room and there was Alyson, talking with

Wesley as if the seizure had never happened. It was one of the oddest things I had ever seen. I followed Alyson to the hallway.

"Dr. Wille thinks he'll be fine. But his eyes. He looked frozen." I was still shaken by the experience, relying on Alyson to put my mind at ease.

"It's very normal after a seizure for the patient to look that way. We'll give him medicine to ward off any new seizures." Her explanation was the same as Dr. Wille's.

Even though it seemed Wesley was fine and he would likely sleep the rest of the night, I called my dad to tell him what had happened and to let him know I would not be coming to the apartment that night after all. Assuming Wesley had a good night, I would be home in time to accompany my dad when he went to pick up my mom at the airport the next day.

I spent the night hardly sleeping, terrified of another seizure, but nothing happened. Wesley slept straight through the night and woke up refreshed in the morning. I still could not get over how odd it was he could be fine one minute, have such a terrifying seizure, and then be fine again a few minutes later. I felt as if the ground beneath my feet and my faith in this ever-rigorous process of recovery was wavering. I did not want ours to be a life of one near-death experience after another. I did not want Wesley to endure seizures and hospital stays. I tried not to let my mind race to a negative place, instead concentrating on taking care of Wesley one day, or even just one hour at a time.

I spent most of the next day with Wesley. We laughed and joked. We were ourselves together. Roger was coming to stay overnight because I planned to spend the night at the apartment after my mom arrived. The logistics of having so many people shuttling in and out and staying in so many places was difficult at times, so a few weeks before, when Tami was visiting, I had rented a car to enable me to get back and forth to the hospital while leaving our car for our guests to drive. By then, Jimbo had taken his Suburban back to Houston and returned our Jeep to us—but not before putting four new tires on it I had not even had the time to notice were needed.

I explained to Wesley again my mom was flying in that night, and I would be back the next day.

"I'll color Easter eggs with Hunter tonight and have an Easter egg hunt with him in the morning. Then I'll be back to spend the day and night with you."

"Okay," he mouthed as he motioned for me to kiss him.

"Sorry. I don't know if I can kiss you yet," I apologized. His shingles were almost completely dried up, and his nurse Brian had already checked with the doctors and cleared us from having to wear gloves and a mask when in his room, but a kiss might pose too much risk. I had to think about Hunter and preventing him from getting chicken pox.

"Hunter," I said, as my one word explanation for not kissing him.

He nodded he understood.

I told him I loved him and left his hospital room. Then halfway down the hall I had a feeling I should not leave yet. I did not know why, but I just was not ready to go. It was like the time months before, when he was in the hospital in Houston, and I had turned around and walked all the way back to his room to tell him of the plans I had made for renewing our vows on our tenth anniversary.

I had learned to listen to that little voice inside we all have but sometimes ignore.

I walked back to his room. When I opened the door, Wesley was surprised to see me.

"Just wanted to tell you I love you again," I said from the doorway and blew him a kiss.

"Love you," he smiled.

I turned to leave again, feeling good I had listened to the little voice.

That night, when my mom arrived, everything felt renewed. I was so relaxed I even had a margarita at the Mexican restaurant where we had dinner. I colored my hair at the apartment, we decorated Easter eggs, and we played Candyland with Hunter. For the first time in months, life felt relatively normal and incredibly hopeful.

Just before I went to bed, I called the hospital to check on Wesley, and his nurse said he was doing great. The twenty-four-hour urine analysis had come back good, so the dialysis line in his leg would be removed in the morning, and Wesley would be getting out of bed that day for the first time. His nurse assured me she would call if anything changed and told me to enjoy my night home with Hunter and my parents.

As Hunter and I said our prayers that night, I thanked God for the good care he had taken of Wesley and for the opportunity we had to save him.

I enjoyed my best night's sleep in weeks.

That Easter morning I made sure I woke up before Hunter so I could set out his Easter basket. Since it was raining, we planned to hide eggs in the apartment for him to find, and my mom had also said she would find an Easter egg hunt to take him to later in the day.

I called the hospital to check on Wesley and talked to Brian, who was assigned to Wesley again for the day.

"He's doing great! We're wheeling a VCR into his room right now so we can watch a movie until you get here," Brian said, sounding cheerful and as hopeful as we all were about Wesley making a full recovery.

"Please tell Wesley I'll be there as soon as Hunter is done with his Easter egg hunt. I'm letting him sleep in," I assured Brian. "You guys wait for me!"

I wanted to be there when he got out of that hospital bed for the first time in six weeks!

"Oh, we will. We won't let you miss it!"

I hung up the phone and started hiding eggs quietly with my mom. I was so excited for Hunter to wake up.

That morning was filled with such hope for the future of our family. Not just for Hunter, Wesley, and me, but for everyone who loved Wesley. We had not endured the months of his illness alone. Many, many people had helped us along the way and supported us in any way we needed. No one wanted to lose Wesley or to watch him suffer the way he had been suffering. We had moved to Birmingham for the hope UAB and a transplant would save us all from having to live one day without Wesley, and I was feeling so grateful we had.

Less than ten more minutes had passed when the phone rang. It was Roger. He was still at the hospital after spending the night with Wesley.

"Hi!" I cheerfully greeted him.

"You need to get here right now!" Roger insisted.

I was confused. I had just talked to Brian a few minutes before, and everything was fine. What could possibly have gone wrong?

"What do you mean? I just hung up with Brian!" I panicked, but kept my voice low, trying not to wake Hunter.

"He's bleeding, and they lost his pulse," Roger told me. I could tell he was trying to remain calm. "You need to get here now!"

I hung up the phone and quickly found my car keys and purse.

"I have to go! Oh my God! It's happening. He's bleeding. His heart stopped again. I have to go!" I cried to my parents.

"Mick, take her. Go! Take her!" my mom cried as she gave my dad his shoes and we ran out the door.

"I'll drive!" he insisted. It was the first time I had had someone with me who could drive me to the hospital in an emergency. I was in no shape to be driving.

As we sped down the highway, racing to the unknown once again, I was terrified. I kept hearing Dr. Wille in my head, saying at some point, there might be nothing more they could do for him. His being gone for the weekend only made it worse.

I barely remember the ride to the hospital. When we arrived, I had my dad drop me off in front of the ICU building and told him where to park the car.

As I ran toward the familiar elevator, my heart was racing. I did not know how we could turn this around.

I ran through the ICU hallway doors. From outside Wesley's door, I saw absolute devastation. I could not bear to go inside—but they would not have let me if I tried.

I could tell by the number of nurses running in and out of the room with bags of blood he was still alive. They had not given up.

"Somebody! Somebody! Please tell me what is happening!" I shouted from the double doors near his room.

A nurse came out and said Alyson would be with me in a minute, then escorted me to the familiar conference room a few doors down.

By then, my dad, Donna, and Roger were in the room. I could barely breathe. Every part of my body was trembling with fear. I tried to think myself into Wesley. I wanted him to know I was there. I wanted him to feel me and know my abundant love for him. If he were capable of knowing where I was in that moment, I wanted him to know my heart belonged with him. How could I find my way to wherever he was? How could I transcend to the place, so distant from me now?

I thought of Hunter at our apartment, disappointed I would not be there for his Easter egg hunt. I sobbed for our little boy and the excruciating disappointment and sadness he would always know if his dad did not survive this day.

Alyson walked in the room, and she looked like she had gone into battle. She was covered in sweat, her hair limp and damp from perspiration, and the protective goggles on her face had specks of blood—Wesley's blood—near her brow.

I burst into tears when I looked into her eyes. The nurse who had had enough hope for all of us in the weeks before this day looked utterly and completely hopeless.

I fell into her arms and sobbed, then mustered the strength to ask her what I did not want to know.

"Can he make it?" I cried.

She sadly shook her head and answered, "I don't think so, Lisa."

I had never cried louder or felt such total despair. I felt lost and disconnected from everyone and everything in the room.

"He's bleeding out. There is a surgeon in the room now, deciding if he can do surgery to save him. He's in cardiac arrest. He's losing blood faster then we can put it back in," she explained.

"Where is the blood coming from?" I did not understand what was happening.

"We don't know. Brian said Wesley started to cough, so he suctioned him and blood started building up quickly through his tracheotomy tube and could not be stopped. His heart stopped soon after. We started compressions immediately and have been giving him blood through constant infusion."

My head was spinning. My mind was racing. I could no longer stand. I started to fall to the floor in tears, but my dad held me up, trying to be strong through his own torrent of tears.

"I'll go back in and come back to tell you how he is doing."

Alyson left the room.

I remember looking but not seeing. I felt my dad but did not look at him. I heard Donna crying but could not go to her. I just wanted Wesley.

Just a few minutes had passed when the doctor came in with Alyson.

He explained everything they had done and what they were still doing to try to save him. Then he looked at me and said there was nothing more they could do.

I did not grasp it. Then why were they still working on him? Didn't that mean there was a chance they could save him?

"I don't understand," I said.

"We can keep doing what we are doing, but what I am telling you is we cannot save him," the doctor explained.

What he was saying knocked me over and forced me to face my most horrific nightmare.

"You're telling me I have to tell you to stop?" I cried, unsure if I was capable of giving up.

"Yes, I'm sorry. That is what we are telling you."

"Oh my God! Oh my God! Oh, Wesley. Oh, NO!" I sobbed, finally looking at Donna.

I could see the same sorrow and panic all over her face.

"What do we do? What do we do?" I cried to her. "Do we let him go?"

I could not stop the tears. I did not want to face this decision alone, yet I knew the decision was already made. It was time to let God have Wesley. The enormity of Wesley slipping from me was screaming inside of my head, and yet I had an overwhelming feeling he was already gone. I knew this was the day, the moment, the tragedy we had fought to avoid. It was here. It was absolute, and there was nothing I could possibly do to change it. Wesley would die today.

"We do. It's time," Donna cried to me, as we held onto each other. "We have to let him go."

I did not want to say the words. I would have let them stand there waiting for my response for hours just to keep Wesley alive longer, but I knew he would not want that. I knew what I had to do for him.

"You can stop," I cried to the doctor. "You can let him go."

I pulled away from Donna and back into myself, knowing the doctor had left the room to tell the nurses to stop compressions and transfusions and to turn off the machines. I needed to be silent in myself as he did this, so I could be present for Wesley. I wanted him to know, wherever he was at that very moment, I was there. No matter the anguish or the panic I felt, I needed to send Wesley out of this world with a clear and present mind. I needed to send him away with love.

I tried not to think about anything but Wesley and Hunter in that moment. I wanted to somehow pull us together with the sheer strength of my will to share a last moment before Wesley was truly gone. I pictured Hunter with his Easter eggs and Wesley watching him as he drifted off to a place only God could show him. I pictured Wesley in two places at once—with me in the conference room of the hospital and with Hunter in our apartment. As I thought of Hunter, I let myself fall apart and enter the abyss. Sadness filled every part of me.

Soon, I would see Wesley for what I knew would be the final time. I heard my dad tell the chaplain to make sure the room was clean.

"Don't let my daughter see his blood." He tried to whisper, but I still heard him.

There was nothing I could do to prepare myself for seeing Wesley. I had to somehow manage to tell him goodbye, even though all I wanted to do was bring him back to life.

I knew I had to leave the hospital and somehow find the strength to tell our son his father had died. Somehow, some way, I had to keep the promises I had made to Wesley and, no matter what, remain the mother to Hunter he had always known me to be—strong, loving, and capable.

I had known Wesley most of my life and loved him all of that time. A part of me went with him that day.

CHAPTER SEVENTEEN

Day One

It was still Easter and still light outside. We were back home in Texas, and it was still the day Wesley died.

Jimbo picked Hunter and me up at the Houston airport. It was the bumpiest flight I had ever been on. At one point we lost altitude rather quickly due to turbulence, but I honestly did not care. It might have been selfish, but I felt if anything happened to Hunter and me on that flight home, then we were meant to be with Wesley wherever he was, and who could question it? It had been just hours since Wesley died, and life felt unbearable, hardly worth living.

At the airport before we boarded the plane, an airline employee named Nancy helped us check our luggage. Unexpectedly, Hunter said to her, "My daddy died today."

She looked at me in shock. When her eyes met mine and she saw the truth, she softly touched my hand and knelt in front of Hunter and said, "I'm so sorry about your daddy." Then she finished checking our luggage and wiped her eyes as we walked away to board the plane.

As we were landing at the familiar Houston airport, I realized no one but Wesley had ever picked me up there. My heart sank, knowing this was the beginning of the million things I would see and hear and do that would forever remind me of him and of his absence.

Family members and a few close friends were already at our house when we got home. My sister Bev was on her way and would arrive late that night. Kelli brought food and drinks, knowing our house had been empty for weeks. I had not eaten a morsel of food all day.

Wesley's sister Jenny and her husband Todd were there. I had asked them and Jimbo to stay the night with us. I stacked our luggage outside our bedroom door, leaving the door closed. It had not been opened since the morning we left for the transplant. Memories of our last morning together in our home, just nine weeks before, were trapped inside. I could not bear to enter our bedroom yet.

The phone kept ringing, but I let other people answer it. I couldn't. I knew I had to plan the funeral, but I was not making any decisions that day. The hospital had told me there was time; tomorrow was soon enough to let them know which funeral home I had chosen for Wesley.

I tried not to think about Wesley in the morgue, still at the hospital. I felt no guilt about leaving before he could be flown home to us. I did exactly what he would have wanted me to do: I brought Hunter home.

My parents had stayed behind to fit what they could into our Jeep and planned to drive it to Texas the next morning. Donna and Roger were staying the night at Rae and Mike's house and planned to drive home the following day. We were all doing what we had to do. I did not consider what everyone else was thinking and feeling as, one by one, they heard the news. Hunter was my only constant concern, and he and his dad made up my only continuous thought. I shared our home with everyone who loved us, and I wanted them there, but I wandered aimlessly from room to room, passing through each doorway and wondering where Wesley was and why I could not feel him.

Food was everywhere. I thought about how Wesley loved to host our parties and how, when I tried to make things simpler, he would persuade me to make them more grand.

"I make the food," he would say. "You make it look nice."

Wesley was missing from everything in the house. During the previous weeks, when the tracheotomy prevented him from speaking, I had endured his silence in the hospital room, but this was our home. This is where there had been life and laughter. I wanted him to be everywhere and in everything we were saying and doing—but he wasn't.

I went outside to sit by myself on the curb of our driveway. I could hear everything and nothing, all at the same time. There was a silence I could not describe, yet every noise seemed louder and more pronounced. With clarity I heard planes flying over our house, a car's tires skid on the pavement blocks away, and laughter coming from the backyard of the house next door.

I could hear the noises of the world around me. Each was distinct and obvious, but Wesley was gone from all of it. I walked in and out of the house several times, each time trying to gather the strength to be in a room that was empty without him. At one point, I stood in the garage, his garage, and sobbed until the back of my throat ached, and my head pounded against the noise of my pulse pounding in my ears.

The evening wore on. People flowed in and out around me, though I hardly noticed them. As it became later, they started to leave, until only a few people were left. Jimbo, Jenny, and Todd were staying the night at our house. Bev arrived after 11 p.m., and it was only then I felt I could enter Wesley's and my bedroom. I knew Bev was there to help me through whatever emotions entering that room would evoke, at a time when I knew nothing of what I was feeling. I did not ask Bev to go into the bedroom with me or tell her I was avoiding it. I just knew when she arrived, it would be safe to do it with her there.

Every home has its own scent, but after spending weeks between a hotel, an apartment, and a hospital waiting room, I had lost whatever scent we had carried with us when we left for the transplant. When I opened our bedroom door and turned on the lights, I remembered it. The room felt familiar in the most primitive sense—its smell, the color of the walls, even the dust on the dresser top. Everything about our bedroom filled me with the memory of us.

I sat on the corner of our bed and stared straight ahead. I thought I would see nothing that mattered, removing myself from the moment if I could. But there it was—the empty space. It was filled with the memory of why we had left, what we had hoped for, and the words I had said to Wesley in front of our house the morning we left for Alabama, "I'm not coming home without you."

In the corner next to our dresser was the imprint in the carpet of his oxygen machine. It was the machine that had kept him alive for months while we searched for a treatment for the disease that even now had not been diagnosed. It was the machine that kept me awake at night with its constant noise, not only the noise it made while performing its necessary functions, but also the noise it made in my head, the fear it represented, and the reality it forced us to face.

Trying to escape the overwhelming emotion of the moment, I studied the pattern of the carpet. Instead of concentrating on the imprint of the absent oxygen machine, I recalled the day the new carpet was laid and hoped the memory would save me.

It had been installed a little more than five years earlier, while I was pregnant with Hunter. To put it in, the carpet layers needed us out of the house for the whole afternoon. Wesley and I drove from place to place, taking our time and eating a long lunch. We shopped, buying extra sheets for Hunter's crib, a baby rattle, and some tiny socks we could not believe would soon be filled with little feet.

We had nothing but time that day as we stayed away from the house. One of the carpet men had told us he had five kids at home. We were in awe of such a number. I wanted three kids; Wesley wanted to take our time with the first. We knew we were having a son. Wesley had selected the name Hunter weeks before the date of his birth was anticipated, and his room was ready down to every last detail, but beyond that we were just anxiously awaiting events to slowly unfold.

When we could think of nowhere else close by to go while we waited for the installers to finish, we headed for home, not knowing if we had been gone long enough. They were still working when we pulled up, so we parked in front of the house and waited.

While we sat on the grass in our front yard, we talked about how amazing it was we were about to have a baby together. Throughout the years, I sometimes teased Wesley, saying, "What would you have said if someone had told you when you were ten years old you were going to grow up and marry Vance's little sister?"

He always chuckled and gave the same answer, "I would've said they were crazy."

By now, we had been together seven years and had seen each other through our fair share of wonderful and difficult times. The early days together were some of the best of my life. We spent those days and nights talking about everything we would be and do. We did not want to fall asleep because we might miss a moment of each other.

In the early months we were together, I found it hard to believe anything would ever compare to what I was experiencing. That first great love turned out to be all I hoped for and more—it was the greatest awakening of my life to that point. To be loved with that intensity is what every woman should know in her lifetime. A love that certain, that committed, is what transformed me from a girl to a woman. Wesley also learned about himself as we unfolded, and our love brought out the very best in him.

When I recall the moments we shared that became our beginning, the feeling of the experience is present, and I am grateful for ever having meant so much to another human being. I was loved, and everything before and after that was a part of exactly who God intended me to be in my life.

I finally looked away from the empty corner in our bedroom where the oxygen machine had been. I had avoided going to bed long enough. Hunter was tired. Bev said she would sleep with us.

Someone offered me a sleeping pill to help get me through the night, but I refused it. If Hunter woke up during the night—any night—crying for his dad or me, I needed to be able to be there for him with clarity. Checking out, even for a better night's sleep on this first night, was not and would never be an option for me.

I slept under the blankets next to Hunter, and Bev slept on the other side of Hunter on top of the blankets. She left Wesley's pillows stacked on his side of the bed untouched. I gave her a quilt to keep her warm, but I wanted Wesley's side of the bed to remain as it was the last night he had slept in it before we left for the transplant.

Bev promised to wake up if I needed her throughout the night, and later, when I said her name aloud, she responded. I could not sleep and could not stand the silence a minute more.

"I'm awake," I said, softly squeezing her arm.

"What do you need?" she asked.

"I don't know."

"What can I do for you?"

"Nothing," I answered. There was nothing she could do beyond being awake with me.

"Are you okay?"

"No." I cried silently, not wanting to wake Hunter.

"I'll stay awake with you," she assured me.

"Okay."

We whispered to each other in the darkness of the bedroom I had shared with Wesley. I no longer wanted to sleep there, but I knew if I did not do it that first night, I never would again. As our whispers stopped, I heard Bev's breathing deepen, and I knew she was asleep again.

I waited for something to tire me, something to lift me out of that room, away from the agony. I waited. Nothing. I closed my eyes. Sleep eluded me. Only tears came. I finally slept, but it was brief. The night went on and on. I waited for the sun to rise. It didn't. More tears. I eventually slept again, but each time I woke up to darkness. Twice more I woke up Bev. Twice more she whispered to me, offering me words she hoped would comfort me. None of her words eased my pain. None of them pulled me from the torment.

It was only by the grace of God I was able to face another day, another night, another thought of life without him. No matter who tried to help, no matter what words of comfort were said, and no matter how grateful I felt for the many years I had spent with him, Wesley was gone from the earth in an instant, and I was infinitely sad.

Morning finally came. Just after 10:30 a.m., I felt a keen awareness Wesley had been gone for one full day. But it was only through
the earth's rotation around the sun I found myself on the other side
of the first twenty-four hours since he had died. It was not through
my strength or my will. It had nothing to do with me. I was no
longer a willing participant in the passing of time. I was its captive,
and only gravity kept me on the planet. I was lost without him.

CHAPTER EIGHTEEN

You're Here, Aren't You?

I hung Hunter's clothes for the funeral in his closet, still stunned by what had just happened minutes before. I needed time to process it, and the funeral was not until Thursday, so I shut the closet door and left Hunter's empty bedroom. How could Christine have possibly known?

It was Tuesday. It had only been two days since Wesley died. He was being flown back from Alabama today. The funeral would be on Thursday. I had taken care of every detail, down to choosing every song, every speaker, and the words I had written that Bev would read during the funeral. Family and friends were in full crisis mode and a constant presence in our house, which I welcomed. Neighbors brought food. The phone rang constantly. I never answered it, but someone did. Our reality was obvious. Ours was a house filled with everything that proved someone who lived there, and was loved, had died.

Hunter was struggling, but had his moments of escape from thinking about the rest of his life without his daddy. Many people focused on him, playing games he liked, taking him to the nearby park, watching his favorite movies. That is the beauty of being five. One minute he was crying and the next he was playing wiffle ball in the backyard, cheering when he got a base hit. I had to chuckle at the way he cheered for himself. Wesley and I were his biggest supporters and, at only five years old, he was already beginning to discover and believe in his own greatness.

I was forced right away to decide how I would handle the job of raising Hunter alone. Just the previous night, our second night home, I had to choose discipline and character over our overwhelming grief.

By then Vance and his girlfriend Tasha and Wesley's sister Amber had arrived. My parents were there as well. They had left Alabama just a few hours after Hunter and I did because they could not bear to stay in the apartment without us. They drove through the night Sunday and were at our front door Monday morning, walking in as Jimbo was leaving at 6:30 a.m. Jimbo wanted to get to the office before everyone else so he could be the one to tell Wesley's coworkers, before they read Kelli's email. Wesley had known most of his coworkers, many of them now good friends, since he had first starting working for Jimbo more than fourteen years earlier.

I had not slept much since returning from Alabama, and with the guests and constant activity at our house, Hunter was also overtired, far from the routine we had maintained even throughout his dad's illness.

It was late, after 11:00 p.m., and Hunter needed sleep, so I took him into Wesley's and my bedroom where he had been sleeping with me, just as he had slept with Wesley and me before we left for Alabama. The rest of the family was still awake in the living room just outside the bedroom door.

With food and drinks being dropped off for us at our house throughout each day, there were things in the house I did not ordinarily buy. We had always provided Hunter with a very healthy diet, and now was no exception. I had not eaten since waking up Easter morning, but I was making sure Hunter was eating well.

When I told him it was time for bed, he did not want to go, so he tried to procrastinate. He said he was thirsty and asked for a Sprite to drink. I offered him water, but he insisted on Sprite. Wesley and I rarely let him have soda unless we were in a restaurant—and then it was a special treat. He had drunk his share of soda during the past few days, and I certainly was not going to let him have any just before bed.

He was not happy about being told no and, being overtired, he started to cry. It did not take long for his tears about being denied the Sprite to become tears about missing his dad. The more he cried out for his dad, the more my heart broke. This was not about the Sprite at all; this was about everything going wrong in our little boy's life and, being only a small child, he did not know how to process his grief or communicate his sadness.

He got up from the bed, turned on the light and insisted, "I want Sprite!"

I walked toward the door, picked him up, and put him back on the bed.

"Hunter, I told you no already. It's time for bed," I insisted, turning off the light and lying back down, expecting him to do the same. Still crying, he got up from bed again and turned on the light.

We were in a tug of war. I so wanted to give in, but I knew I could not because this was not about Sprite. It was about Hunter not knowing how to deal with his feelings and trying to use those feelings to get what he wanted.

I got up from the bed. When I walked toward the door, he walked back to the bed but still would not get in it.

"Hunter, I am going to count to three, then I am going to turn off the light. Get into bed," I told him firmly.

He stood there, crossing his arms, refusing to do what I asked of him.

"One… Two…" I paused, not wanting to turn the light off.

Then, very clearly, I heard Wesley's voice in my head say, "Turn off that light."

"Three."

I turned it off.

Hunter started to cry even louder, so I picked him up and hugged him as I placed him down on the bed and lay down beside him.

"I want my daddy! I want my daddy!" he cried, tears streaming down his tired little face.

"I know, Hunter B. I want your daddy, too."

By then I was silently crying with him, and I knew everyone in the living room could hear him crying out for his dad.

"Buddy, I'll do anything to help you feel better. I'll do anything to help you through this," I promised him, making sure he knew I was there for him in his time of great need.

He cried out again, "I want my daddy!"

"What can I do to help you, Hunter? What can Mommy do to help you feel better?" I asked him, searching for a way to comfort him, praying for God to lift Hunter's despair and let him sleep peacefully.

"You can give me Sprite," he responded, still crying but crying less.

Hunter was a good kid, and we had taught him to respect us. Our words and clear expectations had always been enough. He did not require a firm hand, but when he did need discipline, Wesley could just look at him sternly and Hunter would shape right up.

Hunter was not manipulative, but he was smart. I realized instantly he could use the death of his father in one of two ways: to get what he wanted, because people felt sorry for him, or to strengthen his character and grow in the face of adversity. This was more than a minor struggle over a soda. I fully believed this moment would determine the pattern for our future—how the two of us would continue to deal with Wesley's death and how it would affect my ability to raise Hunter successfully on my own.

Lying next to Hunter now, all of these things ran through my head. I somehow knew if I was ever going to have the disciplinary effect on Hunter that Wesley had, it must start right now. It would have been so easy to just give Hunter the soda and make him happy. He would have stopped crying and gone to sleep, but that would have been a disservice to Hunter, and a huge cop-out as his mother. What would be next? Today it was Sprite, tomorrow and the day after, it would be something else. Before I knew it, Hunter would be a spoiled little kid who got what he wanted because his dad died when he was five and everyone felt sorry for him.

Instead of doing what was easiest, I did what I thought was best, though it was one of the hardest decisions I had ever made as a mother. I wanted to stop his tears and ease his pain, but I knew soda was not the answer. I had to keep my promise to Wesley and to myself and continue to demonstrate good parenting.

"I'm sorry, Buddy, but I can't give you Sprite," I told him as I wiped the tears from his face and settled my own quiet tears. "I love you, and I will do whatever is right to help you through every minute of every day, but I told you no soda and I meant it. You know the rules. They haven't changed."

To my surprise, he settled down and rolled over into my arms. His tears settled and his breathing deepened.

"Good night, B," I whispered to him.

"Good night, Mommy."

"I love you," I said.

"I love you, too," he responded, then drifted off to sleep.

As I held Hunter in my arms and lay in the silence of our new existence, I was overwhelmed again by the constant and excruciating pain of Wesley's absence. I honestly did not know how we would ever survive it.

After I was sure Hunter was asleep, I got up from our bed and went to the living room where everyone was still awake. I could see Bev and my mom had been crying. Everyone had heard Hunter crying out for his dad.

"I wanted to help you somehow," Bev offered, wanting to ease our pain.

"You can't. No one can. This is just part of it," I replied, knowing the road ahead would be paved with parenting decisions I would have to make on my own, with little help or influence from anyone else. This was a part of raising Hunter without Wesley.

A few minutes later my uncle Tommy, my dad's brother, and my aunt Jeri, his wife, called me. I listened as my uncle told me he believed in me and my ability to remain strong for Hunter.

"It's up to you now, Lisa. You know what Wesley would want you to do," Tommy told me.

"You can do this. You'll find your way," Jeri said, reiterating Tommy's words of encouragement to me.

I listened as two people who I had loved very much and had always been close to, told me of their belief in me, yet I questioned any of it could be true. How would I ever find the strength to raise Hunter without his father—the devoted man who had always been involved and present in every aspect of Hunter's young life. I wanted to believe them, but I was weary, so incredibly weary.

After I finished talking with Tommy and Jeri, I walked into

Hunter's empty bedroom and opened his closet door. There it was, hanging on a yellow, child-sized hanger, the suit our friend and lawyer Christine had brought to me earlier that day. She had called the day before, asking what she could do to help. I told her helping us prepare our wills before leaving for Alabama was more than enough, but she insisted she felt helpless and wanted to do more. She asked me what size pants and shoes Hunter wore and offered to shop for clothes for him to wear to the funeral. It had not even occurred to me to consider what Hunter would wear. I realized she was right; he would need something new and appropriate, and I was in no shape to shop. I accepted her offer to take care of it for me.

That morning she had brought a shopping bag with the clothes she bought him. I did not look inside the bag until later in the afternoon. When I took the clothes out, my heart raced and I gasped out loud, although no one was in the room to hear me. I held the small jacket tightly in my arms and began to sob, every breath a struggle, every tear uncontrollable. I was transported back to the dream I had had while dozing on the bench in the surgical waiting room, with Hunter's small hand holding mine as we walked together down a hallway. I stared at the black shoes, the grey pants, the white button-up shirt, the blue blazer, and the green and blue-striped tie Christine had bought. They were the very clothes Hunter was wearing in my vision, although I had told no one about it. There was no way Christine could have known I had seen Hunter in the very clothes she had selected and brought to me. Only God and I knew what I had seen, what He had shown me.

Soon, my tears settled. As I sat down on Hunter's bed, holding the clothes in my lap, I accepted in my vision I had been shown what I did not want to see, and I knew if I was open to being shown more, more would come.

I hung the clothes back up in Hunter's closet and joined our family in the living room. I did not tell them about Hunter's suit. I kept it for myself and quietly thanked God for trying to prepare me that day in Alabama for the pain of seeing Hunter dressed for his father's funeral.

Overwhelmed by the constant roller coaster of emotion, I was growing weary as the hours passed each day. Nighttime was even harder than daytime. The house would start to quiet, and I would struggle in the darkness without Wesley. Sometimes I tried not to think ahead. I tried to concentrate on just getting through a minute at a time. However, I glimpsed into our future without him and the very thought of it would force me into a reality that seemed impossible to withstand. I feared I would never rebuild our lives; experiencing true happiness ever again did not seem to be an option. Happiness was like a distant friend with whom I had lost touch as too much time had passed since our last encounter.

No one tried to make me eat, which I appreciated. When I met with the minister to plan the funeral, he asked me if I had eaten. When I told him no, he said it was okay. He said my body would let me know when it needed food. Somehow, his permission to not eat made it easier to go without food. His validation made me feel normal. He had counseled many widows over the years, and not eating was the least of his concerns for them.

Donna talked with me about a life insurance policy she had maintained for Wesley since he was in the Navy. It was a substantial amount of money that would more than cover the funeral expenses. The rest she would graciously give to me, just as she had told Wesley she would if anything happened to him. We also had two small life insurance policies through his employment contract, and we had a life insurance policy his Uncle JB, Jimbo's brother, had set up for us just ten months before Wesley got sick. JB had encouraged us to get life insurance, but we had said we wanted to wait until Wesley was thirty-five years old before we started setting up life insurance and more aggressively contributing to his 401k. Our priority was my being able to stay home with Hunter until he started school, so spending money on life insurance seemed like an unnecessary expense at the time. JB felt strongly we should get a policy in place, so he set it up for us as a gift and said we could start contributing to it the next year. That policy, combined with the others, and Wesley's social security death benefits, meant Hunter's life would not have to change. I would not have to find a job outside of our home, and he would not have to go to daycare. I could keep running my business and, no matter what happened with it, Hunter and I would still be okay financially. Jimbo also offered to pay for Hunter and me to remain on our health insurance plan through Wesley's COBRA, which allowed us to remain with the same insurance for three more years. Given my medical history and my yearly check-ups, going without health insurance was not an option, but, fortunately, it did not have to be.

These matters were discussed in the early days after Wesley died, but I honestly did not want to think about money—though I can promise you, I would have had to think about it if I had not known it was there. It was not enough for me to retire, but if I was smart with it, money would never get in the way of our grief. Sadly, I had seen the financial plight of others in the years since I had had cancer—people filing bankruptcy due to catastrophic illness, a widow with young children having to find work days after she buried her husband because they did not have life insurance, and she was not able to pay the mortgage or even feed her children. These were the realities many had to face. Combined with a time of tremendous emotional strife, money, or the lack of it, should never have to affect the outcome or the process. Even in these early days without

Wesley, I knew I was blessed to be provided for in this way.

The truth is, my only focus was on Hunter. I could not think beyond what he needed. He was my reason for getting out of bed each day. He needed to be fed and bathed and entertained. He needed to be loved and comforted and parented. He needed his mom and his dad, but Wesley was gone, and it was up to me to provide for Hunter in every way I could.

Just the few days Wesley had been gone seemed like weeks. He felt so far from me. I did not expect him to walk in the house at any minute. I knew he was never going to be home again, but a part of me also felt as if I did not know where he was. God had taken him, I knew that, but wasn't there just a part of him left behind for us? Wouldn't I still feel his breath on my neck or sense his presence in some way? Wasn't our love strong enough for him to transcend heaven and find his way back to us, even just for a little while longer? Couldn't he somehow just find a way to make this transition more bearable? Couldn't he show us a sign he was near and somehow, in time, everything would be okay? I wanted to believe that somehow, some way, he could still be there for me.

It was late on Wednesday night. Our visitors had left and we were down to our overnight guests: Vance, Tasha, my parents, Amber and Bev. I had been outside, just looking up at the stars and wondering what it was like for Wesley where he was. Every thought was of Wesley. I could think of little else.

I finally went inside the house. Hunter was playing Candyland with Vance, and everyone else was watching television. I walked into our bedroom and picked up the phone that was on our bed. I thought about calling Kelli but then decided not to.

I paused for a few minutes, not knowing where to go or what to do, then I walked toward the bathroom and slowly opened the door. That is when it happened. That is when, without a doubt in my mind, Wesley was everywhere.

I stood in the bathroom doorway and, although it is difficult to explain, I sensed he was with me. I did not hesitate. I spoke out loud to him immediately.

"You're here, aren't you?" I asked. "I've been waiting for you. Where have you been, and why haven't you been helping me?"

I stood silent, waiting for him to respond. His response is even more difficult to explain because I did not hear his voice speak to me. I felt his words inside me.

"I've been here all along; you're just in too much pain to know it," Wesley answered, his words deliberate, penetrating my soul.

"I don't understand. I did everything I could to save you. Why couldn't I save you like you saved me when I had cancer?" I asked him, begging for understanding. "How come I survived and you didn't?"

"Because you had to live to have Hunter," he said, his words patient and steady.

"But Hunter needs you, too. You're his father," I argued, knowing Hunter wanted us both.

"Hunter loves us both, but he needs you more," Wesley told me.

"But why the miracle in Alabama? Why the lungs in three days if you were just going to die anyway?" I asked, somehow completely aware of the questions I needed to ask to understand our tragic loss.

"To get it over with, so I didn't die in our living room in front of Hunter," he told me, which immediately reminded me of Dr. Zorn telling me he would not have lasted much longer without the surgery and without the transplant he could have died at home any day.

"But you kept coming back. You died and came back. All of that just for you to die after six weeks fighting for your life?"

"Those six weeks weren't about saving my life. Those six weeks were about preparing you for me to die." His answer resonated in me and I was silent, in awe of his wisdom and his ability to share it with me.

Instantly, the image of Hunter in his suit at Wesley's funeral flashed in my mind.

After just a few seconds, I spoke again. Asking more and more questions. Trying to stay engaged with him, so he would stay with me and never leave. The questions were losing their meaning and, although he was answering them, I knew he would be leaving soon.

"But… But…" I could not find the words to say more.

Wesley stopped me.

"Lisa, it's just earth."

I stopped talking, stunned by what he had said. I realized the conversation I was having was more likely with God, and He was genius for using Wesley and my image of him to communicate with me because Wesley was who I wanted to hear from and would listen to as he explained the message I was meant to hear. I also realized I could have even possibly been feeding myself what I wanted to hear, what I wanted Wesley to say to me. But when he said the words, "It's just earth," I knew it was not coming from me. I had never heard, nor had I ever spoken such words before.

"It's just earth," Wesley repeated. "For as long as you're alive, you're never going to completely understand it, so don't even try," he explained to me, now giving me the answers I needed in order to begin to believe it was possible to go on without him. "Don't let how I died change how you live."

I stood silent. I needed to really hear what he was saying to me. I needed to understand. I needed to feel the power of what was happening.

I did not speak for a few minutes. I knew there was nothing left to say, but I did not want him to leave me, and I knew I could not leave him.

"I cannot leave this room. I'm not capable of leaving you here. Something is going to have to happen. Hunter is going to have to call my name. The phone is going to have to ring. Something," I insisted, unable to walk away from our encounter.

I paused, waiting for something to happen. It was almost an awkward silence, him making sure I understood, me not wanting to say a word for fear he would leave. I had not even noticed I was still holding the telephone in my hand.

It rang, and I answered it.

"Lisa, I'm sorry it's so late. I've been wanting to call you but was afraid to call because it's later there. I was just sitting with the phone in my hand for the last five minutes and finally made myself dial." It was my cousin Krystal, calling from California.

"It's okay. Don't worry," I quietly responded as I backed out of our bathroom, smiled into the empty room, silently thanking Wesley for coming to me and for making Krystal call. I kept my word and left the room when the phone rang and slowly closed the door.

I do not remember what else Krystal said, except she loved me. I just remember knowing I was blessed. I was grateful for being open enough to receive Wesley and be provided with the opportunity to have answers to questions I might have carried with me the rest of my life without ever feeling peace. I might have questioned God for years to come about the outcome of Alabama and why things happened the way they did. I could have always been stuck in a place between what God needed me to know about Wesley dying and leaning on my own understanding.

I knew there was a long, arduous road ahead. A visit from

Wesley was not going to ease my pain. He was still gone, and that would always leave an emptiness impossible to fill. But what I did know after that conversation in our bathroom, what I was absolutely certain of, was if I was open to what I could learn and how I could heal, it was possible for me to exist without Wesley. I did not have to know all of the answers or even God's plan for my life now that Wesley was gone.

"It's just earth" to me meant it was supposed to hurt—I was supposed to feel helpless and terrified. It meant I was human, and even if it took until the day I died to completely understand what Wesley now knew and God knew all along, then that was part of the human experience.

At that point, I was nowhere close to anticipating happiness or expecting the grueling, sinking feeling I had had since I said goodbye to Wesley in that hospital room in Alabama to lift. But where I was, I believed, was where God wanted me to be—and so was Wesley. If I could learn to trust in what God used Wesley to tell me, then I could begin again, eventually. Just the idea of this reacquainted me with something I never expected to retrieve, especially so soon—hope. Hope had shown itself to me again, letting me know it still existed, inviting me back to trust in it again when I was ready.

CHAPTER NINETEEN

Training Wheels

The day after the funeral, I could not bear to get out of bed. Hunter was still occupied with our family and friends who were gathered in our home, so he was entertained and cared for during my absence. Focusing on the funeral arrangements had obviously been a distraction to me because the day after the funeral, I hit a brick wall. Even though I had felt immense and overwhelming sadness and grief in the minutes, hours and days since Wesley had died, there was even more pain waiting on the other side of the day we celebrated Wesley's life and put him to rest.

I felt paralyzed in my grief, unable to move from our bed, unable to eat, unable to shower. I missed Wesley with every part of my body, mind, and spirit. My eyes, my ears, my very skin longed for him. For one day, I stayed in bed and wept for my husband, knowing I would never see, hear, or feel him again in my lifetime. I was overcome.

Hunter came in and out of the bedroom throughout the day. He would jump up on the bed to snuggle with me then race out of the room to play with Vance and my dad or to read a story with my mom. While I was sleeping, Amber unpacked everything my parents and I brought home from Alabama. I was relieved I did not have to do it. I could not face the boxes filled with memories of our failed attempt at saving Wesley's life.

When the day was over, I mustered the strength to walk into our bathroom, turn on the water of the shower, and step inside. I washed my hair and my body. Then I combed conditioner through my hair and rinsed off. As the steam filled our bathroom, I thought about Wesley's last shower the day we left for Alabama. I turned off the water, wrapped a towel around my head, and slipped on clean pajamas.

"Mommy, you're back!" Hunter cheered as he ran to me for a hug when I entered the kitchen.

"Yeah, Buddy, I'm back. Mommy just needed a day to rest," I assured our son as I promised myself I would never take to bed for an entire day again.

Not long after the funeral, people started going home. One by one, family and friends had to resume their lives. Some left by airplane, others by car. I dreaded the goodbyes, but even more, I dreaded the loneliness the goodbyes represented.

The funeral home had provided me with thank you cards, but I could not bring myself to fill them out even though I had so many people to thank. I decided I would not send thank you notes, knowing I would never expect such a gesture in return and hoped people would understand.

I was thankful my parents stayed with Hunter and me. My dad would soon have to return to work, but for now he would remain with us.

I decided to go to Northern California to spend a week with family and friends. We would leave the week following the funeral. A second memorial service had been planned there, where Wesley and I had grown up and where much of our family still lived, but I canceled it. I could not bear the thought of Hunter suffering through another service. Instead, Tommy and Jeri planned a gathering at their house, inviting our family and friends to join us and pay their respects.

I sent Hunter to preschool for the week we would be in town before leaving. I knew he would be better off, playing with his friends and learning from his teacher in a familiar environment than being at home.

Everything felt empty without Wesley. When I needed to talk, I often called Roger, knowing his first wife had died seventeen years ago. He told me it gets better with time but I would always miss Wesley. I cried to him many times in the early hours of the morning before Hunter woke up, and he did his best to comfort me.

Even though Wesley had been sick for a year and had not been able to do many basic tasks or some of his regular chores, like mowing the lawn, I still noticed the absence of a hundred little things he used to do despite his physical limitations.

I quickly grew frustrated trying to reset the timer on the sprinkler system—something he had always done. I tried to mow the lawn, but the lawnmower would not start. We had hired a neighbor to take care of the yard most of the previous year when Wesley was sick, so the lawnmower had not been started in a long time. I tried over and over again to pull the cord and get it to go. After many tries, I feared I had flooded the gas tank.

I looked up at the sky and said to Wesley, "If the lawnmower doesn't start this time, then I give up!"

I pulled the cord one more time, and it started. I looked up at the sky at Wesley again, then began pushing the lawnmower across the tall, thick grass. I held on tightly with both hands, crying as I thought of the many good times we had shared together as a family in our yard. Even the simplest chore, like mowing the lawn, brought sadness.

I finished mowing the lawn and—after searching for the instructions—reset the timer on the sprinklers. Then I tried to adjust one sprinkler head in the front yard that had always given us trouble. Wesley used to do something to make it go in the right direction so it would spray the yard instead of the house, but I had never paid attention to how he fixed it. I tried to adjust it myself, but it was not working. In frustration, I kicked it a few times and started to cry again. To my surprise, it started working.

I missed Wesley in the little things, but I also felt him there.

Hunter still struggled most at night before bed, but now that he was getting more sleep and back in a routine, he did better. One day, as I was helping Hunter tie his shoes, he asked me if his dad had made it to heaven yet.

"I think so, Buddy. I'm sure God was with your dad when he died and took him straight to heaven," I answered him, having truly no idea if that was how God did it or not.

"Oh," he said, almost seeming disappointed.

"What's the matter, Buddy?" I asked him, wondering about his sad face.

"I was just kinda hoping God took half of Daddy with him and left half of him here with us."

"What do you mean?" I pressed, wondering what was going through his five-year-old mind.

"I saw Daddy," he told me, very matter of fact.

I was stunned, almost unable to speak.

"When? When did you see Daddy?" I asked, trying not to seem shaken, even though I was.

"I've seen him a few times. He watches me," Hunter explained.

"Does he talk to you?" I asked.

"No, he just smiles at me. Sometimes he is sitting in the corner reading a book," he said.

"What is he wearing when he visits you?" I asked him, wondering if he would have a detailed answer.

"His jeans with a hole on the knee and his black Superman T-shirt," he answered, seeming sure of what he had seen. "I know why he's here."

"Why is he here?" I asked, fascinated by his certainty.

"Because he's split in half. God took his soul, but his invisible spirit stayed here with us."

I hugged Hunter and sunk into our embrace.

"Buddy, if ever a daddy loved his son enough to be both in heaven and on earth, it would be your daddy," I assured him, validating what he believed were visits from his father.

"I know, Mommy," he said, squeezing my neck then running for the front door. "Let's go to the park now, Mommy!"

The two of us walked the short mile to the park near our house. We planned to meet friends there for the day. On our way, I had an idea I wanted to share with Hunter.

"Buddy, when you feel your daddy, that's real," I began, not sure yet of the right words to say.

"Yep!" he excitedly responded, as if he already knew it.

"Your daddy will always be alive in you and me because he loved me so much he married me and wanted to have a baby with me. And he loved you so much because you are his son and he was a lucky, lucky man to have you as his son," I told Hunter. "And just because someone dies, it doesn't mean everything they brought to our lives dies with them. You are still who you are because he was here, even if just for five years of your life."

"He stays here for me?" Hunter asked, beginning to understand what I was carefully trying to explain to him.

"He lives on because of you. A part of him stays here inside of everyone who loved him," I told Hunter, pointing to his heart and mine.

"You mean my daddy's invisible spirit is alive inside of me?" he asked with excitement.

"That's exactly what I mean. Just like we are walking to the park together now—he's here because he lives on inside of both of us. You can talk to your daddy and about your daddy anytime you want," I said. I wanted Hunter to know he could begin to experience his dad in a different way.

Hunter smiled big and nodded his head, confirming to me his understanding.

Our beautiful son could learn at a very young age the power of his own ability to believe in something bigger than himself. There was nothing to prove his dad could not hear him. There was nothing to prove his dad was not watching over him, even if from a corner of the room while reading a book. If these things gave Hunter comfort, then I would believe in them, too.

On that walk to the park, I began to think about how our interaction with someone who is living and breathing in our lives is what we know, what we expect, but it is not necessarily all there is. It was possible, with enough love and faith, we could have a different exchange with someone we loved who was no longer on the planet. I did not need to see Wesley to know he was there and neither did Hunter. Whatever Hunter needed to ease his weary heart, I would see him through. Maybe the greatest gift Hunter was being given in his grief was his five-year-old's ability to see what he needed to see or to see what adults could not. His pure heart had no reason not to believe his dad was there, whether he was or not. Hunter was not scarred by years of doubt and distrust, the way adults can be. I decided to follow Hunter's lead about his belief of his dad being split between heaven and earth and never give him cause to doubt it.

✳

When it came time to go to Northern California, I did not want to go because I dreaded returning home a week later only to once again face this house without Wesley in it. But I knew people were waiting for us. I owed it to them to show up and allow them the closure they were seeking and deserved. My parents went with us, so we braved it together.

Tracy, my dear friend since eighth grade, flew up from Los Angeles to spend a few days with Hunter and me. While the two of us waited in line for the rental car we would share, I tried not to cry. Even standing in line at the airport made me miss Wesley, thinking of all the times we had done it together.

My cousin Corine and her daughter Kayla also came to see us from the Bay Area. Being with Corine made such a difference for me because we had always been close, more like sisters, as our mothers were, than cousins.

I arrived at Tommy and Jeri's for the gathering they had graciously planned. Many people came to offer their support and condolences. My parents and Bev were there, and they helped give me strength to face everyone else. I tried to enjoy the company of friends and family, but many times I had to walk away and collect myself as I tried to be strong.

My parents, Hunter, and I stayed with Wesley's Aunt Lavaun and Uncle Mike while we were there. Lavaun and Mike went about their lives, making trips to Home Depot for a fence repair, making dinner for us on the grill on their newly built backyard deck. I envied their existence and the easy way each day seemed to run into the next for them.

I still was not sleeping well. I would wake up many times during the night, and morning would come with the familiar sadness of Wesley being gone. I had been told that sometimes, in the seconds just before waking up, people are not completely aware and forget about their loss, only to have the memory flood in when they are fully awake. This had not yet happened to me. I was aware of Wesley's death every minute of every day and night, whether asleep or awake. What helped me cope was waking up to Hunter's smiling face and everyday needs.

I spent a great deal of time reading and sitting in a chair alone under a large tree in front of Mike and Lavaun's house. In a bookstore I had discovered John Edwards, a medium who claimed to have contact with dead people. Before his surgery, Wesley once told me if anything happened to him, I would be strong enough to find him. I did not know what he meant, but I thought I would start by reading one of John Edwards' books and see what he had to say.

I felt conflicted reading the book. I had gone to the bookstore looking in the Christian section for a book that could give me comfort or offer explanation, but I got sidetracked and left with one about how to pay attention to the signs of communication from a loved one who had gone to "the other side."

John Edwards' explanations of death and the other side gave me the comfort I was seeking, but in the back of my mind and deep in my heart, I felt as if I were betraying God by seeking answers outside of Him. I felt I was not appreciative enough of Wesley's visit to me three days after he died. Whatever I felt, I gave myself time to feel it. I had not blamed God for Wesley's death, and I felt I deserved some time to figure it out in my own way without being judged by God.

I wanted to believe the signs all around me meant something and were not just in my head. John Edwards' explanation of certain numbers having meaning took me back to the fifth floor transplant ICU at UAB. I had even taken a picture of the number five on the wall of the unit near the elevator.

I had been wearing Wesley's watch since returning to Houston from Alabama. Every day at 5:55 the alarm would sound, for no apparent reason. The watch had not been set for that time when Wesley was wearing it. The first time the alarm sounded, it was right after the funeral. I was driving to the ranch to gather with more friends and family at Jimbo's house. As soon as the tires hit Jimbo's property and the gravel driveway leading to his house, the alarm sounded. I thought, "It's Wesley, letting me know he's coming to the ranch with me."

Despite my struggle between what I knew of God and what John Edwards' had to offer me in my grief, while in California I arranged to see the pastor of the church I attended when I was young. Paster Don had always been a nonjudgmental, compassionate man who had known suffering in his own life. I knew he was capable of accepting me where I was with my inner struggle.

I had not left Hunter since Wesley died, so I wanted to explain to him I would not be gone long and would return before he fell asleep.

I was pushing him on the swing in Lavaun and Mike's backyard, telling him I was leaving soon.

"Will you be spending the night?" Hunter asked, remembering the nights I was away when his dad was in the hospital.

"No, I will be back before you go to sleep, but it will be dark outside by the time I get home," I explained, assuring him I would be back to tuck him in.

"Are you sure you aren't going to spend the night, Mommy?" he questioned me again.

"I'm sure, Buddy. The only reason I had to be away overnight before was because I needed to take care of Daddy when he was in the hospital," I told Hunter.

"Well, Mommy, then you didn't do a very good job," Hunter said. That stung, but I knew he did not mean to hurt my feelings.

I kept pushing him on the swing.

"What do you mean?" I asked.

"Well, Daddy died, and you were the one taking care of him," he answered.

I wanted to cry, but I didn't.

"Hunter, Buddy. It was not my job to save Daddy. It was my job to make sure he was not alone and knew we loved him," I explained, hoping he would understand, even though I was just beginning to understand it myself.

"Oh. Then you did a very good job, Mommy," Hunter said with a smile.

Thankfully and simply, he did understand.

As I pushed him on the swing a few more times before leaving, I held back the tears. I thought about the many things running through his own grieving, confused mind and how he would need to share these thoughts with me without being afraid he would hurt my feelings or make me cry. This very simple exchange between us might have offered him understanding and healing necessary for his own progress. I knew how much Hunter loved me and would never want to hurt me. I wanted him to be comfortable saying whatever he needed to say.

In that instant, I made a rule about my own grief. I promised myself I would never cry when Hunter talked about his dad. It did not mean I would never cry in front of him, or he would never see my own sadness, but I vowed never to cry when Hunter talked specifically about Wesley to me. I needed Hunter to be able to share what he was feeling and thinking. I knew if I cried when he did so, he would think he was hurting me and would stop talking about his dad. I never wanted that to happen.

I walked him inside the house to my mom and dad, kissed him goodbye and left for the evening.

Pastor Don did not judge me for the books I was reading or the questions I was asking. He gave me room to grieve however I needed to grieve. The few hours I spent with him left me feeling at peace with my path and, if need be, God's forgiveness.

Even though I dreaded returning to Houston, I was ready to leave California when it came time to go. I said a sad goodbye to my dad and he went back to work, while my mom, Hunter, and I flew to Texas. Mom would stay with us for as long as we needed her. I do not even remember there being a discussion about it; it was just a given. My parents' only concern was Hunter's and my well-being.

After we flew home, the reality of living in a suburb of Houston without Wesley began to set in, knowing when my mom eventually left, I would be living alone with Hunter. We lived in a safe neighborhood, but I still feared living in a large city known for its high crime in various areas. I called to have an alarm installed at our house but then decided to wait. Since I worked from home, I could live anywhere and still run my business with Christi's help, so I gave some thought to moving closer to Jimbo, Donna, and Roger. They lived just eighty miles away, where much of Wesley's family still lived. I thought about building a house there and starting anew. Everyone says not to make huge, life decisions for at least a year after someone dies, but I had always operated on my own timeline.

I called a home builder and found out what it would cost to build a new house in the neighborhood I wanted to live in. I could afford it. I was not ready to make a decision, but I knew

I did not want to raise Hunter alone in Houston. I also knew I wanted Hunter to remain close to everything that was important to Wesley—his family, the outdoors, the ranch, Texas. I wanted to keep Hunter as close to Wesley as possible, and I believed staying in Texas was the only way to do it.

Nevertheless, the literal absence of Wesley began to set in. When Wesley died, the overwhelming sadness was surrounded by the reality I would never be with him again in my lifetime, but in the first few days after he died, I had not had time to actually miss him yet. We had never been apart for very long. Now I missed him, not just the idea of him.

Weekends were a struggle. Wesley had always made sure we had plans. He would read the local newspaper to find a nearby festival to attend or plan a weekend at the ranch. I missed him every day, but on weekends I missed him and the family we were together even more. While my friends and their families were busy going on with life, I longed for the days when I, too, lived a life free of this mounting grief—when my only concern was making it to the movies in time for the matinee showing.

I tried to go out to dinner with friends, but I dreaded coming home to a house without Wesley. I started to feel isolated, as if no one understood how I felt. I tried to think of anyone, famous or not, who had loved their husband as long as I had loved Wesley and lost him. Ekatarina Gordeeva, the Russian skater whose husband Sergei had died suddenly of a heart attack at age twenty-eight, came to mind. His death was sudden, tragic, and completely unexpected. He left behind their young daughter, and Ekatarina had to raise her child alone without Sergei, her great love and constant companion. She, like me, did not remember her life before meeting him as a child and did not want to learn to live without him.

A few years before, Wesley and I had watched an interview with her on television. She was talking about her new book, *My Sergei: A Love Story*, and old clips of them skating together were shown. It was sad to watch. I remember Wesley getting up and leaving the room, saying he did not want to see it. I did not understand then, but I did now. I had had cancer years before, and although I had fully recovered, he did not want to be reminded of what he had almost lost. He knew he could have been just like Ekatarina, losing the only love he had ever known.

I bought her book after returning from California, trying to cope, wanting to feel understood. By the third page, as I read her words, I felt understood:

I know that, for me, to find the kind of happiness I had with Sergei isn't possible. It's not unbelievably hard. It's impossible, like trying to find the comet that was in the night sky last spring, which passes earth once in seventeen thousand years. No matter what lies ahead, the best years of my life will have been with my Seriozha (Sergei), and those years are now laid to rest.

I turned every page, reading, understanding, knowing I was not alone. Knowing there were other people who had lost just as much as I had.

This helped me decide to attend a support group for widows and widowers. Kelli went with me the first time. I was the youngest in attendance, though there were others who were close to my age.

While I felt comforted when attending the group meetings, I also felt frightened because there were people there who had lost their spouses as many as seven years before. I did not want to still need a support group seven years later. I wanted a path to healing and a road to understanding. I continued with the group and eventually I fully understood the benefit of participating and sharing my feelings with others. I learned to appreciate feeling understood and lending my own strength and support in return.

My mom and I tried to entertain ourselves, and I did a little work when I felt I could, though Christi was still handling the day-to-day needs of the business. I went into a local bookstore and purchased current issues of *InStyle* and *Parents* magazines. My company was featured in both. I had worked on the *InStyle* placement for eighteen months. The *Friends* show series was ending, and the editor I had worked with managed to get it into the magazine just before the series finale that May.

I watched the *Friends* show finale at home, but it, too, made me miss Wesley. The excitement of having our products on the set of the show began before his illness. Now without him to share it, the success the show had brought the company in an unexpectedly short amount of time meant nothing to me.

I had to go for my annual check-up at the cancer hospital just weeks after Wesley died. I dreaded it more than ever before. Wesley had always gone with me to my check-ups and helped reduce my anxiety level just by being there. After Hunter was born, we did not want him to come to the cancer hospital with us, so Wesley would usually stay home with him, and I would go alone. Even that was helpful because I would call Wesley from the phone outside the doctor's office to tell him I was still cancer free. Going to my appointment without Wesley there, and without him to call afterward, was dreadful.

Over the years, I had developed an allergy to the iodine contrast used during the CT Scan. I would experience joint pain in my elbows, knees, and ankles when the iodine was injected into my IV, and each year the pain got worse. This year the nurse gave me Benadryl before my scan to help prevent any further reaction. I did not know it then, but I was at risk of developing anaphylactic shock, or anaphylaxis, a life-threatening type of allergic reaction with symptoms developing rapidly—often within seconds—

including difficulty swallowing, wheezing, shortness of breath, fainting, and dizziness, to name just a few.

Before I could leave after my CT Scan, I had to wait a few minutes after the nurse removed the IV line to make sure the site did not bleed. When the nurse approached me, there was panic on her face.

"Are you okay?" she quickly asked.

"I'm fine. Why?" I asked, confused by her look of concern.

"Because you have a rash from your feet to your neck!"

I looked down and saw the rash she had noticed before I did. It was obvious my allergy was progressing. She told me she would inform my doctor of my allergic reaction before I saw him two days later for my follow-up visit to discuss the results of the tests they had run.

When I saw the doctor, I told him about Wesley. He offered his sympathy, then told me I would need to be pretreated with steroids and more Benadryl before my CT Scan next year. I would not be able to have a CT Scan outside of a hospital in the future.

I had looked up information and read about the allergy after I developed the rash. I knew now what the risks were, and I was not willing to take them.

"I'm sorry. I've been one of the most compliant patients you've ever had. I'm here just weeks after Wesley died because I know I have a responsibility to our son to make sure I take good care of myself. But I'm all he's got and I'm not willing to risk my life with an allergic reaction to see if I'm at risk of cancer after being well for eight years now. There has to be a better way," I appealed to my doctor, assuring him I was willing to remain compliant, but I just was not willing to do it with a test requiring iodine.

He agreed to my wishes. He scheduled me for the following year's blood work and a chest X-ray, and told me we could talk about the possibility of an MRI, if necessary, the next year.

I walked out of his office and glanced at the phone on the wall I had used to call Wesley many times before when he could not be with me at the appointment. I got on the elevator that led to the parking garage and started to cry. I did not stop until just before I got home, forty minutes minutes later.

By the simple force of time, life began to move slowly forward. I had always told Wesley he would be in charge of teaching Hunter how to tie his shoes, tell time, and ride a bike when the time came, because all of these were incredibly difficult for me as a child. But Wesley had not lived long enough to help Hunter through even one of those milestones.

One day, soon after returning from California, Hunter asked me to take the training wheels off his bike. He had been pushing the bike along with his feet for weeks, so I knew he was ready; his request led me to believe he felt ready, too.

I took the training wheels off and tried pushing him, holding onto the back of his bike. He was not enjoying it at all, but he also was not giving it a chance. I tried again and again to help him steady himself and move a few feet at a time without stopping, trying to build up his confidence, but he soon quit trying and wanted his training wheels back on.

My mom was on the phone, watching Hunter and reporting his progress to my dad. When Hunter asked me to put his training wheels back on, I told him to give it more time. He started to cry and begged me to put them back on. I decided this was not a battle I wanted to fight, and I was ready to put the training wheels back on. My dad was furious with me for even considering it.

When my mom handed me the phone, he told me straight up I was making a huge mistake.

"If you put those training wheels back on, you are teaching him it's okay to quit!" my dad shouted, scolding me, as he still did on occasion.

I was aware of the message I was sending Hunter, but I also did not feel like either of us was giving up. I thought it was all right for Hunter to change his mind. The last thing I wanted was for his bike, which he loved so much, to become something he dreaded and then quit riding altogether.

My dad was so adamant about not putting the training wheels back on that I eventually had to respond firmly to him. Hunter went inside the house, so I said what was on my mind when I knew Hunter could not hear me.

"Dad, enough! I'm in this moment with him. I'm doing the best I can and so is Hunter. It was never supposed to be my job to teach Hunter how to ride a bike, but here I am! Here I AM!" I shouted.

He tried to respond, but I handed the phone back to my mom and grabbed a wrench to put the training wheels back on.

A few days later, when Hunter was riding his bike again, I told him he was capable of riding it on his own without the training wheels. I pointed out to him if the training wheels were not on his bike, he could easily push himself down the street and coast with his feet balancing him, able to touch the ground beneath him on either side.

He soon agreed and asked me to take the training wheels off again.

"If we take them off this time, they are staying off. Do you understand?" I asked him, making sure we did not have a repeat of a few days before.

"OK. I understand," he quickly agreed.

Within a few minutes, he was gleefully coasting down the street. Soon after, he had his feet on the pedals, racing back and forth along our cul-de-sac. He was officially riding his bike. My mom and I cheered for him and took pictures. Our neighbor from the house across the street came outside to watch and congratulate him. I cried tears of joy for Hunter, recalling the independence that riding a bike gave to me. I also cried tears of sorrow because Wesley did not live long enough to see Hunter ride the bike we had surprised him with on Christmas morning two years before. As hard as it was, I forced the sadness from my thoughts and concentrated only on the big smile on Hunter's face as he held his two thumbs up when posing for a picture after his first solo bike ride.

We called my dad to tell him the good news.

"As much as you want to make things okay here, you're going to have to let me do what I think is best for Hunter," I told my dad, knowing he meant well, but also knowing he and my mom both had a way of usurping my role of parenting Hunter.

Wesley was always better at standing up to them than I was. Now I would have to learn how to stand up to them on my own. This would begin the ongoing, sometimes silent, sometimes verbal, tug-of-war between my parents and me, particularly between my dad and me, when it came to Hunter. As much as my dad wanted me to be tough like a father, I was a mother.

I admit I wanted it both ways—I wanted their help when I needed it, and I wanted them to leave me alone when I did not. I know it was not always fair and they were trying to help, but there were many times when I knew they never would have interfered if Wesley were still alive, and sometimes I resented it. With Wesley gone, being Hunter's parent was the only identity I had left that was still familiar, and I was vigorous in protecting it—even though my parents were the last two people I would ever need protection from. Their love for Hunter and me was limitless, but I had to find my own way somehow.

Every family has its dysfunctions. Ours is no different, but what

I know for sure is my mom and dad always had the best intentions, and being there was sometimes all they knew to do. Without them, I do not know how I would have managed the year Wesley was sick or the months after he died. Even when my dad could not be there with my mom, they were both more than willing to be apart so my mom could be with Hunter, Wesley and me. My parents spent only three months together during Wesley's year-long illness and the months following his death. I will always be grateful for the wonderful ways my mom willingly tried to ease the burden of our broken hearts everyday she was with us.

On this day, watching Hunter ride his bike, we all celebrated and cheered for him as he cheered for himself, a newly independent boy on his bike, heading to anywhere his little wheels could take him, as long as I was close by.

Later that day, when the excitement was beginning to wane, Hunter said to me, "My daddy's invisible spirit was holding onto the back of my bike today, Mommy."

I gave Hunter a big hug then held his hands in mine. To my surprise, his fingertips were no longer red and tender from biting his fingernails and his fingernails had grown. It was evident in an obvious way Hunter was beginning to feel normal again, and I could only hope his healing hands were a positive sign his heart would also heal one day.

CHAPTER TWENTY

Hero

After Wesley's lungs were removed for the transplant, pathologists in both Houston and Alabama began studying them, trying to find a diagnosis.

I asked the pathologists in each location to perform separate studies without exchanging information about their findings. I requested they send their reports directly to me so I could be sure the doctors in each hospital came up with their own diagnosis and were not swayed by what the others had determined.

Six weeks after Wesley died, Dr. Patel called me at home.

"You're not going to believe this," she told me, trying to prepare me for what came next. "He had Pulmonary Capillary Hemangiomatosis."

The words meant nothing to me. I did not know what it was, and I almost did not care.

"Wesley would only be about the fortieth person ever diagnosed with it. His biopsy in April did not show the disease, so his biopsy is also probably one of the earliest biopsies available to show the disease in its earliest stages," she continued.

"Is there a cure for it?" I asked, needing to know if the second biopsy Wesley had wanted would have made a difference.

"No, there isn't. But we can learn a lot from him. He can continue to make a difference," she assured me.

"Is there anything you would have done differently if you had known what he had?" I pressed further, needing answers to the questions that still sometimes filled my head.

"No. PCH leads to transplant and often isn't discovered until after transplant—or after death, if a transplant isn't received in time," she explained. "Lisa, the disease was there before the garage. He did lose time from the damage to his lungs in the garage, but we can't know how long it would have been before he started to show symptoms—and either way, there would have been nothing more we could do."

I finished talking with Dr. Patel and walked into my bedroom. I opened the top drawer of my dresser and pulled out a sealed envelope from UAB. It contained their pathology report and the conclusion to their study of Wesley's lungs.

I had not opened it because I wanted to wait until hearing from Dr. Patel so I could compare the two findings.

I opened the envelope and began to read the confusing language used by the doctors who wrote the report. Ultimately, I found my way to the bottom of the page where the diagnosis was clearly stated: Pulmonary Capillary Hemangiomatosis.

It was official. The two teams of pathologists agreed.

The cloudiness on Wesley's X-rays were from the capillary-sized blood vessels proliferating diffusely throughout his lungs and airways. It is frequently misdiagnosed and is extremely rare.

I wrote an email to everyone who had been part of the roller coaster of emotions throughout Wesley's illness. Within an hour of sending it, I received a phone call from a friend on the email list.

Throughout Wesley's hospital stay at UAB, I had been in touch with Kim—the woman whose son's transplant I had read about in the *New York Times*—whom I had befriended. She had called to remind me of our conversation months before, when she told me to have Wesley's doctor look into PCH as a possible diagnosis for Wesley because his symptoms and the onset of disease sounded so much like her son's.

I had forgotten about our conversation. I was amazed to learn from her that her son was the thirty-eighth person ever diagnosed with PCH, as far as her son's doctors knew. A woman back East was the thirty-ninth.

I was overwhelmed by all I had learned in just an hour. I took a long walk to try to clear my head. I wandered our neighborhood. I wondered if Wesley knew as soon as he died what had been wrong with him all along. I wondered if where he went with God brought every answer to every question he ever had on earth, the most important one being: What had killed him?

In my heart I knew there was nothing more we could have done to save him. The garage made him sick, but the disease made him sicker.

I finished my walk and approached our front door, looked up to the sky, and quietly said to Wesley, "So now we know."

In time, I would explain to Hunter that what his dad endured would help other people in the future. I could not be sure he understood what I told him, but one day he showed me he did.

A few years after Wesley died, Hunter told me he was studying Martin Luther King, Jr. in school. He told me he was learning about the impact King had on civil rights in our country; even though he died, he died for a good cause and helped people.

He finished by telling me, "My dad is just like Martin Luther King, Mommy."

"He is?" I asked curiously. "How is your dad like Martin Luther King?"

"Because he was the fortieth person ever diagnosed with his disease, and doctors got to learn from him, the way our country got to learn from Martin Luther King. And we are still learning about Martin Luther King in school years later, so I think we'll learn from Dad for a long time, too."

Once again, Hunter surprised me with his ability to understand what many grown-ups could not even comprehend. His thoughts were pure and honest. With everything he knew about the world, his dad died a hero.

And he was right.

CHAPTER TWENTY-ONE

Heading West

My new existence with Wesley, believing he was near, became part of how I coped in my daily life without him. Hunter continued to talk about his dad and his invisible spirit, and I was still practicing the techniques I had learned from reading John Edwards' books.

My struggle had not ended. John Edwards' teachings held me in conflict; I felt I should be seeking God and not the dead, but I needed Wesley. The greatest conflict was not that I did not believe what Edwards was teaching. The struggle was with myself because I did believe him. I wanted God to be everything to me—my rock, my fortress, my shelter in this storm. But more than that, I wanted Wesley back, in any form I could find him.

Over the weeks I learned to pay attention to the signs Wesley was near. Sometimes Edwards' methods worked, and I would spot something like the orange T-shirt with dark blue stripes on the sleeves Wesley used to wear that had been one of my favorites. When I felt weak and needed a sign Wesley was near, I would ask for it—and literally within minutes, a random man would walk in the door of the video store or the supermarket where I was shopping, wearing that very same T-shirt. The number five was also still turning up at interesting times.

We spent Mother's Day with Donna and Roger, which was not easy. Being at their house without Wesley was a painful reminder of the years ahead without him as I remained a part of this wonderful family.

As a gift, my sister-in-law Tara made me a quilt with pictures of Wesley, Hunter, and me stitched throughout it. It was both beautiful and heartbreaking. She included pictures of us I had never seen. Photographs I had not seen before were harder to look at than the familiar ones I was used to seeing in picture frames and albums throughout our house.

After Tara gave me the quilt, Donna placed a carousel photo frame in front of me with numerous pictures of Wesley and the rest of our family that she had sorted through in the weeks after he died. As I looked at each picture, many of which I had also not seen before, I struggled not to cry.

I left the table and went into the bathroom, shut the door, and absolutely fell apart. It was an excruciating moment. Mother's Day, the beautiful quilt, the many pictures reminding me of nearly forgotten times I had lived with Wesley—all of these were reminders of the life I had once lived but would never share with him again.

As I cried in the bathroom, the intensity of my pain grew. I wanted it to stop, but instead it mounted.

"Please help me, Wesley. Please help me," I whispered to him, begging him to lift me out of the torment I felt.

There was a full-length mirror on the back of the bathroom door and I was leaning on it, tears running down my face, my head beginning to pound.

I pulled away from the door just far enough to see my reflection in the mirror. I was still wearing Wesley's digital watch, and when

I looked in the mirror I was absolutely stunned by what I saw. The time shown in the reflection was 5:55.

"How could that be? It's not nearly that late," I thought to myself.

I stood straight up and looked directly at the watch on my wrist. It showed 2:22, which in the mirror's reflection looked like 5:55.

I stood still, not moving a muscle, staring at myself in the mirror.

I forced myself to receive the gift I was being given and allow healing to come. It was no accident I walked into that room, with its full-length mirror, to gather myself. There were any number of other rooms where I could have sought escape and refuge from my feelings. It was no accident I not only chose the bathroom with the mirror but also looked at the mirror at exactly 2:22. There were only two minutes out of 1,440 in the day when I could have seen 5:55 on the watch in the mirror.

Moments like these left me feeling gifted and more capable of facing another minute, another hour, another day without Wesley. When such things happened, I felt obligated to accept the gifts and try to move on from my emotional paralysis. I feared if I did not utilize these moments as opportunities to gradually heal, then eventually they would stop being gifted to me.

✳

At the end of May, when Hunter finished preschool, I started planning a long trip for the summer. It would give my mom a chance to go home to my dad, and Hunter and me a chance to visit friends and family along the West Coast. I bought two plane tickets to Los Angeles, and we headed west.

Our two-month journey would start at Tami's house in Los Angeles and end at Vance's in Washington. My fifteen-year high school reunion was being held at the end of the summer just miles from my brother's home. We had moved to a small town in Washington when I was fourteen and a sophomore in high school. I graduated from high school there but had not returned in many years. I was looking forward to renewing old friendships. Washington was where I had met my friends Rosemary and Darcy years before. I still have the card Darcy gave me on my birthday, my second week in a new school. I was the new girl, and it was not easy. She had balloons delivered to me because that is the kind of friend she was and still is. After I moved away, Rosemary and I wrote letters to each other and decorated the envelopes. During Wesley's illness and since the funeral, both Rosemary and Darcy had been supportive, but from a distance, as many people had to be due to geography. I looked forward to being with them and spending quality time with them and everyone else along the way.

When we landed in Los Angeles, I was relieved to see Hunter's bike had made it there without damage. We gathered it and the rest of our luggage and met Tami where we picked up the rental car I would drive for the next two months. Hunter was excited to see Tami, Mason, and Tami's youngest son Ethan, and I was thrilled to be in the company of my best friend. The palm trees and warm, sunny beaches were just what we needed.

For our vacation, I rented a car so we could have flexibility to travel wherever and whenever we wanted. I packed all we would need. I used the most recent installment of the money I had made from selling the pillow rights to Europe to finance the trip. I brought my laptop with me so I could work as needed, left Christi in charge once again of most daily operations of the business, and set ourselves free to roam.

We planned to stay with Tami for two weeks. I unpacked our clothes and placed the framed five-by-seven black-and-white picture of Wesley, Hunter, and me—our Christmas picture from two years before he got sick—on the nightstand by the bed in her guest room.

We enjoyed lazy days, spending time at the beach, watching the kids play in her backyard, and having long conversations over tea as the boys slept cozily in their beds at night. Tami was the very best therapy for me. She listened, she held me up, and she let me cry until there were no tears left. Then, the next day, we would start all over again, making sure the kids were having fun and Hunter's sorrow over losing his dad could be soothed with everything a five-year-old boy loved.

One day, Tami and I did what tourists do in Los Angeles and bought a map to find movie star's houses. Wesley had been a long-time fan of Ozzy Osbourne, so our first stop was Ozzy's house. His home at the time had a huge wooden gate out front and a button to push that rang directly into their house. Tami rang it. The man who worked as security for the Osbournes answered and warned us to get off the property. He politely explained he could have us arrested if we did not leave, so we did not need much convincing to move along!

Our next stop was a quick drive past George Clooney's house. We were not even sure if we were in the right spot, but we did not care. We certainly did not spot him. We felt like ridiculous school girls as we drove through the Hollywood Hills and wondered who lived where. At the end of our tourist day, we had dinner at The Ivy—seeing no celebrities—and headed home. Our mission was accomplished, which was to feel the wind in our hair, laugh out loud as much as possible, and hope for the possibility of running into John Cusack so we could buy him a cup of coffee. Harmless fun between friends. It was the silliest, most fun I had had in months.

I had not seen my friend Tracy since she met us in northern California after Wesley's funeral, so we also spent a few days with her while we were in Los Angeles. Hunter and I met her at Disneyland for the day. I hoped it would feel like the happiest place on earth, as its commercials promised.

As I drove through the majestic entrance and Hunter cheered with excitement, I felt sad inside because I wished Wesley could be there—at the same time, I also knew we were only there because Wesley was not.

"Can you please give me a sign today that you're here with us? I need to know you are here," I quietly said to myself and to Wesley as we entered the Disneyland parking lot.

It was a fabulous day, such a wonderful place for children to enjoy. Tracy had been to Disneyland more times than she could count, but she still helped make Hunter's first time at the Magic Kingdom special.

Near the end of the day, Hunter and I rode a Star Wars simulation ride. We exited the ride through a souvenir shop and started walking to meet Tracy at a food court nearby. But after we passed through the souvenir shop exit doors, Hunter asked if we could go back inside to look at the toys. I reminded him Tracy was waiting for us and we needed to leave.

"Please, Mommy! I really want to look at the Star Wars toys," he pleaded.

I knew Tracy would not mind, so I agreed to go back inside for a few minutes. As we walked in, we were going against the tide of people getting off the ride who were exiting through the shop. I was caught off guard when a man about my age accidentally bumped into me.

"Sorry about that," he apologized, holding my arm with his hand, making eye contact, then walking away.

I stood frozen.

He was wearing the same orange T-shirt with the dark blue stripes I had seen at other times when I had asked for a sign Wesley was near.

I could not explain these signs, and I refused to dismiss them. They gave me comfort. I found myself wanting more of them, almost relying on them.

The next day, I went to visit my friend Heather Urich to help her with a fundraising fashion show in Beverly Hills. She and her late husband, the actor Robert Urich, had established a fund through the University of Michigan for sarcoma research, and she continues to champion their efforts even after, or especially after, Robert lost his battle to cancer.

I met Robert Urich in 1997 at a survivor's conference at MD Anderson Cancer Center where he was the keynote speaker. I remembered him from television shows like *Spencer for Hire* and *Vegas*. What I remember most about our first meeting was how good he smelled and how charismatic he was. He filled the room and people wanted to be near him.

Through multiple twists of fate, Heather and I became friends after Robert died of cancer. I had gone to Los Angeles to volunteer at the celebrity golf tournament they held each year. When I went, it was just six months after Robert had died. Heather was determined to hold the tournament in his honor—even though it was difficult for her and for everyone who loved him and mourned his loss—because it was what he would have wanted.

At that time, Wesley was not sick yet. The sympathy I showed to Heather had nothing to do with my own pain. There was no way either of us could have known just how much we would share in the years ahead, both as widows and as friends.

Heather and Robert adopted a baby girl a few years before he died, who was now just a year older than Hunter. Heather, of all the people I had in my life, knew exactly how I felt. She was a widowed mother, which, despite what some people think, is very different from being a single mother. Not harder. Not easier. Just different.

Spending time with Heather while I was in Los Angeles was a lot like coming home. She included Hunter and me in their family, I became friends with her older son Ryan and, most of all, I felt understood and welcomed.

I fondly recall one night at her house. She was having family and friends over for dinner and invited Hunter and me to come. Hunter and her daughter Allison set up a lemonade stand outside her house on the sidewalk while Heather poured me fine wine and served delicious food. We were surrounded by laughter and spirits in her home—both spirits to consume and the spirits of the beautiful men who died long before their time and left us to raise their wonderful children without them.

I told Heather about John Edwards and asked her if she had ever been to a medium. She said she had not, but she knew someone who had, and gave me a phone number to call if I was interested. She confessed the idea of it scared her, and that is why she had never gone herself.

It scared me, too, but I could not stop thinking there was more waiting for me if I just had someone who could get me to the other side or bring Wesley to me. I kept hearing what Wesley had said to me months before, "You're strong enough to find me."

Tami and I, sharing the same faith, discussed the idea of meeting with a medium at length. She knew I was struggling with it because of my relationship with God and not knowing if it was the right thing to do. She had her own struggles with the idea, but she agreed to go with me anyway. I set the appointment for the day before Hunter and I were scheduled to leave Los Angeles and head north to San Jose to visit Corine and her family.

That morning, I got up early and left Hunter with Tami for a few hours. I bought a smoothie to drink and found myself in a shopping center parking lot on my cell phone with my friend and web developer Melody. She had been kind and giving to me, both in business and in friendship. She was a woman of strong faith, and she was completely against my seeing a medium. She believed with all her heart it was a gateway to evil. I was not so sure.

As we talked on the phone that morning, she pleaded with me not to go, but I would not promise her. I needed time to decide.

After I hung up with Melody, I called Alyson, Wesley's nurse in Alabama. I had talked with her several times after leaving Alabama. She was incredibly supportive. Little by little she had told me more about the day Wesley died. She told me only what I wanted to know and what I was ready to hear. Somehow, I felt she knew something more about that day than she had told me so far. I decided it was time to know the whole story. It was her day off, so she had plenty of time to talk.

"Roger said he was with Wesley when he started bleeding and tried to tell him it was going to be okay. He said Wesley closed his eyes. Then Roger had to leave the room so the nurses and doctors could work on him," I began.

"That's right," Alyson confirmed.

"But there's more, isn't there?" I asked her, knowing she had something else to tell me.

"Yes, there is," she said with hesitation. "Are you sure you want to know?"

"I'm sure."

Alyson told me Wesley was conscious when she first went to his bedside. She said he looked scared, and she tried to calm him, but he knew he was dying.

"I told him it was okay for him to let go. I told him God would take care of him," she began, as I listened intently to her every word. "But no matter what I said, he still had this look on his face as if he wasn't ready. He was dying, but he wasn't letting go. And that's when I knew."

"That's when you knew what?" I quietly asked, not knowing what she would tell me next.

"That's when I knew I needed to bring you into the room," she answered.

"But you didn't ever come get me. They wouldn't let me in the room." I responded, confused.

"I don't mean physically bring you in the room. I just knew he needed you there," she tried to explain. "I told him it was okay to let go and that you were a strong woman. I said 'Lisa will be okay. And she'll take good care of Hunter. They will be okay. It's okay. You know how strong she is.' All of this was said within just a couple minutes. There wasn't much time."

Tears began to fall from my eyes; I gasped for air as I imagined Wesley taking his final breath, still only concerned with Hunter and me, not thinking of himself.

"What did he do?" I asked her, yearning for her response.

"He looked at me as if he understood how well I knew you," she answered. "He raised his eyebrows, as if to nod his head."

That is what Wesley always did; anyone who knew him recognized the response she was sharing with me. It was how he sometimes said hello, how he said goodbye, how he asked and answered a question. This simple gesture with his eyebrows and a nod of his head was the Wesley I knew—someone Alyson perhaps did not know but was able to describe to me now.

"I kept telling him over and over you would be okay. I told him I knew how strong you were, that I was there the day of his surgery when you told him to stay away from the light but that you would accept it if he didn't come back because you would know he was better off," Alyson continued.

"You remember me saying that to him? That was the morning you were prepping him for surgery," I said, shocked by her recollection of a day that might have been routine for her but was monumental for us.

"I'll never forget it," she quickly answered.

I did not know what to say. I was silent for a moment. Alyson waited for me to speak.

"What were your very last words to him?" I asked her, needing to know.

"I told him I would tell you he loves you," she answered. "His very last thought, his very last breath, his very last concern was for you and Hunter."

"Was he okay in the end? Did he let go?" I asked.

"He was peaceful, Lisa."

I spent several minutes in the car after Alyson and I ended our call. I was silent, replaying the last minutes of Wesley's life in my head. Because of what Alyson shared, I understood there was a moment when Wesley slipped from this life and into the next. I felt grateful he was aware of it and, most of all, at peace.

I went to a nearby park and sat for a few hours, doing nothing but observing children playing and dogs on leashes with their loyal owners. It was quiet, but inside I felt as if my emotions were trying to break free.

Driving back to Tami's on a Los Angeles freeway, the reality of what Alyson had shared with me became too much to bear, and I was forced to set my captive emotions free. As the tears poured from my eyes, I could barely see the road in front of me. I could not drive any farther. I pulled over on a stretch of the freeway safe from the stop-and-go traffic to my left. For the first time since Wesley died, I was downright angry, furious at the world, screaming for the pain to stop.

"I can't! I can't! I can't!" I screamed, with no one but God and Wesley to hear me. "I can't live without him. I can't feel like this the rest of my life! Where is he? Where is he?" I screamed.

Sobbing into my hands, the familiar pounding in my head coming on, I wanted to be where Wesley was. I did not want to die; I would never leave Hunter, but I wanted to reach into Wesley's new world and bring him back to me. I no longer cared what God would think about me seeking the dead. My husband was the dead, and I wanted him back! I did not care that God wanted me to seek Him. I was even willing to go to a woman with a crystal ball who charged a hundred dollars to read my palm if that is what it would take to have him back in any form. I was desperate and I knew it, but I did not care.

My cell phone rang, jarring me from my state of suffering. It was Melody. I did not want to answer it, but I felt forced to take her call.

"Lisa, don't do it!" she told me. "You'll struggle with this choice, Lisa. You know you will. That's why you are struggling with the idea of going. You know where Wesley is?" she asked, barely giving me a chance to speak when I answered the phone.

"No, I don't!" I shouted.

"He's praying at the foot of God for you," she professed, desperately trying to remind me of the faith I had held since I was an eight-year-old little girl. "He's praying at the foot of God for you, Lisa. He's with God!"

I listened to Melody, then told her I had to hang up the phone. I had reached my breaking point. On an L.A. freeway, so overcome by the agonizing reality of my life, a life without Wesley, I poured out my soul and begged God for the strength to go on.

I prayed for peace and understanding. I prayed for God to take care of me the way I took care of Wesley. I prayed for God to fight for me. To stay by my side and devote Himself to my healing, even when I did not deserve his grace. I begged for God to show me out of this darkness and into the light I knew He still had planned for my life.

Slowly, the tears stopped. My breathing leveled. My head stopped pounding. On the side of that freeway, traffic now blazing by me, I hit bottom for the first time in my life. Even when I had cancer, no matter how frightened I was, there was always hope; I was always getting better, and I had Wesley. This was different. This would require me to take a leap of faith beyond anything I had ever experienced before. I had hit bottom and could only go up from there. If I was ever going to begin to heal, I was going to have to allow the healing to come. It was not about the medium, or God, or even Wesley. This was about me. This was about not losing faith in my ability to find my way out of this abyss of grief one day.

When I walked into Tami's house, she was waiting for me. She took one look at me and knew I had decided not to go see the medium after all.

"It's so hard to do the right thing," she told me, wrapping me in her arms, crying with me, sharing my pain, meeting me where I was in that moment.

It was not that I thought John Edwards was wrong or evil, or even that he, and people like him, were not called by God. Anything was possible. But what I knew was true for myself was I would have to give up a part of my belief system to walk into a meeting with a medium and seek out something God was already offering me. He had given me the conversation in the bathroom. Maybe He had even given me the number five and the orange and blue T-shirt, too. I could not be sure, but what I was certain He had given me years before was my faith. I could not depart from it and expect to survive a life without Wesley.

✻

Over the next six weeks, Hunter and I continued to be welcomed by family and friends. I have often thought I could write a book just about those weeks, experiencing the dynamics of the families we were visiting. It was an incredible lesson as I observed with a heightened awareness of what was important. I noticed things many people would not—the way our married hosts interacted with each other, the attention they paid to their children, and the way they seemed to think the next day was promised to them. I felt safe in the company of these strong, loving families, but sometimes I felt sad watching the simplicity in which they experienced every ordinary day of their lives. I missed that for our own family. I actually envied the luxury of taking someone for granted and, at the same time, hoped I never would have done so if Wesley had survived.

My greatest emotion toward the people who welcomed us into their homes that summer was gratitude. Each home, each friend, every member of our family, was dedicated to making Hunter's and my stay pleasant, entertaining, and peaceful.

The drive from one place to the next was often during the late hours of the night and was sometimes lonely. Hunter would sleep in the back seat of the car, and I would listen to music. A few new songs were being featured on the radio. I wondered which ones Wesley would have liked—and which he would have changed the station to avoid hearing again.

A few weeks before leaving Houston for our vacation, I called one of my oldest friends, Trent. I had also met him while a sophomore in high school, and we had stayed in touch sporadically over the years. He and Wesley had never met but had a mutual respect for each other. Wesley was never the jealous type and had no reason to be.

Sometimes during those late drives along I-5, slowly making our way north in California, I would call Trent and he would talk me through the night's drive. We talked about politics, music—anything and everything but my misery. I always left our conversations so grateful, feeling blessed to have such good friends to help get me through. No one friend meant more to me than another—each person we shared our summer with played an integral part in our healing. That summer, spent embracing life and trying hard to remember the joy it had to offer, was an opportunity to grow in ways I had not expected.

When I bought the plane tickets for Hunter and me to leave Houston, I wanted to escape. I needed to escape our empty home. No matter how hard it was, I had to get away from the familiar routine we had once known as a family but was now lost, replacing it with a new place to wake up and new experiences to enjoy. What I did not expect was the healing it would bring. I thought Texas had to be our home because that was where Hunter would be closest to his dad. But through the days and nights we spent far away from Houston and the home we had shared with Wesley, I discovered one very important thing: Wesley was everywhere. It did not matter where Hunter and I were. In Texas, California, or Washington, Wesley would always be with us.

It was not until the fourth stop along our journey Hunter finally commented on the photograph of the three of us I placed on the bedside table in each guest room.

"Mommy, everywhere we go, people have that picture of us next to the bed!" he observed, seeming perplexed.

"That's our picture. I bring it with us wherever we go," I smiled.

The truth was, we did not need the picture to remind us of the three of us together. That was as much a part of our existence as the rising and setting of the sun. We were a vital part of each other's human experience. We would always be what we had worked to build—a family.

Hunter and I spent nearly two weeks at Corine and James'. She and James had been married for seventeen years, and James and I were also close. Their daughter Kayla and Hunter laughed and played and made grilled cheese sandwiches, just as Corine and I had done when we were kids. Corine, James, and I sipped margaritas and talked about Wesley and the fun times we had together. Then we talked about his illness and the day he died, which was on their seventeenth wedding anniversary. Corine still cannot talk about Wesley without tearing up.

"Wesley once told me long before he died he would always be married to you, for the rest of his life," she cried. "He said he would never leave you; you were everything to him."

I knew this about Wesley's love for me, but it was so wonderful to hear it now.

Next, we spent a few days with John and Kirsten and their two daughters. Wesley had met John in a training program years before, and the four of us became fast friends. They had shown up in Texas for his funeral when I had not even known they were coming. They were dear to us both. I loved that when we arrived at their house, their daughters and neighborhood friends ran to our car cheering, "Hunter B is here! Hunter B is here!" Only those closest to us called him Hunter B.

We also stayed for a few days at my friends Noelle and Ken's house. Noelle has always been a wonderful hostess—placing a fresh water bottle and chocolates by the bed each night. Ken would wrestle with Hunter and their son Nolan everyday, and

Hunter reveled in the rough play he had been missing from his own dad.

After Noelle and Ken's, we met up with my mom at Lavaun and Mike's house again. We stayed there for several days, spending time where I grew up and visiting with lifelong friends and family.

One day Hunter and I went to the waterslides alone. There were two boys eating lunch at the picnic table where we were seated. Hunter was fascinated because the boys were there without their parents, even though they were only ten years old and had come with their older brothers who were thirteen.

"Your mommy and daddy let you come here all by yourself?" Hunter asked, in awe of their bravery.

"My mom let me come. She lets me come here all the time," one of the boys casually said. "But I don't have a dad."

Hunter looked at me confused.

"You don't have a dad?" Hunter asked.

"No. He left when I was still in my mom's stomach," the boy bluntly told Hunter.

"I have a dad but he lives far away, so I never see him," the other boy confessed.

Hunter looked at me again, his eyes wide open, shocked by what he was hearing.

The two boys started talking about the fastest slide at the water-park and stopped talking about their personal life, so I followed their lead until they finished their lunch and left the picnic table where Hunter and I were still sitting. Hunter had not said a word since the boys told him about their dads.

"You okay?" I asked him after the boys walked away.

"Mommy, those boys don't have daddies," he answered, still concerned about them.

"I know, Buddy," I responded, rubbing Hunter on the back of

his neck.

"I have a daddy," he told me. "At least my daddy wanted me and tried to stay."

I was in such awe of his understanding of his dad's death. Hunter had always been a kid who got it. I had been told by people who met him briefly or knew him well he was special and wise beyond his years.

Somehow, our five-year-old son was keenly aware of what his dad's absence from his life meant. He knew what we had done to try to keep Wesley alive and no matter where Wesley was, he would always be his daddy. From the beginning of Hunter's new life without his own dad, he took great comfort in knowing he was wanted and loved by him wherever he was.

✳

We left California and headed to Washington. Our final stop on the journey was to visit my brother Vance. He lived near Rosemary and Darcy and close to where my class reunion would be held. The area where he lived was beautiful. The weather was perfect every day of the two weeks we were there. I recalled experiencing the four seasons when I had lived in Washington years before, so different from Texas. Unlike Houston, Hunter and I spent time with friends at the park and stayed for hours without getting a single mosquito bite or worrying about the threat of West Nile virus. Recreation was abundant and Vance's love of the outdoors was refreshing. Vance took pride in the time he spent with Hunter and in what he could teach him.

Spending time with old friends was also enjoyable. Trent had come for the reunion, and reuniting with him, Darcy, and Rosemary brought me happiness. Being with three of my oldest, dearest friends in life, eager to share in the joys and the sorrows of what Hunter and I were experiencing, reminded me again of how fortunate I was to have such support.

It did not take long before Vance asked if I would ever consider moving to Washington to be near him and my parents. He suggested we move in with him. He said he wanted to be a part of helping me raise Hunter and provide him with the male role model he lost when Wesley died. My dad was working in Oregon and would likely spend the remaining years until retirement working along the West Coast. All three of them wanted to be a part of our lives and wanted us closer. I knew much of my ability to cope day to day was in large part due to my mom and dad's devotion to Hunter and me, and their willingness to sacrifice time together so my mom could be with us when we were in Texas, but I could not expect my mom to stay with us forever. At some point, Hunter and I would need to find our way on our own.

The more I thought about Vance's offer, the more appealing the idea of moving to Washington became. Although I had no desire or need to live with Vance, I did like the idea of being closer to where I grew up, near my family and longtime friends. I was able to consider the move only because our journey was ending in Washington. If we had started in Washington and made the trip in reverse, I would not have been ready to consider leaving Texas. By now I knew Hunter and I could be anywhere, and Wesley would always be with us.

I did not know what Wesley would have thought about Hunter and me leaving Texas, but I guess at that point I also realized, sadly, he did not have a voice in the decision. I also knew he would not want me to make the decision based on him. I remembered what he told me before we moved to Alabama for his transplant: "You're the most capable woman I know," he said. I was starting to believe him.

I liked Washington but I did not want to live in the mountains where Vance lived. I am a city girl, but I was a city girl with a son to raise, and I already knew I did not want Hunter to grow up in Houston without his father. I knew we would be leaving Houston eventually, but until arriving at Vance's, the only move I had considered was living near Wesley's parents. It had not occurred to me to move nearer to my own parents.

A few days after Vance brought up the idea of us moving to Washington, I drove to visit Rosemary for the day. She lived about thirty minutes from Vance. As I approached the breathtaking view of her small, but big enough for me, town, I knew what I wanted to do. This was a place where I could live and raise Hunter.

On my way to Rosemary's house, I spotted a realtor's sign in the yard of a random house. I noted the number and called it. A lovely woman named Kay answered the phone. She offered to show me houses later that afternoon, so I delayed my visit with Rosemary and ventured out to see what was available in my price range. I wanted a neighborhood with families, sidewalks, and kids for Hunter to play with everyday, just as he was used to in Houston. That is what Kay had found for me.

As crazy as it sounds, I found a house within three days of looking and made an offer that was accepted. Although many people would have advised me not to make such a quick decision so soon after Wesley died, no one said that to me. My mind was made up. Hunter and I had nothing to lose. I listened to the voice inside me when I chose to sell our house in Houston and move thousands of miles away from the life we would have had if we had stayed.

It was only because we had life insurance I was able to make such a decision. My grief did not have to be complicated by finances. Having the money gave me the freedom to follow that voice and listen to my heart. Just as Wesley's cousin Jay had said, when I signed the papers to receive payment from the life insurance policy his father, JB, had put in place for us, "This money isn't meant to retire you. It's to help get you where you need to be."

I knew all of our friends and most of our family in Texas would support my decision to move. They only wanted what was best for us, and they trusted I could judge that better than they did. I knew Donna would struggle most with it. I tried to break the news to her gently when I called her from Washington just a few days before we returned to Houston at the end of the summer, but there was really no easy way to tell her I would be leaving and taking Wesley's son, her grandson, with me.

It took her time to accept our moving to Washington, but she set aside her own feelings to support what I truly believed was right for us.

By the time Hunter and I flew back to Houston at the end of August, a closing date had been set for the Washington house, and I had contacted a realtor to list the Houston house. Hunter and I would leave Houston by October.

On Hunter's first day of kindergarten, I woke to tears in my sleep, completely aware of Wesley missing that day. Wesley went into his transplant surgery hopeful he would be well again by the time Hunter started kindergarten. He wanted nothing more than to walk Hunter into class without a single tube attached to his body. As I walked Hunter into school that morning, I thought of Wesley and felt sad he could not be there but also allowed myself to feel good I could be.

My grief shifted in the weeks before moving to Washington. I felt so certain I could build a life there that I tried not to let leaving Texas bring me down. I figured if I was choosing to go, then I should not complain about the sadness of leaving.

Hunter and I spent quality time with our friends and family in the weeks before we left Texas. I turned thirty-three that September. Instead of crying at home or feeling sad without Wesley there, I spent the night with my girlfriends at Jimbo's ranch. He spoiled us with his perfectly grilled steaks and deliciously blended margaritas. We swam in the pool and soaked in the hot tub. No kids, no cares, just girls having fun.

Donna and Roger had returned to Alabama to pick up the last of our belongings. Rae and Mike had graciously cleaned out the apartment for us and had arranged to have Wesley's oxygen machine and remaining tanks returned to the oxygen company. Donna and Roger had taken the leftover Flolan to the hospital, hoping a patient in need could use it. I did not know how Donna found the strength to walk back into that hospital, but I admired her for doing it, and I was grateful for she and Roger's willingness to retrieve our belongings and bring them back to Houston for me. I never would have done it myself. I did not unpack the boxes they brought to me from Alabama. I just left them in our garage to be loaded into the moving truck when it was time.

My mom helped me with a garage sale, and I sold many things I would not need in Washington. When it came time to start packing, I invited my friends over to help. I served them pizza, and, room by room, the girls and I packed up our house and stacked the boxes by the front door. They did such a good job I still have not found our passports!

I cannot explain why it was even possible for me to do this so soon after Wesley died, but it felt incredibly right. I still struggled. Packing Wesley's belongings was not easy. I saved many things for Hunter and gave other things to his mom, his brother Wayne, his cousin Jay, and his best friend Mike.

It was near the end of the night when we started packing Wesley's closet. I told my friends I could get to it later, but they insisted on helping. So, one plastic tub at a time, we packed his closet and I saved what I thought Hunter might want to keep. We did the same in the garage. Little by little, our house was emptying, our new destination just days away.

I spent many hours on the phone with Tami and Trent during that time. They were like therapy without the big bill at the end of each conversation. I continued to go to the support group meetings. I prayed. I wrote. I did my best to be present in my decision to move away and take Hunter from the only home he had ever known.

Before I was diagnosed with cancer, Wesley and I had been married two years, and I was homesick. I missed living in California. I missed my parents and my extended family. It was a difficult time of transition for me. Wesley and I were struggling in our marriage after his dad died. Wesley was drinking a lot, and I felt as if I was carrying the two of us. I remember just wanting to go home for a while to be with my family and be taken care of for a change. Within a few months, I was diagnosed with cancer.

At the time, I did not make the connection between what I wanted and what I got from my desire to be home, but when I read a book called *The Cancer Conqueror* as I was finishing treatment, it became abundantly clear to me.

Wesley and I were in California visiting my parents when I was diagnosed with cancer by the very doctor who had delivered me twenty-four years before. We chose to stay in California to be near my family throughout treatment. During that time, everything was about getting me well. Cancer had never touched our family at such a young age and our only concern was getting rid of it and moving on with our lives. It was not until I read *The Cancer Conqueror* a light bulb went on in my head. While struggling in my marriage with Wesley in Texas after his dad died, all I wanted was to come home to my family and be taken care of for a while. Through getting cancer, that is exactly what happened.

I am not suggesting I wished cancer on myself, but I did believe and still do that sadness and strife can make us sick inside and out. Being with my family when I was sick and finding a renewed strength in my marriage with Wesley were all I could possibly hope for in the healing of cancer. When I got well and we returned to our life in Texas, I no longer wished to be anywhere other than where I was. I learned through that experience I could be anywhere as long as Wesley and I were together and we were solid, both in our relationship and as individuals.

My decision to move to Washington made me feel much like I did when returning to Texas after getting well. For some people, the idea of moving away from the place they had lived for thirteen years would be frightening enough to make them stay put. For me, it was an easy decision to make because there was nothing left to fear. My greatest fears had already come true. Wesley was gone and he was not coming back. I knew I needed to live my life with these terrible truths in mind. If we moved to Washington and it was not right for us, it was just geography; We could move back after giving it our best effort. We had nothing to lose as long as Hunter and I were together.

The day came for Hunter and me to leave Texas. My friends presented me with a painting of Wesley and Hunter—the two of them holding hands and walking to a pond near Jimbo's house to fish for the first time when Hunter was just two years old. It was a picture I had chosen to be displayed at the funeral. The girls had managed to sneak it from my house and had asked a local artist to do the painting. They even had had it framed to match Hunter's bedroom. I was speechless when they gave it to me, so grateful for their friendship.

I was sad to leave Texas but ready to move to Washington. My mom, Wesley's sister Jenny, Hunter, and I would fly to Washington while Jay and Wayne drove the rented moving truck Mike had helped pack.

The last moments I spent in our home in Texas, I cried for what was lost there, but at the same time, I gave thanks for what was given to us. We were made in that house—brought from one end of our lives together to the other, our beginning and our end. As I walked through the house alone, I thanked Wesley for the beautiful life we had made and for all he had taught me since the day I met him so many years before. I did not say goodbye to him because I was not leaving him or us behind. This was our house, nothing more. Everything else still lived on inside of me.

As I shut the double doors behind me, I said quietly to Wesley, "It's time to go. I'm not leaving here without you."

CHAPTER TWENTY-TWO

The Longest Winter

Remodeling can be therapeutic. I loved every part of making this new house our home.

Wesley only liked white walls. It had taken a lot of convincing for him to let me paint our Houston walls beige. In the new house, I repeated the beige in the living, dining, and family rooms, but I decided to paint every other room in the house a different color. Even the laundry room was colorful: I painted it apricot. I painted the kitchen blood red. It was just paint; I could always paint over it, kind of like a bad haircut. Once you have been bald from chemo, you realize a bad haircut is nothing a few weeks' grow-out cannot fix.

I painted all but one of the rooms myself, but for weeks I had contractors in my house making the other changes. I knew when I bought the house I would renovate some of it—hardwood floors to replace tile and laminate flooring, new carpet, new paint for the kitchen cabinets. I was determined to have everything done at once.

Hunter quickly met neighborhood kids to play with. Neighbors brought jars of jam and welcome wishes. When one of the neighbors asked my mother when my husband would be arriving, my mom told her my husband had died.

"Oh, I'm so sorry. When I saw her wedding ring, I just assumed," the neighbor apologized.

"She hasn't taken off the ring," my mom explained, trying to make her feel better.

It was awkward for both my new neighbor and my mom, and it was the beginning of us having to admit our tragedy to strangers in our new town.

I knew starting over would not be easy, but it was how I expected it to be. Some tears, some sadness, but for the most part we were glad to be there. My brother and Tasha helped us get settled. My mom stayed for a few weeks. Rosemary was a strong presence in our home, and her son Justin and Hunter quickly became friends. Justin was a few years older, but that would not matter much for a couple more years. For now, they were thrilled to play video games and build with Legos together while Rosemary and I did the heavy lifting in life—longs talks and furniture assembly. I felt hopeful Hunter and I could begin to rebuild our lives and make this house our home.

My mom left a few weeks after we moved in. It was time. Hunter and I needed to start learning how to just be Hunter and me. It was an adjustment for all three of us to be apart, our longest separation since Wesley died, but we had to begin.

Of all the things that helped me adapt to our new life in a new town, Rosemary's friendship was instrumental. She showed up with her mom's drill, ready to help with anything that needed doing. For one project, she spent two hours hanging all of the framed covers of the magazines my company had been featured in to date. Each was hung perfectly straight, measured evenly from one to the next. Rosemary and the fabric of our friendship is in every stroke of paint in the house. Without her, the experience of being there those early months would have been completely different, and even more lonely. She and Justin in our home on a regular basis gave Hunter and me something to look forward to.

Rosemary never met Wesley, but she knew about him because of our friendship over the years. Her respect for what we had together and what was lost when he died was a comfort to me.

She would say, "I never heard you say a bad word about him in all of those years. If you two had problems in your marriage, you certainly never told me."

She was right. We did have problems, but it was pointless to complain to her, because I knew we would always work through whatever we were going through, and we would always be married. I truly believe I would have been married to him for the next fifty years of my life.

As winter approached, I began to struggle more and more with Wesley's death. I had a housewarming party when the renovations were done; we spent time with friends; Hunter and I built snowmen and had snowball fights. We were rebuilding our lives, but it was still grueling. Some days were better than others, but the pain was constant.

Heather once told me grief is like a room in your house that is always there, but after time you visit it less often. Wesley was still taking up the whole house, a house he had never even set foot in. My favorite pictures of us were displayed in frames throughout the house. I was still sleeping with one of his shirts. I cried myself to sleep most nights. Talking with my friends helped most.

A few months after we moved in, I felt my grief was spiraling out of control, so I flew Corine up for a weekend visit, knowing her support would help. Immediately, being with her lightened my heavy heart. I picked her up at the airport and stopped at a convenience store to buy raspberry-filled powdered donuts. We ate most of the box on the drive home from the airport. It was deliciously delightful.

I needed to be surrounded. I needed the love of my friends and the joy of Hunter. I needed. I needed. I needed. I had so little to give. I felt as if I was always taking—because I was. I was fortunate to have people love me through it. I would do the same for any of them.

While Corine was visiting, she and Rosemary talked me into going out dancing. I had never been the going-out-dancing type. I had never even been to a bar until my twenty-first birthday—and Wesley and I were together by then. I had definitely never been out as a single person, and I still felt very much like a widow, but I agreed to go.

The club was packed. Loud music. People on the dance floor. So not my place of interest at the time. If there was an attractive man in the place, I was not paying attention.

Toward the end of the night, Corine noticed an attractive couple who seemed to be having a fabulous time together.

"They look so happy," Corine said, pointing them out to me.

"They're married," I observed, noticing their wedding rings.

"They look like a great couple," she added.

"You should tell them. Really, tell them you noticed how good they are together and compliment them on it," I suggested, remembering being that couple when Wesley and I were at our best.

"Really?" Corine questioned me.

"Really. People should hear these things," I assured her, then nudged her in their direction.

Corine walked up to them on the dance floor and told them what she had told me. I saw them smile and thank her.

Seeing the two of them so happy together made me sad, but I tried to have a good time. We danced and laughed, until "Sweet Home Alabama" played. I did not want to dance to it, so I went to the bathroom alone and stood by the window looking out into the night sky. I watched cars and people passing on the streets, life moving along as if nothing terrible had happened. No one in the building but Corine and Rosemary knew of my broken heart. No one even knew Wesley had ever existed. But I knew. He was still everywhere and nowhere, all at the same time.

I thought about the happy couple on the dance floor as I went to sleep that night, hoping they knew how fortunate they were. I could not have known then the role they would later play in Hunter's and my life or the impact they would have.

The next day, my sadness mounted. I was struggling, feeling hopeless, wanting relief from the constant emptiness in the pit of my stomach and the center of my heart. I felt the grief physically. Even though I was open about my feelings with a few close friends and family, like Corine, I still tried to be strong in their presence. Corine struggled with Wesley's death in her own way. They had been close.

I tried to hide my growing sadness from her. Corine had come so far to see me. Even though I had asked her to come because I was having a difficult time and needed her support, I did not want to overwhelm her. I walked into my closet and closed the door just enough so no one could hear me crying, but I could hear if someone was coming. I did this a lot.

I had been crying for a few minutes when I felt Corine's arms wrap around my shoulders. She did not say a word; she just held me as I sobbed in her arms.

"I... don't... know... how," I sobbed, barely able to speak. "I don't know... how... to live... without him."

Corine just held onto me.

In moments like these, it felt as if the grief would never end, as if it would always be stronger than my will to move past it. I felt overcome and sometimes terrified of how relentless the pain was, wondering if I would ever feel better.

Sometimes I would spend a few days in a row on the couch, only getting dressed to take Hunter to and from school. It was only after periods of respite from this overwhelming grief I realized how bad I had felt and recognized it as depression.

Other times I would take a drive in the mountains. Alone in the car, I would scream, crying tears of rage and panic, begging for it all to stop.

I was so tired. I was so incredibly tired of being sad and lonely. I wanted my old life back. No matter how I tried to move on, nothing changed, not even a little bit.

During that long, first winter without Wesley, there was never a time when I felt as if life would get better. I faked my way through, for Hunter's sake, but I figured the only way for me to live was to learn how to be happy in my own misery. True happiness, I believed, would always elude me now.

After living in Texas for so long, I was not used to the snow or the way many people hibernate during the winter months. The people we had seen running about the neighborhood when we arrived had not been out for months. There was a quiet, white noise outside our house, broken rarely by the crunch of the snowpack under a neighbor's feet while walking the family dog.

One night, Rosemary and I were deep in conversation. She had asked a few details about the last weeks of Wesley's life. The conversation was intense, as I told her of the horrific things that took place in Alabama, and she listened with interest and compassion. Both of us were in tears when we suddenly heard a strange noise.

"BUZZZZZZZZZZZZZZZZZZZZZZZZZ."

"Do you hear that?" I asked Rosemary, standing up from the couch.

"Yes, what is it?" she asked, also standing up, both of us wiping our tears and immediately shifting gears from the emotional, high-intensity conversation in which we had been engrossed to figuring out what the heck that noise was.

"I don't know. I can't even tell where it's coming from," I answered.

I checked to see if it was the refrigerator. It wasn't.

"What is it?" Rosemary asked again.

"I think it's coming from the garage," I told her, walking toward the nearby door that led to it.

Anyone who knows me realizes my garage is almost always a mess. It has just never been a priority for me. Most of the time, it overwhelms me to even think about beginning to organize it. My house is usually clean, but finding anything in my garage is much like trying to find a needle in a haystack.

We walked into the garage, stepping over boxes and tripping on old toys, bicycle helmets, and rollerblades.

"I think it's coming from over there," Rosemary said, pointing to a row of clear plastic storage tubs in one corner of the garage.

The noise got louder as we approach the tubs, so we started digging through them one by one. We would think we had found the right tub, but when we opened it and dug through it, there would be nothing inside making the noise.

"BUZZZZZZZZZZZZZZZZZZZZZZZZZZ," the sound continued.

By now we were determined to find the cause. We forgot all about the heavy conversation we had been having on the couch just moments before.

Finally, I lifted the lid off the last plastic tub in the corner and the buzzing sound got louder.

"It must be in here," I said, as Rosemary and I began digging to find the cause.

After nearly emptying the tub, there it was, wrapped in a plastic bag. I burst out laughing as I held up the bag and showed it to Rosemary.

"Oh my gosh!" Rosemary shouted.

The two of us stood there and laughed so hard we were in tears, about to pee our pants!

In the bag, buzzing for no apparent reason, was a gift Corine had insisted on buying me for my thirtieth birthday two years before. She insisted I should have one, whether I ever had use for it or not. It was a vibrator!

Apparently, a broken vibrator. No matter what I tried to do, it would not shut off. I banged it against the wall, hit it against my leg. Nothing worked.

"It won't shut off!" I shouted, still laughing.

"I'm not touching it!" Rosemary exclaimed.

Finally, I removed the batteries and the darn thing stopped buzzing.

"Well, that's one way for Wesley to get you to stop being sad!" Rosemary laughed.

"What? What do you mean?" I asked through my own laughter, not understanding what an old vibrator packed in the bottom of a plastic tub in my garage had to do with Wesley trying to keep me from being sad.

"It got you to stop talking about him dying," Rosemary answered.

She was right. If ever there was a lesson to learn about lightening up and beginning to let some of it go, this was it. Trust me,

I had never asked for a sign from Wesley like this, but a vibrator from my crazy cousin spontaneously turning on in the garage at that exact moment—well, it showed Wesley still had a sense of humor. It was time, after months and months without seeing the humor in even the most obvious places, for me to begin to embrace laughter and joy again.

When the laughter settled, I said myself and to Wesley, "Okay. Okay. I hear you. I promise to try to live a little."

I had a new understanding of how things could be if I would just get out of my own way; as if in response, the season subtly changed from winter to spring as the snow began to melt and the sun began to shine. Both literally and figuratively, the light was coming in and things were beginning to look up.

My long hiatus from joy and laughter was coming to an end.

CHAPTER TWENTY-THREE

Getting James'd

In my early stages of grief, I thought moving on meant, in part, beginning to date—or at least seeing what was out there. I knew with certainty Wesley would not only have approved but would have encouraged me to explore my surroundings and embrace life.

Wesley had lived his single life to the fullest, though he put it behind him when we got together. Trust me, he left nothing undone. He partied; he dated; he lived the way he wanted to live so when he did finally settle down, he would not feel he had missed anything.

I had not lived that way—nor had I ever wanted to. When Wesley and I committed to each other, I was perfectly content with him, as he was with me. We just came to it from different places, each in our own way.

Wesley had told me about his experiences with a dating service before I moved to Houston. This was back in its primitive form, before the Internet, when people had to physically go into a dating service to record a video and fill out a profile. Overall, his experience was more comical than productive (lucky for me). But it was easier now, and I thought I would give Internet dating a try.

In late February, just short of a year after Wesley died, Tami helped me set up accounts with the two most popular online dating websites. I was not interested in finding a boyfriend, but at the encouragement of a few friends, I did consider I would not mind sharing time with someone, even if just to go to a movie or to have lunch.

I was private and cautious. I lied about my birth date, though not my age, and about the town I lived in, by a few miles. I said I had a child, but did not mention Hunter's name or age. Geography did not matter much to me, so I said I was interested in meeting someone within a hundred-mile radius, uploaded one photo, wrote a few honest, direct things about myself that would weed out the lightweights looking for a pushover, and waited to see what happened next.

What happened next was online dating became a part-time job of answering emails, checking my profile, and looking at other people's profiles. It was too much work and hardly seemed worth it. There were guys who seemed to be decent, but as our email interaction increased, each would reveal something subtle about himself that left me disinterested. Some tried too hard; others did not try hard enough. Then there were the guys who revealed things that forced me to instantly delete them from my account and my consideration. One guy bragged about having a lot of free time because he was independently wealthy and his ex-wife had full custody of their kid, thinking that might impress me. It did not. Another said he did not want to date anyone with kids, unless the woman was not too committed to parenting. Who would want to date a woman who was not committed to parenting? I found there were a few too many guys like that.

Many guys stated on their profiles they did not want to "settle."

I had no idea what settling meant, but I soon learned. My translation, as I came to understand it, was the longer people are single, the longer they stay single, because what they want in a partner becomes impossible to find. The list of deal-breakers gets longer, and before they know it, they do not know how to share their space, let alone themselves.

I was quickly becoming annoyed with the whole process, until I received an email from a man in Idaho. His name was James, and there was something about his profile picture—the cool, easy way he leaned back in his chair next to a lake, with a black Labrador retriever in the background, that made me want to know more. He was obviously attractive, but I also liked that he said he had three kids but did not have them on display the way some guys did. He just looked simple, in an interesting, familiar way.

I responded to his email, and we began to write each other a few times a day. I remained perpetually cautious, and even checked his story out to confirm he owned the business he said he owned, had three daughters, and had been divorced for two years. It took a few weeks, but I eventually gave him my telephone number, and he called the same day. We talked for almost an hour the first time.

The next day, he called again, then the next day, and the next.

We talked for hours—about family, kids, business. Every night, he called me after Hunter went to bed, and we talked into the night, sometimes until 2 and 3 a.m., other times even later. We watched the sun come up more than once while talking on the phone with each other.

What we seemed to like most about each other was being excited about another person again. He had grown tired of empty, dead-end relationships and casual dating after his divorce, and I had no experience with casual dating. I had no experience with dating as an adult, period, so I did not know I should not answer every phone call or reply to every text because, apparently, I would appear desperate or too available. In fact, I thought I was replying to his text messages all along, but I was not—I did not know it, but my calling plan did not even include texting messaging. I was playing hard to get when I was not even aware of it!

He found all of this refreshing. As the weeks went on, we discussed meeting at some point, but I was not ready, so we talked on the phone for several more weeks. If I have one bit of advice for online daters, it is to meet sooner rather than later. The longer you wait, the higher the expectations you build, making it nearly impossible to have a real connection even when there could have been one if you had not waited and anticipated it for so long.

We agreed to meet halfway from where we each lived about seven weeks after we started emailing each other. I was a nervous wreck. We had exchanged numerous pictures by then. I had been truthful about who I was and what I looked like. I just had not sat across the table from a man other than Wesley in more than a decade. Wesley and I had not dated each other. We had a history together.

When James and I finally met, I had a hard time even making eye contact with him. I was incredibly uncomfortable. After weeks of talking on the phone for hours, I felt as if I had nothing to say. He tried to be patient, but I cannot blame him for his disappointment. He anticipated meeting a vibrant, self-assured, capable woman—but instead, he met a terrified woman who was a mere shadow of herself.

I cannot even blame my grief over Wesley on how I handled our interaction because I was smitten with James—or at least with the idea of him. It was not that he did not have the characteristics of what I thought would be my type of man because he did. I just did not know how to maneuver the unfamiliar territory of dating.

We parted ways, and it was sad for both of us. We sat in a restaurant bar, just a few hours before leaving, and talked about what we had learned from the experience and how we could have handled it differently. He was kind and supportive, but the damage was done.

I suffered the long drive home feeling utter disappointment. When I got home, I hit a wall emotionally. I began to question if I would ever be able to move on with my life and share time with another human being of the opposite sex without feeling lost in the experience. What I was feeling was completely normal, but I did not know that then. There are no rules about dating after a spouse dies. People come to it in their own way, in their own time, some sooner, some later. But I felt as if I had failed—and I was not used to failure.

Having no experience with dating disappointments, I wondered why I couldn't just fix it and change James' mind about us seeing each other again. Why couldn't I convince him next time would be better, I would be better? Looking back, my behavior was ridiculous. I should have known my value enough to walk away with my dignity intact and not need to try to persuade him to see me again. The whole experience was a kick in the teeth. I feared I would linger in the wake of James' rejection for months to come— and in some ways I did.

Not long after we met in person, James left for Europe with his daughters for two weeks over spring break as planned, and Hunter and I left for California. We agreed to talk when we both returned and discuss seeing each other again after having some distance from our first meeting.

Two weeks later, when James returned, he told me he did not want to see me again. It was the first anniversary of Wesley's death.

"You're more beautiful in person than you are in your pictures.

You're an amazing woman, but maybe I'm just not ready," James told me, as I listened for the first time as a grown woman to the ever-dreaded, all-too-common, "It's not you, it's me" speech.

I was such an idiot! I had even made notes of what to say to him when we talked. I had always been able to convince anyone of anything. Why couldn't I convince James to meet me for a second date?

As I sat on the floor of the bedroom with my notes in my lap, listening to his rejection babble and realizing there was nothing I could do to change his mind, I had an epiphany: At age thirty-three, I had just been propelled into my twenties—but with a married woman's expectations. I did not have experience with being rejected. This kind of heartbreak was foreign to me.

One might wonder how anything could hurt after losing Wesley pained me to the core of my being, but this was different. This forced me to question what I had to offer. This made me question who would ever love me the way I remembered being loved. I had never spent one moment in doubt of those things before. When I married Wesley, I had signed up for the rest of my life, no doubt about it. I never expected, nor did I want, to meet or care about another man. In many ways, the solid way in which I had lived my life in the family Wesley and I built together—which required work, as any marriage does—was the very thing beginning to get in my way. I had an unrealistic view of how things worked because of how easily Wesley and I had come together and stayed together.

So why not take the wisdom and the knowledge I had and stay true to myself in the face of this jarring discovery, made while listening to this man tell me I was not worth a second date? It's simple. I did not know how. Just like a young woman might return to the same relationship over and over again, even when she knows she should not, I did not have the tools I needed to walk away. I was like a twenty-something woman in the throes of discovery, a lost babe in the woods, a drifter in search of a safe place to land.

I was and had always been a capable woman. I did what I said I was going to do in my life, whether it was marrying Wesley, writing a book, having a baby, or starting a business. I had it together, and anyone who knew me knew this about me, but in this one, very specific area of my life, I had so much growing up to do.

James' parting words that day on the phone stung. His words lingered in the air, causing my brain to swarm with questions and doubt, forcing sadness back into my life.

"Aren't you just glad we met, even though it didn't work out, because now we know we are capable of feeling this way again?" he asked me and told me, all at the same time.

"Glad? No, I'm not! Do you know what today is? Do you realize the progress I have lost on you, and how many steps back I have taken?" I screamed these things in my head as I formed the best answer I could offer.

"No, I'm not glad. Honestly, I wish I had never met you," I said, just before we hung up the phone.

I wish I could say that was the last time I ever talked to James—that I learned my lesson and walked away from a man who did not see the value of me, but it was not.

Not only would I learn about rejection from James, I would learn about the stupidity of calling a man who was no longer interested. Worst of all, I discovered what it meant to drunk dial. And drunk text. Through my learning curve, he remained patient with me because I believe he genuinely liked me as a person and wanted to see me happy. The two of us stayed in touch for a few years. One night we talked again from a mutual place of closure when he told me he had regretted not seeing me again after our first meeting.

"I don't think about it every day, but when I do, I regret not seeing you again."

His realization made no difference to either of us by the time he revealed it because we had both moved on with our lives. I have to admit—it was good to know he had kicked himself a time or two over letting me get away.

*

I put on a happy face for Hunter. I managed to stay afloat just enough for him, but inside I was sinking further into the abyss of grief, unsure of how anything could change my situation.

Regardless of my heartache, I forced myself to not let the disappointment linger for long. I could not see then what I know now. Not having a second date with James was not the root of my problem. James did not matter to me the way I thought he could, he was just a symbol of my ongoing inner battle as I wished myself back to Wesley. Whenever anything went wrong, that is what I did—I wished myself back to the love that helped make me who I was and wanted to remain. I did not want to grow or change or discover anything I could not share with Wesley. Only Hunter received the part of me that projected a future. Despite my limitations as a woman, I masked the pain so I could meet my own expectations as his mother. Hunter would not know the hurt I suffered in silence.

Spring was in full swing, reminding me of all I loved about this wonderful place when I had decided to move here the summer before. The pulse of this town is recreation, family, activity. I welcomed it and found joy in the everyday life of our neighborhood and the friendships that came with it.

Soon I started meeting men who lived in the same town, even one on the same street. Tadd, who lived across the street from us, was immediately likable and friendly. For months we hung out together, never having a single physical exchange. We built a friendship, which made it safe to have him around Hunter. Tadd was a bachelor by all definitions, right down to the motorcycle he kept in his dining room. His bachelorhood made it possible for him to be spontaneous and available.

My dad was working in Washington for a few months, so Hunter was able to spend time with my parents while they lived nearby. He enjoyed it, and it also allowed me to be more spontaneous. Tadd was usually up for anything—movies, dinner, a night out with our mutual neighbors and friends. We would go to barbecues at a neighbor's house. Then he would walk me to my corner and continue walking to his house. Only once out of all the months he walked me home from the neighbor's house did he come inside on our way home. Hunter was gone, or I never would have invited him in. Even then, we just kissed a lot and, after a bit of awkwardness, ultimately resumed our friendship. Tadd and I did no permanent damage to our friendship by kissing on that one occasion. He still lives across the street and has a wonderful family of his own now. We are still friends.

During my brief stab at dating, I started to go out with my girlfriends. I had met supportive women who had equally supportive and secure husbands who did not mind us going out dancing that spring and summer—and sometimes even came along.

It was just one good time after another—dinner with friends, kids playing outside for hours, babysitters while we all went out together. My parents were around often, which made it possible for me to get out more. I never would have considered it if Hunter were not also enjoying himself and being cared for by them. Hunter still came first.

Hunter and I traveled less that summer. We had been to Texas and California a few times since moving to Washington. Now we enjoyed being home. We played outdoors—rollerblading, camping with friends, going to nearby parks. We spent most of our time with our neighbors, our new friends.

Nicki and Jed moved in about the same time we did. Nicki was giving, talkative, and high energy. Jed was a funny and outgoing man and welcomed me as Nicki's friend. Hunter became friends with their youngest son, who was the same age. Soon they added a leaf to their dining room table because they invited us for dinner so often. Nicki would whip up a delicious dinner, then set out bowls of fresh fruit and vegetables to round out the meal. She quickly became one of the closest friends I have ever had, during a time when we truly needed that friendship in our lives—the everydayness of our friendship was something I had never experienced before. We lived just a few doors away from each other, and for months there was not a day that went by we did not spend time together. They felt like a second family to Hunter and me.

Sara, who also lived down the street from us, was easygoing, strong and centered, with a no-nonsense, zero-drama approach to life and friendship. Her daughter Rebecca spent a great deal of time at our house, and we became equally close to her. Rebecca told me I was like a third mom to her, but I never knew who she referred to as her second mom.

Sara's husband Larry was the kind of neighbor I always figured Wesley would be in a similar situation, had we known of a widow needing his help. Larry helped me with everything that needed fixing. When a sprinkler line needed replacing, I usually did not even know about it until I would see him in my backyard replacing it. I had offered to pay him, but he never accepted money. I finally started leaving a six-pack of his favorite beer on his porch, so he could not refuse some form of compensation for his generosity. He was just a guy who did the right thing. Always has been, always will be. Their son Michael was equally helpful, often mowing my lawn during the summer and snow plowing my driveway during the winter. Michael always did, however, accept money for his help, as any teenager would.

Lynn and Bill and their two sons were also neighbors who enriched our lives. Hunter loved playing basketball with the boys in front of their house for hours. Lynn is the one person I know who is more protective of her children than I am of Hunter. I have spent many hours on her couch, the two of us talking about life while Bill prepared cappuccinos in the kitchen.

Hunter and I were so fortunate to be surrounded by these families who welcomed us into their lives without hesitation. These women were gifts to me, knowing new friendships are harder to come by as we grow older.

Many of my friends in Washington, Texas, and California, joked they were living vicariously through me as I began dating more. No matter how happy they were in their own relationships or marriages, there were a few who noted the exciting possibilities of getting to choose a companion again. I must admit, having the opportunity to choose what was right for me now that I was in my thirties, with a renewed sense of myself and the experiences I had been through, was exciting—when it was not miserable.

Learning the terms of dating and what each meant was very confusing to me. Being friends, as I was with Tadd, was obvious and simple to understand, but hanging out, which could mean any number of things, was most perplexing.

My dad suggested I practice dating by going out with guys I had no interest in being with long term.

"Sit across from a few guys over meals. Get used to the exchange between two people," he tried to tell me. "That way, when you meet a guy you actually like, you won't be so nervous because you've practiced."

One night when all of the girls went out, I met a guy whom I considered to be the most attractive man in the bar. I had never met a man in a bar. My friends dragged us out to dance then left us out on the dance floor alone. I managed to maintain eye contact with him, which was progress for me. His name was Matt. I saw him out a few more times while I was with the girls and eventually gave him my phone number. Just to illustrate my inexperience in even giving out my phone number, I asked him if he had a pen for me to write it down, and he answered, "No, but I have my cell phone," as he pulled it from his back pocket. I blushed. He called me a few days later.

Matt was the first guy I had spent considerable time with since Wesley's death. Even though a part of me was still not over being let down by James, I thoroughly enjoyed his company.

He was fresh from a break-up and was clear he was not ready to get involved. His words could not have been clearer, but we kissed a lot, which confused me. I still had a high school-level take on dating. My understanding was if you are kissing me, then you must be my boyfriend. We also had great conversations. He asked me questions about Wesley, and I listened to him as he shared his heartbreak over the girl he had hoped to eventually marry before she left him a few months before.

Matt was good to me—honest, clear about his intentions, always making sure I was okay with how things were going. If I had learned anything from the months of trying to remain in contact with James and getting rejected, it was when a man says he is not interested in being involved, for whatever reason, it was up to me to believe him. If I built it up to be more than it was with Matt, then it was my fault—kissing or no kissing. During the weeks I spent hanging out with him, I did not try to convince him we should be more than we were—even if, in the back of my mind, I felt as if we could be good together if we pursued a relationship.

Fortunately, I had become stronger through experience, so when his ex-girlfriend came back while Hunter and I were away in Texas for a week, and I returned home to the by now all-too-familiar "It's not you, it's me," speech, I was disappointed, but it did not level me again the way it had with James. He told me I had been his best friend in the weeks we had spent together, and he was right. We were more friends than anything else, helping each other through a rough time. Remaining friends with Matt helped with the transition from being friends who kissed to friends who did not.

I soon went back to online dating. It was fun for a while, but I was growing tired. None of it seemed worth the effort. I did meet a few quality men. Another guy from Idaho who kissed me on our second date and melted me like butter. A guy I saw in the grocery store who knew someone I knew, and who ended up calling me. After a few outings and watching his daughter crawl on the restaurant table with no redirection from him, he did not interest me at all.

I met another guy who, soon after I met him, I suspected might be gay. Within an hour of sitting down to lunch, he started telling me his mother had confronted him, asking him if he were gay. (I did not bring it up; he did.) We enjoyed good conversation and a long lunch, but I never heard from him again and was fine with that.

I had a code text with Corine when I went out on a date. (I added texting to my phone as part of the new way of dating communication.) I would often know right away what my interest level was, so if I was not interested, she would get a text from me within the first hour of the date that read: Nope. There were a number of nope dates. Like the guy whose truck was so jacked up with a lift kit he had to be overcompensating for something. He also told me about the golf cart he had spruced up with a $3,000 sound system. Growing up around golf and living on a golf course part of my life, I knew this was not ideal for the golfers around him. When I asked him how the other players felt about his souped-up cart, he said, "Screw 'em. I pay my country club dues just like they do." Later, when he told me his baby's mama was the devil, I figured there were two sides to this story, excused myself to the bathroom and sent the one-word text message to Corine: Nope.

When I became frustrated, I often turned to Trent, who had remained in my life and was a close friend. When dating became a puzzle I could not solve, having a man to bounce things off was just what I needed. Trent saved me hundreds of dollars in therapy—although I did also have a therapist I saw from time to time.

Some would wonder, why not see where things could go with Trent? We did actually spend time together considering being more than good friends, but it was incredibly awkward and was never going to work, so we ultimately chose not to sacrifice our nearly twenty-year friendship and quickly returned to what was familiar to us. He even went with me to New York City for a business trip, and we stayed at the Waldorf Astoria and slept in the same bed, knowing we were going as friends and unwilling to pay for two rooms. We enjoyed delicious meals and walks through Central Park. We lay in bed and watched David Letterman after being in the studio audience earlier that day and never once crossed over from our sides of the bed or across the friendship line we had drawn in the sand. Sleeping in a fabulous city like New York for three nights and never even brushing up against each other in our sleep—now that is true platonic friendship.

Trent once told me I am the kind of girl men marry, not the

kind of girl men casually date. He was also clear when I met a man who was ready for what I had to offer—stability, passion, true partnership—then it would be easy. When I had a hard time believing him, I thought back to the beginning of my relationship with Wesley and how easy it was. When it's right, it's easy, I remembered.

Some of the best advice I have ever received came from Trent. Even if, by his own admission, he had not figured it out yet for his own life, he still had a wealth of information for a beginner like me.

"I'll never have what I had with Wesley," I once told him. "And, no matter what, I'll never have the history with someone else I did with Wesley."

"There are many rich people," Trent began, in his compassionate yet matter-of-fact way. "But rich people come to their fortune in different ways—some through the stock market, others through owning a business and working hard every day. You got rich the rare, least-likely way: You and Wesley won the lottery. You may never win the lottery again, but you can still have great love and be rich."

His words settled into me like a warm glass of milk, easing a restless night's sleep. Trent made perfect sense, and his wisdom made me reconsider my expectations and how to adapt them.

Summer was coming to an end, Hunter was beginning first grade, and it was time to shift my focus.

If only it were that easy.

✳

After dropping Hunter off at school one day, I thought I spotted the woman whom Corine had approached on the dance floor months before to tell how happy she and her husband seemed together, but I did not speak to her. It was not until we met at a birthday party our sons were both invited to a few weeks later I was sure it was her. I reminded her of Corine's compliment, and the two of us became fast friends. Again, I was blessed to become friends with a woman whose husband and marriage I respected. She and her husband changed both Hunter's and my life.

Over the months, I became very close to both Jessica and her husband Corey. There were times the two of them would ask questions about Wesley, and all three of us would end up in tears. Jessica and Corey were solid, good parents and equally committed to each other. I envied them in so many ways, but my envy was so often met by them with such understanding and grace I could not be anything but comforted in their company.

Corey spent time with Hunter, inviting him along with him and his son to do things boys liked to do. It was being on Corey's baseball team that helped Hunter fall in love with the sport. Before Corey, Hunter had not wanted to play. When I took him to sign up for baseball when we first moved to Washington, before we even met Corey, Hunter said, "I don't want to play. There's just a bunch of dads here." It was a sad drive home that day because I knew Hunter was missing out on something he would enjoy if only he gave it a chance.

It took time and a conversation with my dad to get Hunter to play baseball. My father was certain Hunter would love and appreciate the sport once he understood it, and he was right. Since his first season playing for Corey, Hunter has lived and breathed baseball. The sport has enriched his life. To this day, he still tells me he talks to his dad when he is on the pitcher's mound or up at bat.

One night, on our way home from a baseball game where Hunter had been relief pitcher during the last two innings of a critical game, Hunter said to me, "You know I didn't do that by myself, Mom."

"I know, Buddy. You did it as a team."

"That's not what I mean," he explained to me, telling me what had actually happened. "Didn't you see me looking up at the sky when I was on the bump?"

"No, I didn't notice," I answered.

"I said, 'Come on, Dad. Help me out with this one,'" Hunter explained, just as he had when he was five years old and told me his daddy's invisible spirit helped him learn to ride a bike.

Hunter's team won that game, possibly thanks to Wesley.

I still often struggled seeing my future without Wesley, but Jessica and Corey would be there to pick up the pieces then and for months to come, just as my other friends had been doing. Honestly, I am surprised they all did not grow tired of me and my needs. Dating forced me to need even more. More understanding, more advice, more everything. While a few men I had met made it fun to be single for a while, nothing in the dating process made me feel good about myself or my future. I just sank deeper into grief, unsure of how to cross over.

The truth of my struggle had little to do with the men I met and liked or did not like, or even if they liked or did not like me. I just wanted my family back. I wanted Hunter to have a father figure and a positive male role model in someone we could share our lives. I wanted to stop needing my parents and my friends so much and to start a new life. I wanted to meet one of those men Trent told me about—one who would see me as a quality woman. I wanted it to be simple and to be right.

I wanted to put away the book I had bought soon after Wesley died, with instructions about how to tie a slip knot, how to rig a fishing pole, how to fly a kite. I feared I would never be able to teach Hunter what he needed to know to become the man he would have been if Wesley were still here. I was growing tired of the doubts constantly present in my life without him. Hunter was happy. He had my dad, my brother, and Corey to embrace the needs of this wonderful young boy, but I feared what they had to offer would never be enough.

I wanted all of this, while desperately trying to never get James'd again. "Getting James'd" to me was shorthand for setting an unrealistic expectation and being leveled by the reality that came with inviting someone into my heart who had no interest in the invitation. It was about losing myself in the idea of someone else, being forced to realize finding love was complicated, especially when looking too hard for it. I wanted to protect myself, but at the same time I had been through so much already that finding and losing love was not as frightening to me as the idea of not finding love at all.

Finding a man was not my only focus, but in the dark, quiet hours of the night when I lay in my empty bed, I longed for Wesley. I was in too much pain to realize then missing Wesley did not mean replacing him with someone who could take up space where he no longer did. None of my longing for love had anything to do with what I could offer someone or what he could offer me; it was just, quite simply, the result of my loneliness after losing great love and the family that came with it.

By the end of this season of trial and error dating, I did worse than getting James'd again. I got married.

CHAPTER TWENTY-FOUR

Ignoring the Voice

This is the part of my story I would rather leave out because I fall flat on my face. This is the part where I am most flawed and most human.

It is imperative to say I believe when making decisions from fear, no matter what the fear is, mistakes will always be made and hard lessons will always follow. In my case, I was filled with the fear of being alone and never being able to provide Hunter with the family he deserved.

As a single mom, I took excellent care of Hunter. We had a life of stability and routine, and we were surrounded by people who loved us and wanted us to be happy. We lived full lives. We traveled. We skied in the winter and rollerbladed in the summer. We picnicked at the park and played with Legos at home. Our lives were whole in the ways that mattered most to Hunter. When I started dating, he did not even know about it. My life, first and foremost, was about taking care of him. However, as a single woman, I was lost—and getting James'd did not help.

On New Year's Eve 2005, my parents stayed at my house

with Hunter, and I went out with my friends. I had not been out since summer. I was very drunk and sad by 10:30 that night, so Rosemary drove me home. I did not want to go into the house because Hunter was still awake, and I did not want him to see me drunk. So Rosemary called my dad on her cell phone and asked him to come outside. My mom said she would put Hunter to bed; my dad and I would go inside once Hunter was asleep.

My dad came to the car, and I immediately began to weep. I had drunk so much that night I honestly do not remember much, but I do remember my dad crying with me and holding my head in his hands while I cried and called out for Wesley.

"Where is he? Where is he, Dad?" I sobbed in his arms.

"He's with God," my dad answered, beginning to cry himself. "He's with God, and you are going to be okay."

"But I can't feel him anymore."

It was one of the most excruciating nights I had spent since Wesley died. It was the eve of a new year, and while many people were throwing confetti and setting New Year's resolutions for the future, I just wanted my old life back. I was growing weary and losing hope my life could be truly happy again. When I woke up the next day, I felt overwhelmed by my inadequacies. I told myself I was tired of being sad—I did not have the energy to be sad anymore, and I needed to pull myself together so I might have a chance to be happy again. But I was not even certain what happiness looked like for me.

That could have been a real turning point for me, and in many ways it was. I realized, with the help of those who loved me, and a stern talking to from Jessica, I was never going to find what I was looking for while searching in the heap of sadness that lived inside of me every day. Rather than shifting my focus from the sadness to rebuilding my life without the need for someone to fill it up, I just became more focused on having a family. I wanted to give up dating altogether and settle down. I did not realize my motivations because I was too close to the agony of being alone and the fear of thinking it would never change. As a result, when I met a man I thought was good for us soon after my breakdown on New Year's Eve—a man who seemed to be what I was looking for—I let myself justify falling for him. I had met Mike on one of the most popular online dating services where thousands of people find love and happiness everyday. I had hoped I could be one of those people.

Mike had lived three hours away, and we had spent months traveling back and forth on weekends between our houses sharing time together. Eventually, we involved our children and started talking about marriage. I knew Hunter and I could move to where he lived, and I could still run my business, but I would not uproot Hunter and move there without marrying Mike. Ultimately, Mike and I planned a wedding. Three weeks before the wedding I told him I wanted to call it off because I feared I was not ready. Three hours later I changed my mind. Three weeks after that we were married as planned. And three months after that, I knew I had made a huge mistake. I had rushed in.

I was still the same determined woman whose mind could not be changed once it was made up, but this was not a situation where everyone feared my choice and warned me not to marry Mike. Rosemary was the only one who tried to stop me, and it almost cost us our friendship because I refused to listen to her and forced her to support my decision unconditionally.

No one else tried to stop me from getting married. In fact, one night a few weeks before Mike and I got married, I called my dad in tears, still longing for Wesley and fearing I was making the wrong decision in marrying Mike. In my dad's own fear of my being alone, he made his own mistake.

"Just take one more leap, Lisa," my dad told me. "And if it doesn't work out, you can blame me," he joked.

I see now many people—people like my dad, who loved me and wanted happiness for Hunter and me—desired a happy ending. They wanted me to move beyond the constant sorrow and begin to live in a place of joy and contentment. They were also exhausted by the throes of my grief and needed a respite. If there was a chance I could find happiness with Mike, to all of us it seemed a chance worth taking.

I realize some people may doubt me because of the choices I made, but I believe it takes compassion to see someone through when what they do falls short of our expectations. I am willing to accept the judgment that may come in order to receive the grace that I deserve. There was a time when I was not strong enough or honest enough to tell this part of the story because of the failure it represented. I believed I should have been past the mistakes lingering ahead of me.

Mike and I were married for less than two years and only shared a house for ten months—and it was an absolute disaster. Hunter and I were always safe physically, but emotionally we were abandoned from the start. Everything inside of me struggled to find a resolution that resembled who I was and wanted to remain. I wanted Hunter to know marriage was important and the commitment was sacred, but whenever I resolved to stay in the marriage to teach him these values, it felt as if the lesson would be lost in the dysfunction in which we were living.

I believe in marriage and I value its meaning, but I just had not figured out how to be married to anyone but Wesley. Saying that implies this, alone, was the cause of the demise of my marriage to Mike—but it was only one of one hundred pieces that were never going to fit. In Mike's defense, he could have been Mr. Wonderful and it would not have mattered because I was not ready to commit my life to anyone in that way. In my defense, he was not Mr. Wonderful.

I ultimately decided it was better to let Hunter learn from the mistake of me marrying Mike rather than from the mistake of me staying married to him. I was not going to waste Hunter's childhood on a man who did not deserve us. I would take the advice of everyone who loved me and could see the situation up close—including my mom, who told me to get out. I would accept my failure and walk away. My mom called it my "get out of jail free card." After all I had been through, I guess she figured I deserved a second chance. Maybe it was a cop-out, but I love and respect my mother, and I needed to believe she was right—there was somewhere better for Hunter and me than the place I had just signed us up to be for the next fifty years.

Trent once told me, "If it takes you the rest of your life to figure out how to live the rest of your life without the man you planned to spend the rest of your life with, then that's okay."

The truth was never more obvious. I did not know how to live without Wesley—and I did not want to learn. Just as I had done before when things got rough, I had wished myself back to Wesley and a time when I was sharing my life with a man who loved me and our family was his first priority. If I was ever going to learn to live without longing for him, I was going to have to move beyond that place.

Living in a marriage and house with Mike, absent of even the very minimum of love and adoration, threatened my very being. I could not breathe in the marriage, thrive in it, be myself in it. I was suffocating as I gasped for every bit of life that was never going to come. Mike and I went days without talking, weeks without trying, and months without caring. It was never going to be anything more than it was from the very beginning. He agreed to go to counseling: that did not work. I even went to the counselor alone once to see what I could do on my own to turn it around. To my surprise, he told me to get out of the marriage.

"I'll deny ever saying this to you," he said firmly. "But I have to tell you I think you should get out of this marriage and get out now. It doesn't fit and makes even less sense."

"But I married him," I said defensively, looking away from him as I spoke, unable to make eye contact with a man whom I was paying to tell me the truth that was too hard to hear.

"Then unmarry him. For this marriage to ever work, he will have to rise or you will have to fall, and he'll never rise."

He was right. Not only was I at tremendous emotional risk of losing everything I knew about having a healthy relationship, but Mike's personal and business decisions had caused me enormous financial vulnerability. Wesley was not able to leave me millions of dollars when he died, but he left me enough to take good care of myself and Hunter, and I was not willing to risk that for anyone. I might have rushed into marrying Mike, but even so, I had asked all the right questions—I had even asked him about his taxes and his credit. He just had not told me the whole truth, or he had not been concerned enough about these matters to know the truth about his own financial situation.

Imagine my horror when I was thrust into an IRS audit of his business spanning the past eight years just three months after we were married. After getting to know his lawyer and accountant during my exhaustive efforts to help sort through Mike's mind boggling financial mess, each of them told me I did not belong with him or in the middle of his financial chaos. Mike, however, told me repeatedly that we were supposed to be a team, and I was supposed to help him as his wife. If I had been given even a minimal amount of emotional support to help me cope with what I had just been forced to face, I would have been more capable of helping, but Mike was a taker and gave me nothing in return. The financial extremes were also indicative of the way he managed his personal life and his expectation of how I should deal with all matters relating to it. He knew nothing about what it meant to be a team.

Soon after my visit to the marriage counselor, I ended the marriage with no opposition from Mike. I filed the papers myself and went to the hearing alone.

When I walked in the door of the courthouse, the man who took my paperwork joked, "Are you here for the weight loss meeting?"

He read the confusion on my face and quickly added, "Because you look like you are carrying a lot of weight on those shoulders. A lot of weight you can leave behind when you leave here today a free woman."

I smiled at his observation and just how right he was.

As I waited for the hearing and my turn to present the case to the judge, I literally felt gleeful. I felt as if I had another chance to live the life I was meant to live. I wanted nothing more than the opportunity to learn from this and move on with my life in a better and more productive way, no longer consumed by what I did not have but grateful for what I did have. And I had a lot. I had not sold my house when I married Mike, I still had friends who loved me, parents who would always be there for me, and a son who still believed in me with all his heart and would follow me with trust wherever we went.

Where we went next was home. Back to the neighborhood where our healing began. Back into the grace of God.

One day, soon after I decided to go through with the divorce, I said to Hunter, "I need to ask your forgiveness for something, Buddy."

"What do you need my forgiveness for?" he asked, confused.

"I need to ask you to forgive me for the mistake of marrying Mike and moving you away from our home," I began. "I never meant to hurt you or make your life any harder than it already was after your dad died. I wanted us to have a family, and I thought Mike and his kids could give us that family. But I was wrong, so very wrong. You and I are already a family, without anyone else. You and I will always be okay."

"I forgive you," Hunter said smiling. "Can we go home to our old house now?"

"That's exactly what we are going to do," I assured him, smiling back at him.

I also had one of many talks with God and asked His forgiveness. The voice inside I had relied on all of my life was the voice God had given me. The voice had never steered me wrong; only I could be responsible for detouring from the path I knew was meant for me, when I leaned on my own understanding and chose to disregard the gift of the voice. Ignoring it brought consequences that were mine to face. I accepted this and received the forgiveness I asked for from God and from Hunter. Any remorse or shame I carried for my shortcomings after that was a human response to my failure. I have accepted the outcome. More than accepted it, I have learned from it because the lesson is always the gift we give to ourselves after the mistake passes and the pain we put ourselves through diminishes.

Mike had never been married before, and he told me after the divorce he would never get married again. He said he was not cut out for it, and I have to agree. But I was just as unprepared to be married as he was because I was still deeply in love with Wesley— and not just the idea of him, but with the real him. I have tried to never make Wesley more angelic than he was, very aware of how we often immortalize people the longer they are gone from our lives, whether in death or in divorce. I remember what worked and what did not work about the marriage and the life we shared, but at the end of every day, I always wanted to be married to Wesley and do whatever it took to stay married to him. I was happy, and so was he. I would imagine, for Mike, living up to my dead husband and Hunter's dead father was an insurmountable task, because Wesley was still alive and beating in my unhealed, broken heart. It probably would not have mattered how hard Mike tried to live up to the life and love I shared with Wesley, and he should not have had to, it never would have worked because I never could have functioned the rest of my life in his chaotic, seemingly normal to him, life. Wesley in my heart or no Wesley in my heart.

After the divorce, I was happier than I had been since Wesley became sick. I was content with experiencing life less like a widow and more like a woman. I spent months being truly alone with Hunter, with absolutely no interest in dating or even considering dating. I felt peace and restoration from embracing my life as it was and allowing the greatest lessons to come through in their own time.

The truth, I finally discovered, was the life Hunter and I shared was the life we were meant to share. We had people who loved us, but we were the only family we needed to be complete in the way I remembered from when Wesley was alive. The family Hunter and I had become on our own was timeless and solid, just like the family we were before Wesley died. Our new family was much like the family we had been. We resolved conflicts, balanced schedules, never said I can't, and always said I love you and Goodnight at the end of every day.

For years, I had missed Wesley beyond what I felt I could bear, but now I knew I could no longer focus on what my life was missing. I could no longer perform the balancing act of feeling joy about an event or an emotion and yet feeling sorrow because Wesley was not there to share it with me. I stopped feeling sad when Hunter did well on the pitcher's mound at his baseball game because his dad was not there to see it, and just allowed myself to feel the joy of watching him play. It was not easy, and it certainly was not automatic. I had to teach myself that focusing on the past or projecting too far into the future left me with uncertainty and sadness, and the only way to begin again was to remain in the present.

I stopped seeing being alone, without a man to share my life, as temporary, and accepted and embraced all I had to offer outside of a relationship. Hunter and I could miss Wesley every day, but we had to carry on. Even though Wesley's life ended decades before any of us wanted it to end, our family still lived on in each other.

Ultimately, after questioning everything I thought I knew about myself and the mistakes I had made while in search of a family for my son—the little boy who, it turned out, had all the family he needed right here with me and me alone—I went back to where we started and learned one of the kindest lessons of all: grace.

Through much despair, I discovered—perhaps from the moment Wesley took his last breath—it was supposed to be just Hunter and me. Through relinquishing my expectations, I realized loss and tragedy does not change whom we love or how much we love. The love lives on inside us. And in my life, the love lives on in Hunter. His father is forever stamped in the essence of him, and in Hunter, his dad remains.

It took years, but through the mire of grief and the reality of rebuilding our lives, I finally realized the life Hunter and I had was the life God intended. I accepted there was an enormous reason for Wesley being gone, and it was my life's work to bring us through it to happiness and fulfillment—not in spite of Wesley dying but because of it. I stopped questioning whether I was enough for Hunter and discovered Hunter, now nearly ten years old, had been without his father for as long as he was with him—and he was not only surviving but thriving.

That summer, Hunter and I returned to Texas for a visit with Wesley's family as we had every summer since moving away. Only this time it felt different. This time it was not sad. I did not cry when I went to sleep or feel an emptiness starting each day. This time, I was able to enjoy the experience of being in Texas and near people who knew and loved Wesley, without feeling I was leaving him behind when it was time to go home.

On the flight home from Texas, I wrote most of this chapter on napkins and gained a new understanding that was revealed to me from the moment the plane took off as I watched Houston fade below us in the distance. For the first time since leaving Texas and moving to Washington almost four years before, I finally felt Hunter and I were heading home. After years of feeling homeless while living in a beautiful house absent of the man I had slowly learned to live without, the voice I had abandoned for such a long time was rejoicing in the choice to begin again.

After years of learning to let go, and finally setting myself free of the sadness I thought would always be at the forefront of my life, I began to truly heal, and I finally forgave myself. I had searched for love because I thought there had to be an equally deserving and capable man on the other side of Wesley and what he left behind. As I wrote on the napkin, I looked over at Hunter asleep against the window of the airplane, and the most profound thought came to mind: The only man who completes this story is still a boy. His name is Hunter and he is, and forever will be, our son. I needed nothing more than that and, without even knowing it, simply by moving forward, I was making room for every wonderful thing waiting for us around the corner.

I had only known myself as the woman who loved Wesley. It was time to discover who I was without him.

CHAPTER 25

Crossing the Abyss

"Are you nervous?" Gabby asked me as we waited for our cue to go on stage.

"No, really, I'm not," I told her, feeling confident about the hour ahead.

"Me either," she responded, equally confidently. "We're gonna do great!"

The *Friends* show had ended almost three years before, but my plan to get media to pay attention to my company because the show used our products as set decoration was still working. Just six days before Gabby and I found ourselves standing backstage of *The Rachael Ray Show*, I had decided it was time to get back to work in a marketing capacity after a long hiatus. I figured out the email address of the senior producer of the show and sent her an email about my story—and her associate producer called me the next day.

When my first book came out, the publicity firm we hired did a horrible job, so I learned how to do my own publicity. Still, I did not have media training or really know how to respond to the publicity the book was getting. I once sent a gift basket to Oprah Winfrey and Gayle King, Oprah's best friend and editor at large at *O: The Oprah Magazine*. The basket had candles, chocolates, bubble bath, my book, and a card I made that read: *Everything you need to curl up with a good book, including the book*. Gayle called me as she was opening the basket, so impressed with the gift idea. The only problem was, I had not expected the phone call, so I was not prepared for the conversation, and I was less than impressive. I did not even have a pitch prepared, so her spontaneous and gracious phone call to me was an opportunity lost.

By now I had learned to expect success, so when *The Rachael Ray Show* producer called, I knew I had just a couple minutes to convince her I was right for their show about entrepreneurial moms. My pitch worked, and just a few days later, when Gabby (another entrepreneurial mom I had met just hours before) and I were about to go on stage for the show to tell our stories to millions of viewers, I truly was not nervous. Preparation meets opportunity, and I was fully prepared.

A few days after the show, I received a return call from some- one at *Extreme Makeover: Home Edition*, a show I had also con- tacted. They liked my idea of using our products to help decorate an upcoming house they were building for a family in need. We sent a number of products to them and a few months later the show featuring them aired.

Within a week of returning from *The Rachael Ray Show* tap- ing, one of my friends and colleagues, John St. Augustine, heard I had been on the show and called to invite me to be on two shows that were part of *Oprah & Friends Radio*, which he produced. "You must be ready to get back to work," he said. And I was.

Being on Oprah's radio network was the fulfillment of a dream. I had grown up watching her show and knowing somehow, some way, I would be part of the vast platform she had created to help and entertain others. I related to how she viewed herself. Even as a poor child living in Mississippi, she knew of her own greatness, no matter her obstacles. When I checked into the hotel, I stood in awe as I looked out the window at Chicago. I remembered all the times I had heard Oprah announcing "guests of the Oprah Winfrey Show stay at the Omni Suites Hotel, in the heart of Chicago's Magnificent Mile." There I was, in the heart of it myself, preparing for the next day's taping.

When I went to the studio to tape the two radio interviews, a woman in the control room listened to the interview. When I finished, she approached me with her card and asked if I had representation. She said she had a friend at William Morris Agency in Los Angeles who would be interested in meeting me. At the time, I did not understand what an enormous opportunity that was. I was just getting back to work, and everything was happening so fast. I took her card but did not call. I used to regret this, but I have learned enough to know everything comes to us right on time.

Leaving Chicago, I fell apart. I spent the entire ride to the airport on the phone talking to Bev and sobbing about Wesley, wishing he were alive to share this with me. I had not let missing him interfere with the joy of the experience, but my emotions could no longer be stifled when it was over. When the limo driver dropped me off at the airport, he tried not to be intrusive after hearing my conversation with Bev, but he kindly put his hand on my shoulder and said, "You take care of yourself, honey. You're going to be just fine. You'll see."

I wanted to believe him.

It seemed miraculous how every door was opening, as if this little part of my world had been waiting for me to come alive again and get out there and do something. It reminded me of how important it is to know sometimes simply making the decision to move forward opens our lives to opportunities that otherwise could not penetrate the emotional and financial walls we build around us. My story had not changed, nor had my ability to tell it. What had changed was my willingness to share the story.

The company I had started just a year before Wesley became sick had never been my dream, or what I considered my purpose in life. I always knew it was a vehicle for better things to come. Consequently, when a potential investor heard about my growing business and flew out to meet with me about developing a product line for stores like Target or Macy's, I was quietly reluctant. I had met plenty of entrepreneurial moms who were wildly successful, but their success had come at a high price. Those women who managed to balance success with their home life often had a supportive partner at home taking care of the family, making sure the kids were okay.

Had Wesley still been alive, this opportunity may have looked more appealing to me because he could have offered the balance it would have required for our family life, but on my own, as a single mom to Hunter, I was reluctant. When the investor talked about my needing to be in China on a regular basis while developing the product line, I thought about the women I knew who struggled with the balance and were miserable about it. I did not want to be that woman or that mother, so I was relieved when the deal started unraveling. I happily let it go.

Those discussions came at an economic high point, but soon the economy took a downturn, and my customers were having to choose between ordering high-end children's products or filling up their SUV gas tank. I felt the business had served its purpose, so I shut down the website and closed the business. I had a new plan in mind for myself, a plan that would truly set me on a path to know and embrace my purpose. I was crossing the abyss of grief and letting go of the limitations I had placed on my life and experiencing rewards at every turn.

For nearly half of Hunter's life, I had worked from home. As far as he knew, people were able to stay home and work in their pajamas if they wanted. He knew nothing of a work ethic outside of our home, and I knew I was the only one who could teach him. It was time for me to leave the house.

For several months, I had thought about doing my own radio show. I had developed an interest after being interviewed on numerous talk radio shows when my first book was released, but being on Oprah Radio increased my motivation. I promised myself I would have a show by December 2007, within six months of setting my goal.

By January 2008, though, I had done nothing to work toward achieving my goal, but in February, I finally moved ahead. I produced a demo CD and got a meeting with the general manager of seven radio stations in the market where I live. After an hour-long meeting, he decided to give me the opportunity to produce and host *The Life with Lisa Show*. It would be a guest-oriented show covering topics I related to in my own life—motherhood, health, entrepreneurship, marriage, family, and community. He also offered me an additional part-time job that would be created for me, community service director for all seven radio stations.

I committed to part-time employment, ensuring Hunter would remain my first priority. With this job I would still be able to pick him up from school each day and be at every school and athletic event. My new boss understood I had promised Wesley to take care of Hunter for both of us, and it was a full-time experience I would not trade for any job opportunity.

One of the greatest benefits of my new venture has been that it belongs to both Hunter and me. Hunter is involved in the community aspect of my work, learning to reach out to those in need who can benefit from our help and empathy. He enjoys coming to my office and often sits in the studio quietly listening as I interview guests during my live show.

"Mom, how did you get your radio show?" Hunter once asked me.

"I paid attention," I told him.

"To what?" Hunter asked, looking confused.

"To life," I answered.

He smiled big at me. I love it when he smiles big.

I always tell Hunter he has the right to ask for anything—but it is best to have earned the right. If he comes to me and asks if he may go outside to play basketball with his friends, I do not grill him with "Is your room clean?" or "Did you do your homework?" I assume he knows my clear expectations and these things are already done, or he would not be asking. It teaches him to be responsible for himself without me having to nag him about the obvious.

When I asked for my radio show, I knew I had lived through enough life experience, both joyful and arduous, and worked through enough adversity and triumph, to have earned the show I wanted to produce and host. Of course, the general manager of the radio station also had the right to turn me down. Fortunately, he did not. But if he had turned me down, I would have kept pitching the show idea to other radio stations until I got the opportunity I knew I deserved.

In the past decade of my life, I have been a wife and mother, a cancer survivor, an author, an entrepreneur, and a widow. I have met countless survivors like myself, both in illness and in life. My message has remained the same, one borrowed from Henry Ford: "Whether you believe you can do a thing or not, you are right." I had torn this quotation from an early issue of *O Magazine,* and it has been taped next to my kitchen sink, both in Washington and in Houston, since 1999.

It holds true in all areas of life. I consider this statement and its possibilities every day. Whether facing a life-threatening illness, changing careers, going on a first date after fifteen years of thinking I would never have to, or being enlightened by the child I hope to inspire each day, there is possibility at every turn. I have always believed in finding the balance between what I have lost and what I can gain from the experience of life. And if I help others along my own journey, then it is the right life.

CHAPTER 27

Thoughts From My Father

Someone who meets my dad casually might never see the side of him I know or that he shares in the pages that follow. This side comes out only when I write a book and ask him to write a chapter or to people who are lucky enough to be born to him or to love someone born to him. He is a man who fills a room, often with his politics and always with his opinions. While he is not perfect, I love him. He and my mom have both been there for me since the day I was born.

I love my dad for the times he held me in his arms while I cried with a broken heart, and he did his very best to put me back together. I love him for the commitment he shows to my son, and for the memories he holds of Wesley. He is my dad, and I think he is capable of helping more people than I may ever encounter myself with the beautiful words he shares here and with his soft, soft heart.

Here is my father's chapter:

There are many short stories to tell in a long story.

The first memory I recall of Wes is an old one. He was eleven years old.

His father, Alton, was one of the best friends I've had in life. Donna and Alton had divorced years before and Alton had remarried Laverne. I met Alton when he and Laverne moved to California to be near Laverne's family. They had two daughters. His two sons with Donna, Wes and Wayne, later moved to California from Texas where they had been living with their mom and Jimbo, in order to live with Alton and Laverne. Our neighborhood was filled with kids, including my own, Vance and Lisa. Our neighborhood had dead-end streets, no sidewalks, big yards, and huge, majestic valley oak trees, with a 96-acre field bordered by our street and the Sacramento River.

Our kids' freedom was theirs to lose if they ventured beyond where they could hear my wife Carmen yell for them or Wes's Aunt Lavaun's whistle to call the kids inside from a long, unsupervised day of play. Things were different then. We never had to worry about our kids. There was safety in numbers and dead-end streets.

Wes and Wayne lived near us for a few years, until Alton and Laverne decided to move back to Texas. None of the kids was too happy about it, but Wes wanted to move back. He was proud to be a Texan, and he missed his mom and Jimbo. His heart was always in Texas.

About a week before they were scheduled to move, I saw Wes walking down the street on my way home from work. His head was down, his hands were in his pockets, and he was kicking rocks as he walked. He was the kind of kid who liked an audience, and he was prepared to put on his act for anyone who might happen by. Unfortunately for him, I was the one who came along; I kept on driving. I remember thinking it was a good act, but I paid him no more attention.

I didn't know then he had already stolen Lisa's heart, and further down life's road than a man can see, he would steal ours.

It wasn't as if he went away and we never thought of him again. We spent weekends, holidays, and special occasions with his family, the extended family who still lived in California. We all became lifelong friends, so we always knew where Wes was in Texas, and we heard the news when he joined the Navy.

When Lisa was a teenager, she begged me to let her go to Texas to visit Alton and Laverne and their kids for Thanksgiving. She had to have her mom on her side for this one to get by me, and she did.

I've always said a son can look his mother straight in the eye and lie to her, and she will believe him. A mother doesn't want to think her son will lie to her. It wasn't until I was much older I realized daughters do the same thing to dads. Now I'm not talking about stealing, doing drugs and alcohol, or running with the wrong crowd, or that kind of lie, because we had good kids. I'm talking about the kind we talk about later in life and maybe even laugh about. Lisa didn't lie to me about Texas, but she didn't tell me the whole truth either.

Lisa made her way to Texas, and guess who was there visiting his parents while on leave from the Navy? Wes. This is when their story changed. Before this visit, Wes only knew Lisa as a little kid—she was only ten when he moved away. She was just Vance's little sister, and although our families were close friends, she meant nothing more to him than that. But by now she was nearly sixteen and he was turning eighteen, and instead of being a kid, she was becoming a beautiful young woman. The seed was planted for both of them. Years later I found out they kissed for the first time during that visit, and it used to make me mad, like it would any dad. Now I just laugh at the thought because every single thing in this life happens for a reason.

Later, as adults, they fell in love, and Lisa soon moved to Texas. Her mom and I didn't want her to go, but we knew there was no stopping her. Nothing ever stops Lisa once her mind is made up. By then Alton and his family had moved back to California again. Alton was thrilled they were together. He was so happy. He and Lisa were very close. She'd get mad at me when she was growing up and go to him with all her troubles. As a man with a son, I imagine any dad would be thrilled to have my daughter as a daughter-in-law. We were all there when they got married a few years later.

Lisa and Wes visited us often from Texas. In December 1995, they flew to California for a visit during their winter break from college. The day after Christmas, Lisa was diagnosed with cancer. Our family had never been through worse. Wes never left her side. All of us fought for her, prayed for her, and helped her get well. Lisa beat the cancer, wrote a book to help others, and she and Wes had the miracle child they named Hunter. We were all healed.

When I wrote the chapter for Lisa's first book, looking back at our experience with cancer as a family, it was all about triumph, the strength of the human spirit, and the victory of overcoming our greatest fears. Battle faced, battle won.

Alton would never see the battle Lisa fought, or the honorable man his son was throughout it because he died a year after they got married, a year before Lisa got sick. He never met our grandson Hunter, the grandson he and I share. He never read a single page of the story that was Lisa's to write all those years ago. To this day, when I'm watching Hunter pitch during a baseball game, I wish Alton were there. Nothing would have been more fun for the two of us than that.

As a man who has been married for forty-three years, the father of two wonderful grown children who exceed my own capabilities, and grandchildren who make it all worth while, my most frequent prayer is for the safety and the happiness of my children and their children.

When Wes got sick and wasn't getting better, I knew the balance of happiness and safety I prayed for my family every night would never be the same. I knew my daughter would never be the same. The story as we had known it so far was being rewritten.

There was nothing Wes wanted more than to marry my daughter and have a son. He took great pride in his family, and the two of them together built a solid life. As time went on and Wes became sicker, he got angry. As much as I hated to watch what he was doing to himself and to my daughter in his anguish, I knew it wasn't his fault, and Lisa knew that, too. He was just a man with a body that wasn't allowing him to live the way he wanted to live, and he knew he would never grow old and see his son grow up. He was only thirty-five years old. I don't know what that was like for him.

We were there for them as much as we could be. My wife Carmen did what she had done when Lisa was sick—she selflessly showed up every day in every way she could. She was in Texas for weeks at a time, helping with Hunter so Lisa could take care of Wes. I only visited a few times that year because of work. Carmen told me about what they were going through, but it was worse for her to see it up close.

Nine months after Wes got sick, Carmen and I met Vance in Texas to spend the New Year's with Wes, Lisa, and Hunter. We tried to celebrate New Year's Eve, but in the back of our minds we were haunted by the secret fear it might be Wes's last.

Late that New Year's Eve, Wes and I sat talking in their Jeep after a few shots of whiskey. The car was parked in the driveway of their house and we weren't going anywhere. Wes was so incredibly angry and enraged that night. He was venting his fear and disappointment. This young, driven family man was in a rage. He knew he was dying, and he wanted no part of it. I would have let him beat on me if it would have somehow helped ease his despair. I just tried to receive his rage; I would like to think I was there for him. Wes and I took away some of the darkness that night. I would later realize that was our own, private goodbye. The morning we left to go home, Wes slipped a note into the Jeep for Carmen. He thanked her for her help while he was sick. The note is still one of Carmen's most treasured possessions and, as she, too, would later realize, it was their own, private goodbye.

My daughter is like a pit bull. She's a fighter, and I have never seen anyone fight harder than she fought for Wes. He knew he was safer in life and in death with her on his side. She loved and cared for him beyond measure. After his transplant, when she finally said she needed me there, I got on a plane, and I did what she needed me to do. She didn't ask me to stay with her or need me to hold her hand. She didn't care what was happening to her. She needed to save Wes, and she needed me to take care of Hunter when she couldn't.

You attract what you are. Lisa has always been surrounded by the most amazing people. When I arrived in Alabama, just a few weeks before Carmen could join me, Lisa's best friend since junior high school, Tami, was there with Hunter and had been for two weeks. Lisa came home when she could, but she needed people she trusted to take care of Hunter. He had never been away from her and Wes for long, hardly more than a night or two with his grand-parents. Wes and Lisa were good parents, and they took good care of Hunter with little help from anyone else. Their absence from Hunter at this time in their lives was hard on them all, but it could not be helped.

Before Tami left to go home, she gave me maps to locations throughout the city with the best activities and restaurants for kids. She hadn't just sat around watching television. She had taken good care of her best friend's son.

The night after Tami left, I couldn't get Hunter to sleep. He was lost without his parents. Lisa would come home to their apartment during the day when she could, but Wes wasn't doing well and she couldn't risk leaving him alone at night at the hospital. Finally, around 3 a.m., I asked Hunter again what was wrong, and he finally answered, "I miss Ms. Tami."

I knew he missed his mother even more. To help him get to sleep, I promised Hunter his mom would be home the next night. When I told Lisa of the promise I'd made, she asked me to never again make him a promise about when she would be home. From one day to the next, Wes's condition made it impossible for her to leave his side. She came home that night, but she was torn by her choice, as she had been every day since Wes' transplant weeks before.

She kept the promise I made, but after that night home with Hunter, she didn't sleep at the apartment again for several more days because of the complications Wes was suffering. Carmen arrived on a Saturday afternoon, the day before Easter. Wes was finally doing better and about to get out of bed for the first time the next day, so Lisa decided to stay home with us, celebrate Easter the next morning, then go to the hospital for the rest of the day.

Just after 8:30 a.m. on Easter morning, the hospital called to say Wes didn't have a pulse, so I drove Lisa to the hospital as fast as I safely could. She had been through this before. The phone call, the drive to the hospital, not knowing what she would find when she arrived. But this time, she seemed to know it would be the last time. And it was.

I listened in horror as the doctors told Lisa there was nothing more they could do for Wes, and she told them to let him go. I stood next to her as she said goodbye to the shell Wes's spirit had left behind after he died just moments before. My daughter had lost her husband. Hunter had lost his father. We had lost a son.

I felt helpless as I stood next to Lisa. Through her agonizing pain, she couldn't even see me. I couldn't help her. There were no words I could say; there was nothing but death. Wes was gone.

I placed my hands firmly on her shoulders. As much as I wanted to be strong for her, I think she was holding me up as she said goodbye to Wes. I watched her as she rubbed the eagle feather tattoo on Wes's ankle, the tattoo just like the one on her ankle. It had a private, special meaning for them, although I don't know what it is, and it wasn't my business to ask. That moment became a part of me, as much as the day she was born. It has never left me, and it never will.

Lisa asked me to call a few people before we left the hospital. I told her it could wait, but she insisted it couldn't. I called Vance, then Kelli, then Wes' best friend Mike. His was the hardest call for me to make. When he answered the phone, he was excited to hear from me. The reason I was calling didn't dawn on him. When I told him Wes had died, I broke his heart. By then, no one believed Wes would live a long life, but we didn't think we would lose him so soon. So much pain.

Lisa and Hunter got on a plane for Texas that day. Carmen and I stayed behind to drive their Jeep home with as much as we could fit in the car. The rest would have to wait. We'd planned to spend the night in the apartment and begin the ten-hour drive the next morning, but we couldn't bear to stay there without them. We drove through the night and arrived at Lisa and Wes's home just before dawn.

Family and friends had already begun to gather. My constant thoughts were of Lisa and Hunter. What could her mother and I do for them? How could we ease their pain? There were no answers. As hard as it was for Carmen and me to witness, only Lisa could find her way through the loss of Wes. I could only pray that somehow, some way, my daughter would find happiness again.

Throughout the days after Wes died, we all did all we could for one another. After the funeral, Vance, Wes's cousin Jay, and I finished that half pint of whiskey Wes and I had started a few months before, the night we sat in the Jeep. The bottle is at the bottom of Jimbo's lake now, where we put it that day as we drove away from the place Wes loved so much.

In the days after Wes died, people assumed Lisa would move back home to California and leave Texas, but Lisa said Texas was her home. Her mother and I knew telling her anything different would be futile. Lisa was still the woman with her mind made up. We knew if she chose to leave Texas, it would have to be her idea.

Damn, if she didn't take Hunter on a two-month voyage and find her way back to where she had started years before, on the West Coast, where she put her feet down and began to build a new life. Raising Hunter was her focus and her joy. Her friends were there, and so were Carmen and I, as much as we could be, but there came a time when Lisa asked us to leave. She knew she needed to find her own way, and she and Hunter had to learn how to live without Wes. We couldn't help her with that, so we went away and came back as often as it seemed right to return.

As much as I knew Lisa was hurting, and even though I couldn't imagine her life without Wes, I knew she would eventually fight her way back, though it would take a very long time. What can I say about my daughter? She's a fighter. Get cancer, beat cancer. Want to be with Wesley, go and get him. She was and still is capable of anything and everything.

I think maybe the way people get past such excruciating times is they have to act their way through, each of them playing a role they hope to eventually fulfill. Carmen and I tried to be strong parents for Lisa and a consistent presence and influence for Hunter. Lisa tried to be a good mother first, and learned to be a woman without her husband only second, after giving Hunter what he needed of her. The rest of Wes's family and friends, they all had to find their way, too.

Somehow, through the sorrow and pain, we survive. This hole we thought we could never crawl out of, we do. The despair that lingers even today softens as the little gifts of life accumulate. Eventually, the mourning process becomes the healing process.

Today, Lisa has survived. Even more than survived, she has prevailed. Wes would be so proud of her, never having to worry a day about the son he left behind. Hunter is twelve now. He's bright, funny, and a Little League All-Star. It's been seven years since Wes died. Seven years... I think we have learned to live with our loss, but I still think about him, now with more smiles and less pain.

Sometimes, when I notice a picture of him on the wall in our home, I think, "Damn it, Wes. Where are you?" and it still pisses me off he's gone. But instead of sinking into sorrow now, I kind of accept it, take a deep breath, and try to be thankful for all we have.

I said there are many short stories to tell in a long story. As our lives continue to unfold and the story keeps going, I still pray for the same thing every night: for the safety and the happiness of my children and their children, because this gift is the true joy in my life.

Lisa asked me months ago to write this chapter. I didn't want to, but I did it for her. In the beginning I dreaded it because I didn't want to go back to the dark place where this part of our story lives. But what I found along the way, while writing it all down, is this story is also one of triumph, just like the chapter I wrote for Lisa's first book. For me, it has been a reminder of how fortunate we are to have so much love in our lives that helps us endure.

I shudder to think of the people who have to go through something like this without family or friends. How do they find their way? I think that's why Lisa does what she does. I wrote one chapter, but she wrote a whole book. She didn't do it for herself, as I'm sure it wasn't easy for her. She did it for the people she may never meet who will be strengthened by the people and process that gave Lisa the strength to heal and move on.

I am not qualified to speak for or of God, but I do speak to Him. I do believe Jesus is our savior and our God is loving and true. I have felt God's love and protection. I have felt comfort in the sorrow and despair of life. I have seen the miracle of birth and watched in awe as the sun sets—all are miracles. The miracle to save us all is the gift of faith. I still have faith all will be right.

Just walk into the light, Wes.

Love,

Dad

CHAPTER 26

Big Love

Sometimes waiting for the ending of a story is the hardest part. Not knowing how it ends can make the beginning either wondrous or tortuous. So can wanting something wonderful to remain, or something horrible to heal and bring us back to life.

Wesley's death was the end of many things for me. It was the end of Hunter's life with his father. It was the end of knowing Wesley was here to see me through the hardships of life with his strength and his discernment. It was the end of believing nothing bad could ever happen to him and our family would always be okay.

What I could not realize in the grief of losing Wesley was it was more a beginning than an end for me. I could not see the gift of surviving the loss of him; I could only see the burden of it. It took years for me to understand I was capable of more without him than I was when he was here, simply and truly because of the experience of losing him. With loss comes lessons, with fear comes strength, and with agony comes hope. None of this was obvious to me in the months and even years after Wesley died, but I learned my own truth along the way. In every corner of my heart, I wanted to prevail. I wanted to heal. And I wanted to be more than a widow. I wanted to be whole again, even after—or especially after—all the tragedy losing Wesley brought to my life. It took a long time to find myself in the complicated maze of grief. It was not until I accepted the lessons of loving and losing Wesley that I truly began to appreciate everything he was to me, both in life and in death.

It was during this time I received a phone call from Wesley's brother Wayne.

"I think you might want to sit down for this," he told me. He reassured me he did not have bad news, but what he had to tell me might be overwhelming to hear.

"Okay," I said, walking with my cell phone to the private hallway in the back of the studio where I worked. I preferred privacy to sitting down.

"A guy named John just started working here with me. I don't know him well, and he knows nothing about Wes," Wayne said to me. "I'd heard he communicates with dead people."

My heart immediately began to race.

"When we were working together yesterday, he looked past me and said, 'You have a visitor. He says he's your brother.'"

My teeth began to chatter, as always happens when I am nervous or excited.

"I was skeptical, because I am not too convinced of these things, but he was very convincing. The whole conversation took about twenty minutes and from the start it was like he knew Wes. He said Wes was a strong force and that he was demanding John's attention. Wes wouldn't leave him alone."

I did not speak. I just waited for what Wayne would say next.

"He said things about Wes that only people who knew him would know. He said Wes loved to fish. Then, Lisa, he talked about a big, black dog!"

"Huck," I whispered. Our black lab Huckleberry Finn had been stolen a few years before Wesley got sick. He was the biggest black lab we had ever seen. By now he would have died of old age.

"Yes! Huck!" Wayne exclaimed, trying to tell me everything John had told him without missing a single detail. "He told me Huck is with Wes."

I started to cry quietly, remembering when we first got Huck, a wedding gift from Wesley's Aunt Charlotte and Uncle Jim.

"He told me Wes was fishing in his underwear, which didn't mean he was actually fishing in his underwear. It meant he was vain. He asked if Wes was overconfident in life." We both began laughing at John's incredibly accurate depiction of Wesley.

"This is the part you might want to sit down for, Lisa," Wayne warned me.

I stood quietly in the hallway.

"John told me he was getting the description of a woman. He said she is a relative but not blood related. He asked me, 'Is there a woman who is part of your family—she's been in your life for a long time and is like family but she isn't of blood relation to you? I'm not sure why she is family but not related. Does this make sense to you? Is there a woman like this you know of in your family?'"

Wayne and I both knew John was talking about me.

"I didn't want to tell him anything that would help him figure it out, so I just told him, 'Yes' and gave him no details about who you were," Wayne said, beginning to cry himself.

"She took your brother's death really hard," John had told Wayne.

"I told him you were Wes' wife, and we all grew up together," Wayne told me.

"She took it the hardest. Your brother wants you to know this," John went on to tell Wayne.

I began to sob as Wayne told me of John's message from Wesley. Unlike the reservations I had felt before, when seeking solace in the works of John Edwards soon after Wesley died, this time I felt no guilt when receiving what Wayne was sharing with me. I had not sought this out. I had not asked for it. But I received it. With all of my heart I received it.

Somehow, Wesley had managed to penetrate my spirit in an indirect way. Although I sobbed and was overwhelmed by the thought of Wesley truly still being around and still capable of making his presence known, what Wayne told me did not set me back or make me sad. In a way, it came at the perfect time—when I could receive it and not lose the progress I had made in my life without Wesley. Before, such a discovery would have sent me searching for more, back to the time when all I could think about was Wesley telling me I was strong enough to find him. Now that I was strong enough, he had found me.

I received the gift Wayne shared with me, and I let the rest go.

Three years ago, when I grabbed airplane napkins to write what I thought would be the final chapter of this book, I felt healed. I sensed the hardest parts of Wesley's death were behind me. I knew I would always miss him, and I did not have to stop loving him, but I felt a shift in the essence of who I was and who I was not. Who I was, was a capable woman who had found renewed strength. I found strength in my work and in the nurturing of other people in need. I found strength in the time that passed and in the good that could come when I was willing to learn from the unexpected in life. I found strength in the continuous and unconditional love of my beautiful son.

Who I was not anymore, was a widow. I was no longer defined by whom I had loved and who had loved me, and the terrible, tragic fact he had died. I was no longer a prisoner in the agony of grief, no longer a captive of this planet, barely holding onto what I could not let go of—Wesley.

Wesley died in the ICU in Alabama six weeks after his transplant because he was supposed to die then and in that way. He could have died many other ways and on many other days, but he did not. The six weeks he spent fighting for his life were as much about preparing me as the time was about preparing him, only it was impossible to know it then. At the time, all I felt was the enormous hole nothing and no one could fill. I would spend much wasted effort trying to fill that hole and to reconcile the loss. It was only after I accepted Wesley's death and all that came with it I was able to truly begin to heal and feel grateful for every circumstance of his death.

Soon after I got off the plane from that trip to Texas three years ago, everything in my life changed. It is important to say the shifting of my focus and my healing came before everything else I am about to share with you. No one thing made the difference; everything came together at once to manifest the entire blessing.

I have heard it said many times love finds us when we stop looking for it. Whether it is true or not for everyone, it certainly was true for me. And it happened when I least expected it and only because I left late one night on my evening jog.

Hunter rode his bike while I jogged, and we usually went two miles around our large neighborhood. We had started late, and it was getting dark outside on a summer evening in early August, so instead we stayed close to home and went five times around our block for the two-mile run.

One street over from ours—a street I never drive because it does not lead to home—there was a hot guy outside with his children as Hunter and I passed by. He had his golf clubs on his back, and his children were playing in the front yard. He said hello, and I said hello as I jogged by.

I had already planned to go around the block five times, but Hot Guy did not know this. When we passed by his house again, he smiled at me and made a comment about the second lap. I asked him where he had golfed that day, and he answered as I jogged past, with Hunter alongside me on his bike.

The next time I rounded the corner onto his street, I noticed he was nearer his house, away from the sidewalk where he had been on my two previous laps. I also noticed when he spotted me about five houses down, coming up the street again, he started to walk back toward the sidewalk.

We made small talk again, but I kept jogging. The next lap I decided to pay attention as I turned the corner on his street to see if he would make his way back to the sidewalk when he saw us coming. He did it again. As I jogged by the fourth time, I smiled at him and told him I had one more lap to go.

When Hunter and I made our way down his street for the last time, he was standing on the sidewalk waiting for us. But this time, as I passed his house, he called out to me, "Do you live around here? I haven't seen you before."

I stopped, turned around and met him at the sidewalk to talk with him. In a matter of a few minutes, he told me he was divorced. He asked what my husband did for a living, and I told him he had died four years before. (Wesley's death was much more relevant to his question than my divorce from Mike.) We talked for a little while longer. Then Hunter and I finished our jog and went home.

The next day at work, I was talking with some of my male friends before our production meeting, and I told them about "Hot Guy" down the street, as I called him. One of them told me Hot Guy was hitting on me, but I was not convinced. I told them I would jog by again that night and see if he was outside again.

That evening, Hunter and I left earlier, so we went on our usual route and only went around the block one time at the end of the run. This time, Hot Guy was waiting at the sidewalk for us when he saw us coming.

"Why are you always outside on the sidewalk when we come by?" Hunter innocently asked him.

Hot Guy looked away and blushed.

We talked for a little while. Then he invited me to hit a bucket of golf balls with him the next day. I told him Hunter and I were leaving on vacation and would not be back for a week and a half. He was also leaving town shortly and said maybe we could get together when we both returned.

Hunter and I left on vacation, and I honestly did not think much more about Hot Guy. For the first time probably in my life, I felt no need for the company of a man. We returned home and after a few weeks, my friend and neighbor Sara convinced me I should at least start a friendship with him, given we were neighbors and had things in common like golf and children. I was reluctant to leave my newfound independence and lack of a romantic life behind, but I was not against making a new friend. I had not been by his house since we returned from our vacation, so that night Sara and I walked around the block—but he was not outside.

About an hour later, however, I was looking out my kitchen window and saw Hot Guy walking with his daughter. Hunter was outside playing catch with a tennis ball against the garage door, so I went out there to casually say hello as he walked by. He joined me by my front porch, and we talked for a little while. He again mentioned getting together to hit a bucket of golf balls. I gave him my number, and the next day he called. And the next day. And the next.

It took weeks for me to agree to go on a date with him. I was in a very different place in my life than I had ever been. I was not afraid of being alone, and I was taking care of myself without the fear of thinking I needed the love and support of someone else to make me complete. Because I was content with my life as it was, I did not answer every phone call from Hot Guy or accept every invitation when he invited me to his house for dinner or to play a round of golf. Looking back now, this is probably why it all worked out as well as it did. By the time I went on a date with him, the night before my thirty-seventh birthday, I knew I was going out with him for the right reasons. Because I enjoyed our conversations on the phone and the few times he stopped by my house or invited me briefly to his, I knew I would enjoy a date with him.

"Who is this man who won't give up on the idea of taking me to dinner or watching a movie together?" I wondered.

I accepted his invitation to dinner and spent hours that night delighting in conversation with him. I enjoyed the way his mind worked and decided by the end of the night I did want to know more about him. I stopped referring to him as Hot Guy to my friends and starting calling him by his name: Brian.

Slowly and surely, this was our beginning.

When it's right, it's easy. There were no games, no doubts, no need to interpret actions or motives. It just felt good to both of us in every way. He was a grown-up. A man of his word. When he opened the car door for me, I once giggled and said to him, "Let's be who we are from the start. Please don't try to impress me with opening the car door for me unless you plan to keep opening the door for me, because I don't want to have to wonder in a few months what I did to make you stop opening my door."

To that Brian replied, "I'm the guy who opens your door."

A few weeks later, I opened the car door myself without thinking, and he said as he laughed, "You know, tell me now if you don't want me to open your door for you because in a few months I don't want to wonder why you won't let me open your door anymore."

He has been opening the car door for me ever since.

Brian and his children bring humor and joy to my life and Hunter's. I went from having one child to sharing my life with two more, much younger than Hunter. At times life is comedically chaotic, but somehow, between kids and work and sports and having to be so many places at once, we still make time for each other. When we tell the story of how we met, Brian swears he was not looking for my house or using taking his daughter for a walk as an excuse to find me. He also claims when I saw him out my kitchen window and went to my front porch to greet him I did not just casually say, "Hi." He claims I flirtatiously hollered, "Heyyyyyyy!" We end up laughing about it every single time. He knows the truth.

Meeting Brian and falling in love with him has truly been one of my greatest life lessons. I am so thankful my life was open to meeting him, and I was not blocking him because I was wasting my life on the wrong man. I am equally grateful I was not looking for love when love found me. My not being interested in a relationship—which had nothing to do with Brian—led to our coming together. I was content with who and where I was, which was the exact place to be when an honorable, exceptional man like Brian showed up in my front yard.

Brian coming into my life did not heal me. His love did not save me. I had done the work I needed to do in my life to bring myself to a readiness for what we now share. Even if he had not come along, I would have been just fine—but I am so glad he did come along. How amazing is it he lived around the corner from me, literally moving in the same month Hunter and I did years ago, but we never met until the timing was right? While I was suffering the loss of Wesley, he was heading for a difficult but necessary divorce;

neither was by our choice, and yet all we can be is grateful to have found each other.

One of my widowed friends, whose husband died about two years after Wesley, once asked me how long it takes to be ready to move on with life because she could see I had moved on and was happy. I told her what I have learned about time and grief and how complicated it can be. I have learned time is the great healer I have always heard it to be, but without doing the work and truly allowing myself to heal, all I had was the passing of time, a compilation of years of sorrow and continued grief that were never going to get better.

How long does it take to move on? There is no simple answer to that question. For me, it took more than four years; for others it may take more or less time, but no matter what, what we do with that time makes all the difference.

Hunter will live the rest of his life without his father. There was nothing fair about what happened to the three of us. It was a sad and tragic thing to happen to our family that forever changed us. I look back at Hunter's life and the family he had in the three of us and, although it was only a fraction of his life, it was everything. As he grows older and becomes a man with children of his own, he will have a greater understanding of the love his father had for him. The circle of life will teach him what he cannot yet understand completely. He will not only learn from what he lost when his father died but from what he gained with the gift of having Brian in his life and experiencing our new family.

I believe in beautiful beginnings. I believe in big love, the kind of love that helps get a relationship through the rough spots because we know somewhere in our beautiful beginning the love we signed up for still remains. That is the only kind of love I am capable of having. Sometimes we choose a partner based on what is happening right now, as I did with Mike, without considering what is to come. I know now part of why I married Mike was because I did not expect to ever truly love again. It was not that I felt as if I did not deserve true, enduring love; I just figured I had had my turn.

Wesley and I were able to take care of each other in our times of greatest need and life-altering crises because we fully committed to each other, and we were capable of getting through the no-matter-what's of life. I feel the same way about the love Brian and I share. I believe in us and the man who tells me he waited for me his whole life and will always do his best for us. When Brian got down on one knee and asked me to marry him, I said yes with a full heart and excitement about our future together. I will grow old with him, and when hard times come our way, we will find our way back to the part of us that remains—our love and commitment to each other, whatever life brings. I share it all with Brian today. My beginning and my end. I have crossed the raging sea of grief, been beaten against the rocky reef, and slowly made my way safely to shore. I live on a new island of hope, rewriting my story, no longer defined by what I have lost, but propelled by what I have gained, including Brian and the big love we share.

I still feel Wesley in the moments I quiet myself enough to receive him, and he comes to me in dreams, although not as often as before. The dream I have most often is of Wesley and Hunter playing catch, while Brian and I stand by watching. Wesley does not speak, he just delights in his time with Hunter. When they are done playing, he looks deep into my eyes, telling me without words he still loves me. I feel his gratitude for the care I have taken of our son. Then he quietly shakes Brian's hand without a word between them. The two men nod at each other as if to agree to love both Hunter and me and take care of us from where they are, respectively. Loving these two men in my lifetime has taught me of God's love for us. There is enough for everyone.

While I write this chapter, I am sitting by the pool at Jimbo's new house on the ranch. I brought Brian to Texas to meet Wesley's family and share with him where Hunter and I came from. Now, I am just yards from the lake adjacent to Jimbo's house, the lake where Jimbo and I spread Wesley's ashes soon after he died. I look to my right and I can see in the distance Hunter with a fishing pole and Brian helping him cast into the very waters where a part of Wesley will always remain, both figuratively and literally. The ranch was one of his favorite places on earth.

It is only in this moment I realize how primally connected we are, the four of us: Wesley, Hunter, Brian, and me. It is not just the earth or the water or the sky that connects us. It is the love. It lives on, in everything and in everyone. Like the two of them shaking hands in my dream, we share a moment when everything is as it should be.

And I know this is where I belong.

The DON'T WAIT Project®

As I wrote the final chapters of this book, I feared the sadness readers would experience reading each page. When Wesley died on Easter, after he was doing so well and expected to make a full recovery, I knew readers would be as shocked and horrified as we were. Many people, even our family and closest friends, would be learning the enormity of our daily fight for his life for the first time. Even I was overwhelmed recounting the magnitude of our struggle. As the one person closest to it, who lived through it all with Wesley, I knew if I was overwhelmed, others would be as well.

Recently, I read *All Aboard*, written by my new friend Debi Tibbles, whose son died of pediatric brain cancer. As I turned each page, I could hardly bear to keep reading. I would stop for a few minutes at a time and find myself in our kids' rooms, watching them breathe as they slept, caressing their cheeks, whispering my love for them quietly into their ear. I would text Debi and tell her I was having a hard time reading her book, knowing from the moment I picked it up her son would soon die, but she assured me it would get better.

"Keep reading," she would tell me. "I promise, it will be okay."

She was right. In the end, even in the tragic midst of losing her son, she has found her purpose and healed her family.

After weeks of wrestling with the sadness my book might bring to others, I woke up from a deep sleep at 5:30 a.m. one morning with an idea about the book and how I hoped readers could benefit from our experience. After walking with me through what we had endured, I wanted people to be able to close the book, then take the emotions it evoked in them and do something with their reaction.

I thought about the years it took me to write these pages, but also, once I decided it was time to share the story with others, how the words flowed out of me like the melting snow from the mountain caps near our home, feeding into the nearby vast river, sustaining life in the habitat where we live. I questioned my timeline and wondered if I had procrastinated but was quickly reminded of the relevant steps it took me to get here—raising Hunter, rebuilding my career, healing our lives. I did not wait to write this book; the story had to reveal itself to me in its own time.

In the early hours that morning, I wondered about the things we put off in our lives, assuming there is always tomorrow, or giving up on today. I thought about how someone like Debi, who lost her son, had managed to rebuild and become better than she would have been without both the gift of her son and the tragedy of losing him. I thought about the people in our country who are losing their jobs and being forced out of their homes, realizing for many people, it has been a lesson in the difference between what we want and what we truly need in this life. A bad economy cannot take from us what was not ours to begin with.

I wondered what all of us are waiting for when it comes to healing ourselves and rebuilding our lives. How could we change or expand our thinking in simple ways that could have an enormous effect on our outcome? How could we begin to do what we often wait too long to do? Then, with clarity it came to me—create a project that would propel people to stop waiting and start living.

As these thoughts ran through my mind, I jumped out of bed and began searching the Internet to find out if anything like what I was considering already existed. A fire of excitement and purpose was igniting inside of me as I got down to business in a hurry.

I immediately told Brian everything I could think of as ideas filled my head. Within days, I put together a two-page proposal and received enough corporate and local business sponsorships to fund the entire first phase of the project. Quickly, we hired two attorneys, one to form the nonprofit and another to handle trademark filings. Together, Brian and I created what is now called The DON'T WAIT Project®.

The DON'T WAIT Project® means different things to different people. We have started by advocating for organ donation registry. While 90 percent of the U.S. population supports organ donation, only 30 percent of people are registered. We are not trying to change anyone's mind who does not agree with or believe in organ donation. We are just attempting to encourage the people who do support it to commit and register to be a donor.

We also encourage families to have their affairs in order by establishing a will, designating a legal guardian for their children, and having even modest life insurance policies. For years I have been told by men and women, "I don't know how you survived losing your spouse. I couldn't do it." The cold, hard truth is, someone has to die first. If you are married, there is a 50 percent chance you will go through what I went through. You will lose your husband or your wife, and you will have to find a way to survive it. Denying this and putting off being prepared for it only makes it harder when faced with the reality of loss one day. Preparation still meets opportunity, even in the instance of death. If we are prepared for death, we have the opportunity to grieve without money hindering our privilege to grieve properly and in our own time.

The project is not just about the serious side of life, but it is also about doing the things we put off that bring us joy and allows us to get through the responsibilities and burdens life sometimes brings. It is about creating the balance we need. How many times have you told yourself you want to take your family on a much needed vacation, away from the stress and the worry of everyday life? How many times have you thought about calling an old friend but put it off and still have not made that phone call? How many things in your life are you leaving undone, putting it off until tomorrow but tomorrow never comes?

The DON'T WAIT Project® can be as simple as a new way of thinking, a new approach to what we already know. The possibilities are endless. If your marriage is broken, DON'T WAIT® to get help to fix it. If your grandmother gifted you her heirloom china, DON'T WAIT® to use it as a tradition in your own home. If you have always wanted to take a family vacation and can afford to do it, DON'T WAIT® to build those lasting memories with your family. If you know you need a mammogram but have put it off, DON'T WAIT® to take responsibility for your own health. If you are tired of being physically out of shape, DON'T WAIT® to join a gym and begin exercising.

Phase one of the project includes the launch of this book and a website where we receive stories from people impacted by the project. It includes the DON'T WAIT® pendant designed exclusively for the project—a conversation piece about the project and what it means to the people who are applying its principles to their own lives.

Phase two of the project is a book sharing DON'T WAIT® stories provided by everyday people whose lives have been bettered by the project: a donor recipient's mother registering to be an organ donor; a single mother returning to college; a family bonding over a much needed, long overdue vacation; an ordinary man who dreamed of becoming a pilot. The stories of triumph and hope go on and on.

Finally, phase three of the project is where the long-term philanthropic opportunity comes into play. Operating as a 501c3, the project helps those in need through an application and a nomination process. Whether we help widowed mothers provide school supplies for her children or help pay COBRA premiums for a patient who is facing catastrophic illness and financial hardship, the project enhances the lives of people in need throughout communities in America.

Much of what has happened in my life has led me to The DON'T WAIT Project®—leaving my business behind for the radio show and the community service director position, learning about nonprofits and forming my own with Brian, fundraising with the help of corporate sponsors who are innovative thinkers and willing to spend marketing dollars in creative ways. Again, making up my mind and listening to the voice inside of me has brought me to a crossroads and a certainty about my own life only these experiences could teach me.

We sometimes spend so much of our lives focusing on what we do not have, we are too blinded by the inadequacies to see the gifts that are our own. I am as guilty of it as anyone who will ever read this book. I fell down so many times I questioned why I should bother getting back up again. But the truth is, it is the getting up that makes us stronger. I once read: *Get knocked down eight times, get up nine.* It is painfully yet incredibly true.

Maybe you will live to be 100 years old. Maybe you will live to see your children have children. Maybe you will die in your sleep holding the hands of those you love. That would be wonderful, wouldn't it? It could happen, but it is not guaranteed. Consider, from where you are right now, what is your DON'T WAIT®? And if you do not have one, not a single one, because you are living the exact life you know you are supposed to be living, every minute of every day, please share with the rest of us how you do it because you can change the world. I mean that.

However, if you are like me, flawed with shortcomings, not always living the life only you were meant to live, or even knowing what that life is, then DON'T WAIT®. The message is not to suggest you live each day as if it were your last because then you would not go to work, you would probably keep your kids home from school—who knows how many distractions would come by truly living that statement? Instead, live each day as if it is your first. Be flawed and uncertain, but also be a glorious work in progress. I say it all the time: If you can breathe, you can do anything.

One night during Wesley's illness, he and I were sitting in our family room together talking about the things he struggled with every day—the many things we take for granted. He was no longer able to shower himself, read our son a bedtime story, or go to work at the job he loved. He was saddened by how much of himself he had lost in such a short time and questioned if he would ever return to the man he was before he got sick. He wondered if he would ever get the opportunity to be the best version of the man he knew himself to be. Would he heal? Would he survive? What would he do with the gift of healing if it were given to him?

"Maybe you should talk with God about that. Maybe it will help you," I told him, suggesting his feelings could be best dealt with in prayer.

"Lisa, there isn't one more conversation I can have with God from our bed I haven't already had with Him," he told me as he pointed to our bedroom. "There is nothing I've left unsaid."

Wesley was never a religious man, but he knew God and came to know Him better in the final months of his life. Wesley was right. Whatever he and God had worked out, it was out of Wesley's hands. Now I realize that besides what he did not leave unsaid, there was also nothing Wesley left undone. Was there more he wanted to do? Yes, there was more. There was a lot more, but it was more of the same—more time with Hunter, more time with me, more time, period. As young as Wesley was, and as much as he had endured, he died knowing he had given his life the best he had. To me, there is no other way to die, and there is certainly no better way to live.

Many times I fondly recall the eight-year-old girl who sat perched in the pine tree in front of Wesley's grandparents' house, and I am fully aware my ability to believe in and follow my own purpose is the balance God promised me. We are all promised this greatness.

I no longer need the book I bought soon after Wesley died about how to tie slip knots and skip rocks on water. I was terrified I lacked the ability to shepherd our son through life on my own, until I realized the gifts I had to offer Hunter were enough, even if my talents were different from his father's. The truth is, I never did need that book. Tying slip knots, rigging fishing poles, flying a kite—these things Hunter would learn from the incredibly giving people we surrounded ourselves with, each with his or her own talents. What I knew, I offered to Hunter with abundant love. What I did not know, I learned. What I still struggled to learn, I called upon others to help us with by widening our lives and letting love in.

I no longer try to fill up a space that is not mine to fill. Wesley was big to me, a force of love and fortitude that was gone when he died. Today, when I hear a song he might like or Hunter does something that reminds me of him, I can smile instead of feeling sad. Now, rather than missing him and focusing on the empty space his dying left behind, I can only be thankful for the impact he had while he was here. In the end, I am grateful for the effect Wesley's death had on my life because it is a direct indication of the impact he had on me when he was alive.

I believe I will be an old woman crossing over from this life to the next before I truly understand why Wesley died when he did and how he did. I stopped asking the questions that could not be answered seven years ago, three days after Wesley died, when he visited me in our bathroom in Houston and told me everything I needed to know about his death. He wanted me to live and find happiness without him, and I have. In this wonderful life I now live, I have discovered strength in finding myself on the other side of something I did not know how to survive.

As I type the final words of a book that took me years to write, Brian is near me, aware of my work and my reasons for needing to tell our story. We have just left Los Angeles, where we met with several people about our project and received tremendous positive feedback and support. It was my first time returning to Los Angeles in nearly seven years—since my emotional breakdown on the freeway as I struggled to live my life without Wesley. What a revelation it was to be on the same freeway with Brian and know the emotional and spiritual distance I have traveled. What a gift it is to know this love—to live it and breathe it, to appreciate every part of it, even the parts that are flawed and imperfect. I am in this for life, my home is with Brian and our children, and God willing, I will watch every last hair fall from his head, his hardworking hands wrinkle with old age, and his eyeglass prescriptions change with time. I will grow old with him and love him until my own final breath.

I would live every day of my life the same again in order to bring Hunter into this world, and I know Wesley would agree. The cancer, Wesley's illness and death, the heartache following both—I would do it all again. I have no doubt Wesley believed his greatest contribution was what he left behind—our son. After cancer, I said that more than the reason I survived, Hunter is the reason I was born. Now I believe he is both. He is the beginning, middle, and end of my purpose, with a million gifts in between. He has taught me what I am capable of and inspired me to reach deeper inside myself than I knew I could. Reaching inside for strength and reaching out to Hunter to give him what he needed, I sometimes surprised myself. To my amazement, I managed to teach Hunter what I thought would be impossible for me to teach him—even how to tie his shoes.

The more I live and the more I love, the more I know none of us is meant to remain in torment, departed from our own purpose. I expect to learn from loving and losing Wesley for the rest of my life. I expect to be propelled by the experience and delivered from it in a way that is only possible when I remain open to the work and progress ahead of me.

The work ahead for The DON'T WAIT Project® is the hopeful reminder we are all capable of healing our lives, embracing our purpose, and leaving behind big shoes to fill.

About Lisa Bradshaw

Lisa Bradshaw is a mother, cancer survivor, entrepreneur, and the founder of The DON'T WAIT Project®. She hosts her own terrestrial radio show, *The Life with Lisa Show,* and has been a guest on national television and radio, including *The Rachael Ray Show* and *Oprah Radio*. Her designs and her story have been featured in numerous magazines, including *InStyle, Parents, Better Homes & Gardens Kids' Room* and *ePregnancy*. Bradshaw is a sought after speaker on topics ranging from motherhood to patient advocacy and entrepreneurship to organ donor registry.

Seven years after the death of her husband, Lisa is now stronger, happier and eager to share what can be gained when one is willing to learn from the unimaginable. Lisa lives with her family in Washington.